ANCIENT ENERGIES

OF THE EARTH

An Extraordinary Journey into the
Earth's Natural Energy System

DAVID COWAN

WITH ANNE SILK

Thorsons
An Imprint of HarperCollins*Publishers*

Thorsons
An Imprint of HarperCollins*Publishers*
77–85 Fulham Palace Road
Hammersmith, London W6 8JB

The Thorsons website address is:
www.thorsons.com

Published by Thorsons 1999

1 3 5 7 9 10 8 6 4 2

A catalogue record for this book
is available from the British Library

ISBN 0 7225 3800 6

All photographs by David Cowan unless otherwise specified

Text illustrations by Jeff Edwards

Printed and bound in Great Britain by
Creative Print and Design (Wales), Ebbw Vale

David Cowan would like to dedicate this book
to his parents,
Robert Hogg Cowan
and
Joan Anderson Duff

Anne Silk would like to dedicate her work to
Dr Cyril W. Smith
with thanks for all his encouragement

CONTENTS

FOREWORD

This book relates the story of a remarkable exploration into the mysteries of the living Earth – the further our understanding, the deeper these mysteries become.

David Cowan set out on a path of exploration which has led him into unexpected depths. Our generation has realized that the Earth is an organic, living whole, not merely a complex lump of dead minerals with a film of life over its surface, but truly a living creature with its own breath and bloodstream, glands and sensitivity, thought and consciousness. The concept of Gaia, the Earth goddess, has been revived in our time to explain the uncanny intelligence of the Earth in meeting attacks on her life energy through industrial development. Now, in his study and exploration of 'ley lines' and standing stones and circles, David reveals a fascinating clue which throws light on many strange mysteries. The phenomenon of 'cup-marks' carved in rock by ancient man has never been adequately explained. David puts forward the hypothesis that they are connected with ley lines or, more correctly, energy leys, those paths of energy which are linked in a great network over the face of the country.

Alfred Watkins, discoverer of ley lines, called his book *The Old Straight Track* (Abacus, 1927). Now we know that some ancient trackways were established on artificial lines of Earth energy flowing between sacred points on the Earth's surface. The temple sites of Neolithic and Bronze Age man mark those points where divine energy crosses the surface of the living Earth.

Now David has made the discovery that cup-marks are used to link up and form the great network of lines of flowing Earth energy. His theory has taken him on an astonishing and crippling journey of over 3,000 miles on foot through the Highlands of Scotland. In the process, he has touched on many mysteries and legends and much ancient knowledge. This book tells his story and will, for many, open up the secrets of these great hills. The Highlands remain one of the most glorious areas for exploration on many levels, offering great widths of wild and wonderful country which can only be traversed by those who know how to use their boots. This book reveals another aspect which will further our understanding of this mysterious country.

David is to be congratulated on the courage and persistence which went into this exploration, which was undertaken, apparently, when he was in some distress from the demanding and arduous task to which he had committed himself. I urge you to read his story and follow up the clues which he gives.

SIR GEORGE TREVELYAN

INTRODUCTION

DR CYRIL W. SMITH

A plausible impossiblity is always preferable to an
unconvincing possibility

ARISTOTLE, POETICS, 9

The writings of the ancients, Aristotle, Ptolemy and others, which had been translated into Arabic and carefully preserved, were translated back into the *lingua franca* at the meeting points between Western Europe and Islam, the Universities of Cordoba and Seville. This injection of a tradition older than the extant traditions of wise men became a powerful intellectual force leading eventually to a Renaissance extending throughout human endeavours. This force for change intensified where it became clear that neither tradition's accounts could withstand an appeal to nature through experimentation; and through dissemination by the printed word, science as we now know it was born.

Today, we may be in the midst of a different Renaissance. We do not find it necessary to invent a god to take responsibility for each unexplained natural event; neither is it acceptable to deny the existence of the 'Earth Energy' phenomena as described in this book by David Cowan and Anne Silk, just because they do not fit into the paradigm that modern science has created. There is a realization dawning that a human can enjoy closer integration with the natural, and not-so natural environment through capabilities which seem to defy scientific explanation but, which although formerly

IX

available, have now atrophied through lack of use as life has moved away from close contact with nature.

Anne Silk combines the clinical experience of a professional optician and Fellow of the Royal Society of medicine having a real interest in the total welfare of her patients, with a true historical sense of the former human environment as befits a Fellow of the Society of Arts and a geological sense of the world long before life appeared and began to evolve.

Geological time has hardly moved when compared to the development of life and the human race, which has taken place in a dynamic environment of geophysical activity on or near the surface of a planet whose crust has natural spherical resonance frequencies in the range of milli-Hertz and whose iconosphere has natural Schumann Resonances which closely match the brain-wave spectrum. Specific frequencies from throughout these ranges are of biological significance, being able to stimulate chakras and acupuncture points and bring to living organisms an awareness of their geo-environment. For example, the 7.8 Hz frequency of the Schumann Resonance in a person's environment will stimulate the heart chakra and the heart acupuncture points (He9) on the hands. It also occurs as a natural resonance in melatonin/pineal extract. The pineal gland is an end organ of the sympathetic nervous system and its melatonin secretion and circadian phasing are influenced by dark/light and stress. Light does not penetrate far into the human body and melatonin is the chemical messenger for its day/night information.

The fact that chemical analysis can be done by spectroscopy is evidence for the duality between frequency and chemical structure. Furthermore, in highly coherent systems such as living organisms, the constant parameter is no longer the velocity of radiation, but is the distance over which its coherence is maintained. The result is that there can be many frequencies with proportionate velocities of propagation and all with the same coherence length. For example, events stimulated by high frequencies can appear simultaneously in the brain-wave spectrum.

In 1988, I was comparing notes with Anne Silk concerning the wide range of eye problems that electromagnetic frequencies were triggering in the hypersensitive patients that I was testing. Here, she reports on her own clinical experiences of finding electrical sensitivities among some of her own patients, on how they were affected and how they felt. One thing that many of her patients had in common was that they had been exposed to some form of geological (geopathic) stress.

In this book, she considers the five traditional senses of man plus two more – electric and magnetic sensitivities. Before discussing dowsing as a sensitivity, she opts for the Russian term 'Bilocation' in preference to the Roman 'augury', the old German 'da sein' (now 'Rutengänger'), the English 'dowsing', or the American 'witching'. She then considers what might be happening in 'distant sensing' or 'map-dowsing'.

When I was considering the possibility that ley lines emanating from stone alignments and radiating out over water could be used for navigational purposes, I remarked that a π-shaped (Stonehenge-like) geometry would concentrate the Earth Fields within its gap. Anne was able to produce a photograph from maritime archaeology showing a boat with just such a π-shaped structure at the stern exactly where the helmsman would stand.

Anne Silk discusses the possible effects of seismic disturbances, natural and man-made, and relates the legacy of Dr Tom Lethbridge, archaeologist and dowser, Keeper of Antiquities at Cambridge University, in connecting unusual effects with what is actually happening and surprisingly finding in it a description of the Roman spirit of a place, its *Genius Loci*.

She also considers electrical effects associated with such phenomena as ball lightning and earth lightning and unidentified aerial phenomena in general; effects in quartz and quartzite; Pliny's account of volcanic tubes; spontaneous combustion; strange effects at mud springs; crop circles seen as Chladni patterns; and the 'devil's footprints in the snow' phenomenon. In addition to electrical phenomena, she considers types of magnetism for their possible contributions to anomalous effects including magnetostriction, magnetic resonance and the work of Prof. H. A. Burke of MIT.

Quantum computing is now a rapidly developing science. In this, the basic memory unit does not switch between the 'one' and 'zero' states, but has a certain probability of being in each state simultaneously. That is, it has a grey-scale rather than rather than being black and white. One of the implications of quantum computing is that the memory can be accessed in its entirety without having to scan through all the locations in a time sequence. This seems much more like the way that living systems read the information in their environment with all its Ancient Energies of the Earth.

ACKNOWLEDGEMENTS

Permission to use the picture of the nuclear submarine was kindly given by the *Glasgow Herald*, that of the Cailleach and her family by Robert Money, Crieff, the footprints of 'the Jersey Devil' by The Fortean Picture Library, the island of Boreray by Colin Baxter and the Dwarfie Stane by Charles Tait Photography, Orkney.

Grateful thanks to Sharvie Price and Pat Toms for taking the time to read and advise on the early proofs, to Robert Money for his help to make me computer literate, and J. R. S. Photographers of Perth for help and advice spanning several decades.

Thanks are also due to Hamish Miller of Hayle, Cornwall, for permission to use the updates of his book *Sun and the Serpent* (Pendragon Press, 1989); Bob Brydon, Edinburgh, for sharing his experience of ball lightning; and others who have told me of their experiences which science still has to understand.

DAVID COWAN

Acknowledgements to William Corliss of the Sourcebook Project in the USA, always a mine of factual information; to the medical physicist, the late Dr William Sutherland, whose work led me into the study of geophysics and with whom I had the privilege of working on natural subtle energies in relation to health and ill-health; and Dr Alice Walker of the British Geological Survey in Edinburgh, who has unfailingly helped me with my queries on geophysics.

Any errors or omissions in my sections are mine alone.

ANNE SILK

introduction

For many years, walking the length and breadth of much of Scotland, the ancient and hoary standing stones and circles have exerted their attraction to me. Often on a lonely hillside I would pause and study these decaying remnants of our misty past, thinking sadly that their function in bygone days was, and always would be, almost totally unknown. The best scientists and archaeologists in the country had studied these artefacts for almost a century, yet found few clues to illuminate their function. Therefore, I thought, they were obviously destined to remain a puzzling enigma forever.

There were, however, certain individuals who could see in such ancient sites a knowledge beyond our present science – Watkins, Thom, Stukeley, Underwood, Michel, Hamish Miller, Paul Broadhurst and a few others ignored contemporary thinking and began to see their function in a different manner.

Largely due to their intuition and dedicated hard work, scientists are now becoming increasingly aware that standing stones and circles are emitting strange and subtle energies. Much has already been done in monitoring these emissions scientifically, notably by members of the Dragon Project, who used a wide range of scientific equipment and even a few people sensitive to Earth energies, and there is no doubt that an increasing amount of literature will stem from these studies. With modern equipment at their disposal, scientists are now able to measure magnetic fields, ultrasound, radioactive anomalies, etc. However, when they have all of the results, they will still largely be unable to find out exactly what these Stone Age relics were used for and how they worked unless an attempt is made to rediscover our forgotten past *using the same methods the Stone Age builders used* to find these energies and follow them, learning *en route* the qualities which the different types of energies possess and discovering, through folklore and personal experience, what effects they have.

That is the essence of this book. There is little use here for modern and sophisticated equipment. That will be covered adequately by the scientists themselves. Instead, I will use nothing more than the simple divining rod, used for centuries to find underground water and minerals and now being used by a few enlightened people to tune into the song of the megaliths once again.

I have walked more than 3,000 miles over an intensive eight-year period, following the remnants of this ancient energy from a variety of sources, over some of the most difficult terrain in the country, to recover a working knowledge of the complicated energy patterns emitted by standing stones and circles. Anyone wanting to follow my example should do so in the full knowledge that it is an exhausting task, one which requires stamina and stubbornness – and also one which is so interesting that it can easily become a life-long fixation.

We are at the gateway of a new millennium and there is a noticeable change in our culture. The general public, and some scientists, are becoming much more aware of the hidden side of nature, seeking knowledge beyond the scientist's test tube. This book, I hope, is just a part of the recovery of the knowledge of our forefathers. Like any other country with standing stones and circles, Britain has an ancient and powerful knowledge just waiting to be rediscovered by any able-bodied person, providing they are not imprisoned in the mental strait-jacket which our science, for all of its benefits, imposes upon its subjects.

In all likelihood, the maps presented here show territory unknown to the reader, but nevertheless deserve close study, since they form the microcosm of the system of telluric energies which covers our globe. They reveal the beginnings of a working understanding of our Stone Age culture, a reawakening of our senses and the recovery of a long-lost knowledge.

EARLY RESEARCHERS OF EARTH ENERGY

Alternative Theories on Ancient Enigmas

DAVID COWAN

Knowledge is of two kinds – we know a subject ourselves, or
we know where we can find information on it.

DR JOHNSON IN A LETTER TO WILLIAM STRAHAN, 27/3/1775

ALFRED WATKINS

In 1921 Alfred Watkins, Hereford businessman and magistrate, expert on local folklore and antiquities, inventor and photographer, was on a visit to Blackwardine. According to tradition, he pulled up his horse to survey the landscape below. It was then he became aware of 'a network of lines, standing out like glowing wires across the country, intersecting the sites of churches, old stones, and ancient sites'.[1] This was to be a significant step in the rediscovery of our past.

Alfred Watkins' 'vision' was no accident, as he had spent years in study and had a wide knowledge of classical mythology and local archaeology. Indeed, it is more likely, according to his son, that the insight actually occurred when he was looking at a map.[2] As far back as the 1820s archaeologists had described ancient monuments as forming 'lines across the landscape', while in the late nineteenth century, at the age of barely 15, William Henry Black had spoken of 'grand geometrical lines across the country'.

Watkins believed that ancient man used straight tracks for the transportation of flint and salt, which were generally available in coastal areas.

He suggested that staves were used to mark out these straight lines, marking stone circles, cairns, ponds, mounds, notches cut into hills, ancient tracks and other sacred sites upon which castles and churches were subsequently built. Ponds, Watkins argued, were to act as flashing reflectors for beacons. Cairns were alignments to distant hills, but not always on the summit. Mounds were made to be seen from a distance and standing stones were placed at the crossing-point of two tracks, with their spine, if any, indicating the direction of a ley. Stone circles and holy wells were initial points of a ley, and hill notches invaluable sighting-points.

Figure 1: A standing stone, one of many scattered across the country. This one is St Adamnan's stone, in beautiful Glen Lyon, Perthshire.

Ancient homesteads, Watkins surmised, ought to be included, but he decided against this, as they were too numerous, and it was difficult to say which were old and which modern. (Later I will explain the positioning of some of these sites and their relationship to cup-marks, which are fundamental to the workings of energy leys.)

Unusually perceptive, Watkins summarized the work of the builders, the early surveyors, or 'Dod-men' as he called them in his book *The Old Straight Track*:

> *I feel that ley-man, astronomer-priest, druid, bard, wizard, witch, palmer and hermit were all more or less linked by one thread of ancient knowledge and power.*[3]

He emphasized the straightness of a ley:

> *It should be noted that these and other alignments are, and must be, exact and precise through the mark points. 'Close to' must never be accepted. The sighting method is just as exact as the aiming of a gun, bringing the two sights and the objects in line.*[4]

Archaeologists have used this idea to reject the concept of leys, pointing out that even the finest line drawn on a 1:50,000 OS (Ordnance Survey) map is in the order of 11 yards (12 metres) wide on the ground.

As my investigations have uncovered, however, energy leys are comprised of a large number of individual vertical sinuous waves with their own specific wavelength and amplitude – in fact, a stream of energy – and so appear to weave across the surface of the planet like a serpent. Bronze Age man and his successors, I am sure, did not intend energy leys to be absolutely straight, probably caring not at all for such a level of accuracy, and for modern man to insist on it effectively stymies the recovery of this knowledge.

Nevertheless, there *are* lines of ancient sites, therefore those who propose that straight leys exist must be correct in their conclusions that there are energy leys which do fall within acceptable limits and which will reward researchers with leys accurate enough to satisfy the demands of archaeologists.

A book by Nigel Pennick and Paul Devereux, *Lines on the Landscape* (Robert Hale, 1989), takes the concept of leys as archaic alignments much further and argues that straight leys do exist, but as alignments of burial-grounds. In *The New Ley Hunter's Guide* (Gothic Image Publications, 1994) Paul Devereux describes straight roads as 'faery and spirit paths'. He argues that ancient cultures across the planet believed that the souls of the dead could only travel in straight lines.

These books should encourage archaeologists to take a closer look at the enigma of leys. It will probably take some time, however, before they will be prepared to admit that the leys have life, have energy flowing through their veins, and can provide a fascinating insight into our ancestors' beliefs and practices. But our understanding of ley energies may yet reshape our own culture in ways which cannot even be guessed.

OTHER EARLY RESEARCHERS

Watkins laid the foundations for others to follow and much more understanding slowly came to light. As knowledge of the ley system developed, a major disagreement erupted amongst researchers. Some now see the archaic track as simply a line of ancient and holy places (sometimes evolving to the present day, where, for instance, a church may be built near a standing stone, incorporating it into its fabric), while others see the same line as an energy ley, a straight line alive with an as yet unidentifiable form of energy.

Some researchers consider the energies to be simply the Earth's electric field, that is, the voltage gradient which exists between the negatively charged planet and the positively charged ionosphere. This gives voltage without appreciable current. There are others, however, who say that this theory is untenable.

Whatever the source of leys, it is obvious to me that they are circuits of energy which do have a source and a distant target. After many miles traversing the country in a straight line they may return, running parallel to the source, whence once again they start the circuit afresh. This gives, in effect, two or more energy leys side by side.

A great deal is owed to the archaeologist Guy Underwood in the further evolution of the rediscovery of the Earth's energy system. In the 1930s Reginald Allander Smith of the British Museum suggested to him that underground water might have a connection with the siting of ancient monuments. As a result, Underwood taught himself water divining.

Lacking sensitivity, he designed his own 'geodetic rod', with which he surveyed a number of sites. He discovered different patterns, each having a unique shape, which he described as 'Primary Geodetic Lines, including Water Lines, Track Lines and Aquastats, which appeared to have wave motion; had great penetrating power; to form a network on the surface of the earth; to affect the generation and the growth of certain trees and plants; to be perceived and used by animals; to affect the opposite sides of the human body, and to form spiral patterns'.

Underwood's main theory was that all prehistoric sites were situated with respect to the various coils, spirals and twists of these patterns. Churches, he claimed, were carefully constructed to allow aquastats (a form of energy derived from water) to pass through spirit holes, founts placed on 'blind springs', stoups and altars. This view has since been modified, as some buttresses, doors, etc., actually *cause* the effect, rather than are placed there because of it. Churches and other ancient monuments, however, have certainly been carefully positioned over powerful points of Earth energy.

Guy Underwood also realized that the 'Earth force' affected animals and vegetation. This was investigated by J. Havelock Fidler, a scientist who had spent a long career in agricultural research. One of his many experiments involved measuring plants' rates of growth when exposed to the radiation from a 'charged' stone.[5] This was, I think, his most interesting contribution to the field. His discovery was that stones (neutral stones, untouched by hand) can be charged, both by hammering and heating. (This was later to play an important part in my recovery of the knowledge of petroglyphs. Hammering or percussing a rock or boulder – carving a cup-mark, for instance – causes the stone to emit a much enlarged 'telluric shadow' of that engraving, as we shall see later.)

J. Havelock Fidler further postulated that the designers of the energy system interred their dead in certain places in order to insert the psyche of a particular person into the telluric pattern as a 'guardian spirit'. He argued that this was delivered initially by normal interment and later, with the discovery that the spirit grew weak and faded, by cremation, where the 'psyche' was fixed.

Professor Alexander Thom, at one time in the Chair of Engineering at Oxford University, discovered that stone circles appeared to have been constructed to precise geometrical formulae and also that stones in a circle were set apart at a specific distance, 2.72 feet (0.83 metres), which he called the 'Megalithic Yard'.

A knowledge of mathematics and astronomy on the part of the ancient builders was also postulated by Professor Gerald Dawkins, who wrote *Stonehenge Decoded* (1978). He pointed out that Stonehenge and Callanish in the Isle of Lewis appeared to be huge astronomical calculators, situated at advantageous positions for certain lunar and solar observations.

As more discoveries are made in the layout and workings of stone circles and standing stones, some authors are crediting the builders with almost superhuman powers of strength and knowledge. This is unlikely to be an accurate description. They simply had a different culture.

Archaeologists have recently been able to provide a picture of the megalithic builders from their skeletal remains. It appears that they were slightly smaller than we are today, the male averaging 5 feet, 7 inches (171 cm), and lived for a comparatively short time. In Orkney, for instance, the average age at death was a mere 25 years old and in other areas around 30–35. So the builders of such massive structures were little more than teenagers, slightly built, with delicate features and physically smaller than their modern counterparts. What strange path would our own civilization take, if few of us survived to be adults and it was left to teenagers to carry on our culture?!

THE SUN AND THE SERPENT

In the last few years others have picked up the gauntlet of exploration, notably Hamish Miller, an experienced dowser, and Paul Broadhurst, who have both investigated the St Michael's Line, which runs across southern England. This is not the traditional straight energy ley they had initially expected, but various tortuous streams of energy through Glastonbury Tor, Avebury and Silbury Hill, amongst others. This line has similarities with the cup-mark leys described in this book, with some differences, one being that the St Michael's Line tunes into holy wells, which cup-mark leys avoid. Basically, there are two currents of energy in the St Michael Line, crossing at important node points.

In a similar manner, using divining rods, I have followed energy leys of different types, which have been intelligently controlled, focused and manipulated across our country. This has given me an insight into an undiscovered world of subtle energies which has been woven into extensive and complicated circuits, using the energies emitted from standing stones and circles and volcanic plugs for a purpose which I can only guess.

Hostile to the very idea that ley lines even existed to begin with, I became amazed to find active energies forming vortices which can cause severe illness in the population. Apparitions, poltergeists and even demons began to come to my attention. Shunned and ignored by the scientifically-orientated general public, such 'beings' nevertheless make their presence felt to some unfortunate individuals.

As my knowledge grew, so did my awareness that our culture is over-dependent on science and is badly out of balance. Delving back into our past can throw light upon our ancestors' understanding of Earth energies and on the ancient mythical warriors who understood them – and who never did die, according to folklore.

REFERENCES

1 Alfred Watkins, *The Old Straight Track*, Abacus, 1927
2 Tom Williamson and Liz Bellamy, *Ley Lines in Question*, World's Work
3 Watkins, op. cit.
4 Ibid.
5 J. Havelock Fidler, *Ley Lines: Their Nature and their Properties*, Turnstone Press, 1983

LISTENING TO THE PLANET'S PULSE

The Strange Energies from Standing Stones

Laugh not so lightly, O King, for in these stones
is a mystery and healing virtue.

MERLIN SPEAKING TO ARNELIOS IN *THE HISTORY
OF BRITAIN* BY GEOFFREY OF MONMOUTH, 1136

My initiation into the mysterious world of Earth energies came from an unusual source – the BBC television programme *Tomorrow's World*. One evening in 1978 Henry Lovelock, an inventor, showed a 'terahertz generator', a device which, he hoped, would enable aircraft and ships to navigate a very precise course. It was simply a box which emitted a form of energy. The twist in the tail was that Lovelock used a pair of divining rods to find the energy.

The following weekend I took with me on my usual hill-walking expedition a pair of divining rods of the same type used in that programme. These were angle rods, very simply fashioned from two metal coat-hangers.

My walk that weekend was high in the hills above the beautiful village of St Fillans, Perthshire, one of the most scenic areas of Scotland. To the north of the village the Hydro-Electric Board had constructed a number of dams, underground tunnels and water pipes, so it was an excellent place to make my first attempt to discover underground water.

It was with a mixture of curiosity and almost total disbelief that I tracked across a partially buried pipe with my angle rods at the ready, to find that the rods, apparently of their own volition, turned downhill.

Following their direction with some hesitation and with growing amazement, I followed the pipes for some distance, until I had traced the pipeline down to the hydro-electric station.

The following *Tomorrow's World* programme showed the construction of the terahertz generator. It was nothing more than a box with an electric light bulb inside it, shining through a window of clear quartz!

Once again the *Tomorrow's World* presenter used his divining rods to detect the energy from the 'black box', and then switched it off. To everyone's astonishment, the energy could still be found, streaming across the room. He moved the box, still switched off, to a different location and the energy could still be traced in its original position. He said that in a previous trial, the waves could be detected even several days later.

This was quite an astonishing revelation, but little did I realize then that it was only the beginning of a long series of astonishing revelations for me, which now span many years and several thousands of miles of tough hill-walking.

Coincidentally, at the same time a book on water divining and allied subjects appeared on the market. Written by Tom Graves, it has since been reprinted as *The Diviner's Handbook* (Destiny Books, 1990). The contents ranged from water divining and finding drains to discovering oils and minerals, looking for lost objects and people, and the compatibility of food and medicine to people. The final chapter discussed 'ley lines', an unknown energy travelling across the country in straight lines from standing stones to stone circles, churches and burial-grounds. To me, back in 1978, this seemed quite ludicrous.

ENERGIES FROM STANDING STONES

The following weekend I walked across the heather-clad moors of Dunruchan Hill to the south of Comrie, where a few years previously I had found a number of standing stones set out in a row. Approaching one of them, a huge stone, I took out my divining rods and proceeded to walk round it. I was surprised to find a faint reaction in the vicinity of the monolith. Following the rods carefully, it soon became obvious that they were picking up a spiral of energy. I walked for some distance, further and further out from the stone, then tried the other standing stones. They all produced the same reaction. Deeply puzzled, I returned home. Obviously, a

Figure 2: Seeking the energies from one of the five standing stones on Dunruchan Hill, Comrie.

great deal of work would have to be done to solve this mystery. Little did I realize then exactly how much hard work and how long it would take!

Another standing stone, this time at Lawers Farm, a few miles from my home town of Crieff, Perthshire, caught my attention. I resolved to discover more about this curious energy by spending several weekends working around it. With my back to the stone, I fixed my eye on a point in the far distance and walked towards it, holding the divining rods. Every few yards they would cross, indicating the presence of some form of energy. Since there must surely be a relationship in the distance between each reaction, I reasoned. I marked each one on the ground and measured the distance between them, only to find that there was no correlation whatsoever.

The following weekend I returned and with no clear idea in my mind, tuned into the energy from the stone. Without realizing it, this time I had actually tuned into one of the many waves emitted by the stone and my rods took me in a wide, sinuous line, rather like the movements of a snake. This explained the odd figures I had been getting the previous week. The sinuous wave did travel to the point I had walked to the previous week, but on that occasion I had simply walked straight towards it, the rods crossing when they chanced to encounter the wave.

Vowing quietly to myself that I would eventually get the measure of this strange business, I continued for a few more weekends, discovering in the meantime that there were more than 40 waves coming from this stone. There was little more to be found here, as it happened. The only item of real interest was that four of these waves travelled to a nearby priory, each of them picking out a corner-stone of the old building, whilst a fifth spiralled up the path and entered the priory. Later I discovered that the priory had been built above an underground stream. The path followed the stream as far as the road and the stream continued on underneath the monolith. The builders of the priory had cleverly incorporated the sub-surface energies into the design.

The reason for the dearth of discoveries here was not difficult to understand. For many centuries farmers had been tilling the land and removing stones as agriculture had intensified. Now the land was quite different from the way megalithic man had left it.

But my confidence and knowledge were growing rapidly, and it was time to progress to another standing stone, this time at Stonefield Farm, to the north of Crieff.

Figure 3: The standing stone at Stonefield Farm, near Crieff.

A Working Standing Stone

This monolith seemed rather different from the previous ones. It had a faintly ominous feel, whereas the others had a natural, balanced feeling. I spent some months mapping out its waves of energy, which travelled to a rather peculiar artificial mound, now badly destroyed, with 28 boulders at its circumference. These boulders returned the waves back to the standing stone. One boulder, which had rolled down into low-lying ground, had yet another wave pivoting over it. I returned this boulder to its proper place at the periphery of the mound and the wave obligingly followed. Apparently, these 29 boulders were all charged in some manner to attract the energy from the standing stone. Perhaps the synodic lunar month, 29.5 days long, has some bearing on this discovery.

WATER DIVINING AND DOWSING

Now I had some experience of locating energy using divining rods, I was able to look at the subject in a new light. There are many different types of Earth energies, with different properties, and those who work on them are prone to give them different names, a problem presently being addressed by the British Society of Dowsers' Earth Energy Group. To find these energies, however, there is really only one way, and that is to learn the ancient art of dowsing.

Using Divining Rods

Most people think of the tools of the dowser, water diviner or biolocator as the traditional 'V'-shaped hazel twig. In fact, there are over 200 different types of divining instrument, but for following the various types of telluric energy, the best of all is the simple angle rod, a length of wire, some 16 inches (40 cm) long, with another 6 inches (15 cm) bent over at right angles to form a handle. Made from heavy fence wire, or even from metal coat-hangers, these rods are extremely sensitive, even in the hands of a complete beginner. For working outdoors, they should, ideally, be made of the heavier fence wire, which is much less influenced by rough terrain and wind.

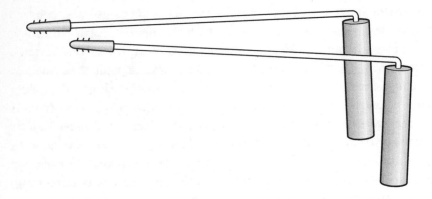

Figure 4: A simple pair of divining rods.

Some people find it an advantage to have handles of some description, while others prefer to feel the bare rods turning in their hands. For handles, ballpoint cases may be used, or 1 inch (2.5 cm) diameter dowelling rod bored down its length to take the short ends of the instruments, or even several cotton reels glued together. For safety's sake, the bare ends must be protected with rawlplugs or taped over with electrician's tape so that they will not penetrate the body in a fall. In all cases it is essential that the rods move freely in their holders.

Do not be misled by the simplicity of this instrument. The amount of knowledge which you can obtain from it is astonishing.

Like any other dowsing instrument, these rods work because they are in a fine state of balance. Try holding them perfectly level in front of you, in a comfortable position, just above waist height, facing away from your body. Now, gently raise the tips, so that they are slightly above the horizontal, and you will find that they go out of control and swing back towards you. The rods are at their most sensitive position when the tips are a few degrees below the horizontal. Lowering the tips further makes them less sensitive.

If you are fortunate to have a standing stone in your neighbourhood, try using the rods there. Choose a fairly calm day to begin with, to avoid any chance of the wind influencing your results. To make the rods more sensitive, give each a brisk rub lengthways with your hand before commencing work.

Every standing stone has at least two veins of water (or fissures) crossing beneath it at different depths and the energy from these travels vertically to the surface. It can be found entering one corner of the monolith and exiting via the diametrically opposite corner. This is the raw material each standing stone uses, via, presumably, the quartz crystals in its structure, to form an energy ley, a straight corridor of waves between ancient sites.

Programme your mind to look for energy around the standing stone. We are surrounded by a maelstrom of energies of various types, and it is by tuning one's mind into a specific form of energy that results can be obtained. This is very easy, for we do this naturally every day in conversing to friends at a party, for instance, when you can easily listen to what one person is saying, even if that person is some little distance away. In dowsing, the acknowledged way to tune into one specific type of energy is to hold a sample of what you are looking for. For instance, a water diviner might hold a bottle of water in their hand, thus 'programming' their mind to pick up nothing else but radiations from water. A slightly more professional approach is to use a Mager disc, a wheel with coloured segments. Holding this with the divining rod in the hand, more experienced dowsers can put their finger on a colour, blue, for instance, which to them means water, and find nothing but water, or perhaps the black segment, and tune into an unhealthy underground stream or energy ley which may be causing ill-health to those who live within its influence. After some time most people will find that they do not need props of any kind, as their subconscious minds have become sufficiently clear to discover precisely what they are seeking.

Silently commanding the rods to move in the direction of any energy which may be emitted, walk across the face of your standing stone. Specify clearly what you are trying to tune into – woolly-minded dowsing gives woolly results. Try and make your mind as detached as possible and relax. The rod tips should move slightly away from the stone. Carefully turn and follow the rods in the direction they indicate. With just a few minutes' practice you will gain confidence. The energy you find should be a wave, a sinuous snake-like line emitted vertically from the stone *(see Figure 6)*. It is important to note that you must be walking to make the rods work – they will not move when you are standing still.

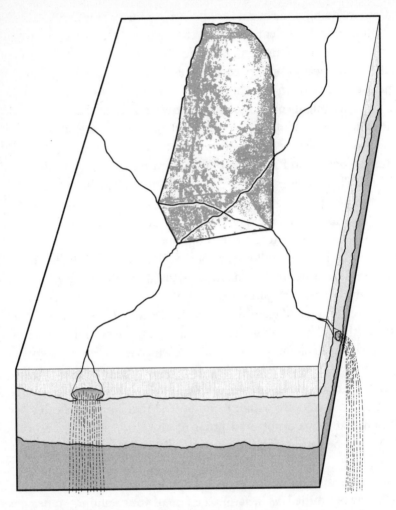

Figure 5: Standing stones are carefully situated above crossing underground streams.

Some people discover that one rod points in one direction while the other points at right angles to it. This is simply failure to 'programme' the mind properly. What usually happens in this case is that one rod follows one wave and the other tunes into another, crossing wave. Simply repeat to yourself firmly that the rods must follow one individual wave and they should 'come to heel'. After a little time you will gain confidence and the conscious instruction to search for telluric energy can be discarded as the subconscious mind will take over, enabling you to walk any distance

Figure 6: The structure of a wave. This cup-marked standing stone is at Kilmartin, Argyll.

without concentrating on Earth energy at all. Sooner or later it will be possible to use one rod only, which gives more accurate results.

After some weeks' practice, I found that I could follow an individual wave with my arm outstretched to one side of my body, then traverse across the wave to the other side, the divining rod faithfully following the sinuous wave without any deviation at all. In other words, no matter where my body was in relation to my hands, the rods precisely followed the wave. Some form of energy flows up the divining rods to or from the person operating it. Do not try to analyse this phenomenon, unless you are particularly interested in this facet of the art, just use it.

The traditional forked twig used for locating water is useless in following energy leys, as the operators have to set their grip continuously, and the twig will show wave direction and amplitude only with great difficulty. There is no harm in trying this type of divining rod initially, however, if you find it easier to use.

Figure 7: Plan view of one of the double waves from the Chieftain.

As you become more proficient, you will discover that it is quite possible to use the rods with their tips pointing sharply downwards, their most insensitive position. This is very useful in adverse weather conditions, a high wind for instance. Sometimes I have used rods with no difficulty at all in winds which literally snatched the breath out of my mouth and drove me to seek shelter behind the nearest rock or dyke.

There are a number of books which go into the subject of dowsing in detail (some are listed in the Further Reading section at the end of this book) and it is a good idea to read as much as you can on the subject to enable your mind to accept what is, certainly, a very strange art.

A Tunnel beneath a Dungeon

Some of the easiest things to find are tunnels, as the American army discovered in Vietnam, when locating underground complexes built by the Vietcong. Some years into this fascinating research, I followed a ley to Meggernie Castle, Glen Lyon, Perthshire, and met the gamekeeper and his wife. They asked me to locate a tunnel which was said to pass from the castle to the nearby river. When the castle was built this tunnel had been incorporated into its structure and the unfortunate inmates of the dungeons were ultimately tossed into it, their bodies being swept into the river. This gruesome tale seemed impossible, however, as the castle is only a few feet higher than the river and any tunnel leading to or from it would be full of stagnant water.

The 'keeper's wife pointed to a deep depression on the flat, expansive lawn. This, she said, was another tunnel, partially collapsed, running westwards from the castle to a small burial-ground. I could practise locating the tunnel there.

A wide, sinuous wave of energy was emitted vertically from the partially collapsed tunnel and this ran towards the old burial-ground, but unexpectedly curved past it and ran beneath the castle and on to the river, to disappear at the riverbank. Retracing my steps, the wave, almost as if it were bouncing from one wall of the tunnel to the other, ran from the river, beneath the castle and back to the river, further downstream, in a crescent shape, to give a good flow of water beneath the dungeons – a very simple solution to a perplexing problem.

Figure 8: Meggernie Castle in Glen Lyon, where the river was diverted below the dungeons to dispose of its unfortunate residents.

ANNE SILK

Anne Silk has long been interested in the reasons why some, but not all, see or hear phenomena and why these phenomena are very often specific to place. With a professional background in optics and a lifelong interest in geophysics and for the past decade in electromagnetics, she believes many of the visual, acoustic and tactile reports are explicable by the laws of physics, with eddy currents in the brain from natural high-amplitude energies. The human brain may be thought of as a tiny part of a global and natural Internet, responsive not only to endogenous (internal) signals, but also exogenous (external) signals. The human body is very sensitive to static electricity and geomagnetism and in these facts lies the answer to the question: phenomena – or physics?

In 1939 I was, with many other children, evacuated to Cornwall to escape the bombing of London. At play, other children told me about the 'jewels' to be found on the nearby beaches. So many happy hours were spent poring over handfuls of sand and tiny pebbles looking for the coloured 'jewels'.

Soon I had collected tiny green, gold, red and, rarely, blue crystalline treasures, hoarded and gloated over in a small box.

'Rubbish,' said the adults. 'That's just broken glass rolled in the waves.' But the sharp eyes of the optician-to-be knew glass from crystal even then. Many years later, to my great delight, I read in a text on geophysics of the gemstones to be found in certain parts of Cornwall. Tourmaline (green like an emerald), pyrite (fool's gold), chalcedony (a form of quartz ranging from white to grey, blue or black), quartz and serpentine (green) are just a few of the many gems and minerals which have developed as millions of years ago magma welled up through cracks – faults in the granites of the West Country. This was my first intimation of the wonders Nature could produce from her energies far below. The old legends were indeed true.

Then there were the ghostly outlines of buildings which appeared in the grounds of my boarding-school in Hertford – but only in frosty weather. Quite invisible normally, the outlines of ancient walls were clearly marked on the ground, to the wondering eyes of schoolgirls looking down from the height of the dormitory windows. This led me to think back in time to earlier people, their mode of life, their thoughts, and marvel again how natural energies (in this case very cold weather) could show us such a 3-D image. And then there were the special places – but you must read on to find the reasons why a place can so affect us...

We do not think of our bodies as being magnets on two legs, but nevertheless this is so, and, like all magnets, the system will respond, in a greater or lesser way, to an ambient magnetic field, whether man-made, like an electric shock, or from the Earth, as with walking across an active fault. Remember that all flowing electrical current has a mirror image of itself at 90° to the direction of flow – this is the magnetic field. Our nervous system is a giant electrochemical matrix. Our brains are effectively 3 lb (1.4 kg) power stations constantly sending electrical signals down the neurons to our toes, fingers, gut, etc., along intermediate channels, the nerves, blood vessels, cell membranes, bioelectrical closed circuits, myelin sheaths and muscles. We may think of these as the power lines of our bodies.

There are many sites where clumps or chains of magnetosomes (like tiny bar magnets) only nanometres in length will all dance and swivel to the call of a local magnetic field. When such magnetosomes are suddenly 'zapped' by an electrical shock, or lightning, or maybe the charge in the quartz (piezoelectricity) of a standing stone, the rotation of the particles is affected, as is the electric potential of cell membranes, neurotransmitters and synapses, and this in turn affects the chemistry of free radicals, extremely energetic particles which zip around the body. As Dr Galt, at Gothenburg University, states, the particles are 'free to rotate like a torsion pendulum'. With an external magnetic field, which may be in the local environment, a 'sick office' or an RF (radio frequency) hotspot, an enhanced sensitivity follows. Imagine a grandfather clock with a biomagnet as the pendulum, but now, instead of a gentle side-to-side motion, it revolves as well. Impossible? No, at microscopic cell level this is happening.

ELECTROSENSITIVITY

This is the term applied to the problems of a growing group of sufferers found in technologically advanced countries who have the ability to affect, and are themselves affected by, electronic and electrical equipment. Electrosensitive (ES) people are also found in areas of high natural geomagnetism, for example the Highlands and Islands of Scotland and parts of Wales, Cornwall, Oregon, California and Iceland, to quote but a few. This syndrome has been derided by many in the medical profession, but is taken seriously enough in Sweden, Norway, Germany and Austria for ophthalmologists, dermatologists and immunologists to have set up special clinics to treat those affected.

So what is ES? On the equipment side, it means that the individual can, quite unwittingly, wipe bank cash machines after touching the control panel. Computers can crash, radios will crackle and TVs can even change station and crackle loudly when they pass by, due to the enhanced radio frequency energy emitted by the stressed body. Such individuals can also stop watches or cause them to run fast or slow when in use and give big electric shocks to people they touch. Some I have known have even had such a high charge that a mini-lightning flash is visible when, for example, they attempt to kiss or embrace. Dr Michael Shallis was one of the first scientists in the UK to draw attention to this effect, though he received little acknowledgement for his pains. But as, over the years, many ES people have contacted me, and I have met very many of them, it is obvious, when their symptoms are compared from their personal notes and reports (remember that they are unknown to one another), that this is a real syndrome which is, with a very few notable exceptions, not at all well addressed by GPs.

In interviewing these ES people it appears that certain factors are common to all:

- The person has had an electric shock, perhaps from a live wire or powerpoint.
- The person has been struck by lightning or been in a lightning 'splash'.
- The person was born in or now lives in an area of high geomagnetism, a geomagnetic anomaly area, where the magnetic field can range from a few tens of nanoTesla (nT) over deep metamorphic basements to several hundred nT over basic intrusions and several thousand nT over magnetic ores. Igneous rocks, basalt and some ironstones are noted for such anomalies.
- The person carries a very high electrostatic charge.

(All of the above can send currents flying around the body, triggering great eddy currents in the vessels, brain, brainstem, etc.)

When someone who is ES passes close to a device which is itself emitting an electromagnetic field, albeit small, the two may be imagined as 'talking' to one another, the positive poles being attracted magnetically to the negative poles, and interference and malfunction are the extreme results.

From my own records of ES people, both men and women, whom I have interviewed, it is clear that there is no joy in this phenomenon. Rather, it is a source of embarrassment and disruption. Imagine not being able to stroke your cat, as it is terrified of your touch, or kiss your partner, lest a shock be transmitted as lips meet. Other symptoms are sudden acute pain, specific to place, with no logical reason, sudden nausea, extreme weakness, the sensation of ants walking on the skin or water dripping on the head. Some of these are skin effects from the electrical field while others are due to magnetic fields (to which the skull is totally opaque) causing eddy currents deep in the brain.

THE SEVEN SENSES OF MAN

Classically, man has five senses. Twentieth-century research adds two more: electricity and magnetism. The full list is:

- Sight: visible, infra red and ultraviolet
- Hearing: audible sound, ultrasound and infrasound
- Smell: variable sensitivity
- Touch: variable sensitivity, neuropathies reduce
- Taste: variable sensitivity, illness affects
- Electrical: We all emit and are sensitive to, electricity. Excitotoxins can trigger, in the brain of fit, normal people, motor, somatosensory, autonomic or psychic symptoms, with no impairment of consciousness. Hairs rise, fingers, toes and lips tingle, hallucinations of sight, smell, taste and touch can occur.
- Magnetic: We all emit and are sensitive to magnetic fields, whether they are man-made or natural (seismic). We have magnetosomes in the brain, thymus, lungs, spleen, liver and ethmoid sinus and in haem in the blood. The pineal, hypothalamus, Ammon's Horn in the hippocampus and the ethmoid sinus are all highly magnetosensitive to very small field strengths, as is the limbic system.

Our direction sense, biolocation (dowsing) ability and the ability of some to affect compasses, electrical and electronic equipment appear to be related to our electrical and magnetic senses.

BIOLOCATION

In the Middle Ages the Germans named this *da sein* ('It is there'), and before them the Romans knew it as 'augury' and its users as 'augers'. Unfortunately, in the UK it is known as 'dowsing', a word with somewhat negative connotations since we 'douse' fires to put them out. In the US it is known as 'witching' or 'water witching' by some – hardly a better phrase. The Russian twentieth-century term 'biolocation' is the most accurate and logical, and describes exactly what happens – the human body can locate objects.

Having been used for many centuries to detect underground water and minerals, dowsing has now become much broader in scope, with individuals specializing in discovering oil reserves, tracing geological faults and locating the origins of unhealthy radiation from a variety of sources. It is also used in archaeology to find underground remains and the foundations of buildings.

A Marvellous Device

However, dowsing needs a sophisticated vehicle. This marvel was developed long before *homo sapiens* began to walk upright. It had an electrochemical structure with exceedingly complex wiring and built-in indicators for heat and cold, which enabled it to tell when it was too hot for its own correct function, or too cold for its safety. It could automatically adjust itself for humidity, had sensors for particulate matter, an inbuilt compass for direction finding and could easily tell if it was light or dark. Some of these built-in sensors darkened to protect the invention's vehicle if the sun gave out too much ultraviolet energy, and it could tell if a surface was hard or soft. Its automatic sensors also knew just how much liquid it needed to function, and most models could sense water, even though it could not be seen. This marvellous device could even sense subterranean metal ores and through its complex sensors locate all manner of objects, both natural and man-made, including metals. You, the reader, have the latest version – it is, of course, the human brain.

What Is Going on in the Brain in Distant Sensing?

Natural Earth energy bands are in the same frequencies as those of our own brainwaves. Within the brain, certain areas, like the pineal and the hypothalamus, are extremely sensitive to magnetic fields, to which the bones of our skull are totally transparent. The temporal lobes, the limbic (edge) zones are also magnetosensitive to magnetic fields, however sourced. Eddy currents, from Lenz's Law, are set up in deep layers of the brain, thus stimulating areas biochemically and electrochemically.

In high magnetic fields, slow waves of the brain *increase* their rate of firing. Slow wave nerve cells increase in *coherent* activity. Such eddy currents in local tissue can rhythmically depolarize deep neural structures which are normally accessible only by surgery. These effects will vary between fat and thin people, whether standing, sitting or reclining, walking barefoot or shod, or standing on grass, granite, quartz or on a non-conductive surface.

The most ancient and therefore most essential part of the brain is the vestibular apparatus with the cerebellum and its philogenetically most ancient section, the medial area. Is it possible that this part of the brain, once vital for existence, is slumbering, waiting to be awakened by the art of biolocation? It is indeed curious that so many people who have either received an electric shock or been near to, or even hit, by a lightning strike seem to develop faculties which they did not exhibit before. In fact, medical research is now being undertaken into sub-clinical electrical effects. We now know that profound but yet subtle effects can be produced in the brain and body. One of the pointers to field effects are the natural magnetosomes found in the brain, ethmoid sinus, thymus, spleen, lungs (of smokers) and liver.

In the sensory perceptions of dowsers four factors are paramount:

1 Magnetite particles, magnetosomes in the body.
2 Minute gravitational anomalies due to the Earth.
3 The speed at which the brain and body traverse such areas.
4 The natural magnetic field of the Earth, which has enormous local variations.

Every living thing on Earth is subject to a multitude of forces – gravity, magnetism, planetary forces, the Coriolis effect and the sun – to which we must now add man-made fields. We have some idea of the rise and fall of the tides and sunspot activity, but are in the main far less familiar with the subtle energies from flowing water, buried ore bodies, the oscillation of the planet itself and its interaction with energies from beyond and above the Earth.

Living systems will normally react to these infinitesimal changes connected with the lithosphere and atmosphere with climate changes. However, if the ambient fields reach sufficient strength – and this response will vary with different individuals – there will be a nulling or negating effect on the biolocator's response. Many a TV documentary in a crowded studio has been a disaster as the combined magnetic fields from TV cameras, lights and humans override the subtle effects on the brain of the dowser; this is known as 'magnetic saturation'.

Few people realize that simply by walking across the ground, and thus cutting across the natural geomagnetic field of the Earth, they are producing electromotive force, voltages in the body from the application of Faraday's Law. By moving very slowly at the rate of 1 metre a second, an internal field of 4 microVolts/metre is generated (equal to 2 milliGauss). But if one runs very fast at a speed of 8 metres a second, the internal electric field is 400 microVolts/metre (or 200 milliGauss).

This is one of the reasons why exercise of any type is good for the system. But there is another curious effect and that is that when the body and head rotate or twirl and when the head is moved constantly up and down (as with some faiths at prayer), these actions generate currents in the brain. For example a fast nod taking 0.16 seconds will create an electric field in the brain of 4 microVolts/m or 2 milliGauss. Rotations, like the spinning dance of the Sufis and many Native American tribes and African tribes also generate a significant electrical field in the head and brain. Together with the rhythmic pounding of drums and the beat of music, altered states of mind will occur. And what if the dancing takes place in an area of high geomagnetism? What non-linear effects may be seen?

Even labyrinth walking can produce strange mental effects as instead of moving backwards and forward, the slow head movement now follows the direction of the body, side to side as the person walks.

HOW IT WORKS

There are almost certainly two modes for the biolocation process, both located in the brain. The first is the response of magnetite to minute field strength changes from deep flowing water (ion potentials), minerals, rocks and ore bodies, etc.

The second is what Prof. Erwin Laszlo, leading scientist and philosopher, calls the 'Psi phenomenon' and Robert Sheldrake the 'morphogenetic field'. Most people are familiar with the Internet, which enables instant communication between people world-wide. Think now of your brain, that 3 lb (1.4 kg) of grey matter, nerves and neurons, as the Internet of nature, a distant location system and even on occasions communication channel between yourself, other people and objects. Both Laszlo and Sheldrake, together with many other serious researchers, believe that the ancient methods of communication over distance, as practised by the

Australian aboriginals and the Kogi people of Columbia, for example, can be activated by many people, especially at times of high emotion.

In Arabic there is a word which is of great significance: *baraka* (spirit). I believe that this refers to the 'spirit' of an object, implying association with its maker. When we say we feel 'drawn' to an object, perhaps an antique, or an image, we sometimes say 'It speaks to me.' And so it does, but in subtle ways, quite beyond its artistic or practical usage.

Professor Laszlo writes that we have to open up our minds to this sensitivity. If people are 'shut off' and claim that it does not exist, they will not be aware of it. They will walk through life, so to speak, with their mental eyes closed. Open up your awareness and this information channel will flow – your very own Internet!

Both macro- and microscopic effects of the electromagnetic radiation, which is all about us, are determined in humans and animals by the direction and magnitude of the fields inside the head.

Now for a little quantum physics! As light is now known to be both a wave and a particle, so man is both physical and spiritual. We can no more separate the one from the other than water can flow uphill.

The letters M A P mean to most of us a cartographic representation of roads, towns, hills, etc. But within every map of this type there lurks another, albeit unseen. This is the Magnetic Anomaly Point, the summation at a point in space, on or under the ground, of the totality of magnetic fields, including seismic, solar, planetary, local and magnetic fields.

When geophysicists speak of 'percolation theories' and dowsers of 'veins of water', both are addressing the same subject. Porous rocks and reservoir rocks (those holding water in strata) exhibit permeability to liquids and act as conduction fluids for Earth (seismic) energies. We know that springs emerge on the spring line, a junction between rocks at discontinuities. In the same way, oil seeps from shale along lines of weakness and, over millennia, mineral-laden fluids seep up from the magma far below, metal ions being deposited as the superheated liquid cools, and we find seams of gold, tin, silver, copper, and so on.

Electrofiltration potentials on the Earth are created by the combination of flowing water, both above and below ground level, and the filtering actions of rocks, chalk sediments and aquifers. Depending on the body resistivity of the dowser (high resistivity = poor dowser, low resistivity = good dowser), response to the natural electromagnetic gradient of any traverse will be poor, good or excellent.

This is complicated by the fact that what is known as 'dip' is also involved – the angle of a MAP to the central core of the Earth, that dynamo which drives all life, in conjunction with solar energy. This dynamic movement is now considered to be the major cause of continental drift or plate tectonics, a theory first postulated a mere 40 years ago and now the subject of major research by Earth scientists.

To return to the magnetic field. The average magnetic field of the Earth in the UK is 50 microTesla, but it varies tremendously, often over very small areas, depending on the deep rocks below ground (ironstone, basalt, haematite, etc.) and nowadays also on the presence of TV and radio transmitters, together with any other equipment which emits electromagnetic fields in order to carry its signals. The field also varies around the steel cores of modern buildings.

BEWITCHED

The New Builder of September 1991 carried a strange story regarding building works at Castle Mall in Norwich, where a £125 million shopping mall was being built beneath an ancient castle mound. On a 164-feet (50-metre) stretch outside the old fortress gates, workers found that steel piling sections were rejecting each other in a manner similar to the like poles of a magnet. It was impossible to get welds to take and some cracking of underground sections was discovered. Expanded Pilings, the installation company, quickly found that the piling casings seemed to be strongly magnetized. The casings, however, only became charged (with magnetism) when brought on to the site and further investigations showed that 'previously cast piles were found to be affected, together with their steel reinforcement'. A search of the area failed to find underground cables, generators or substations capable of producing magnetic fields strong enough to affect the work. Attempts to degauss the casings (neutralize their magnetic field) were unsuccessful but welding was eventually restarted using industrial magnets to counteract the force.

The source of the magnetism remained a mystery, but Geotechnics managing director George Ballard was recorded as saying that a electric or magnetic source nearby was inducing a flux in the casings. A look at a map of Norwich shows clearly that Anglia TV headquarters is located 135 yards (125 metres) from the site and BBC TV 820 yards (750 metres) away. Was it the reactive fields of the nearby television stations or a power surge or over-voltage from a lightning strike (maybe some distance away) which affected the metal casings?

Further, 'Chips' Barber, writing in *Ghosts of the West Country* (Jarrold Publishing, 1996), reported a similar occurrence when building work was being carried out at St Anne's brewery in Exeter. Here, metal pilings which had been lying flat on the ground 'jumped about in the air', terrifying the workmen carrying out the building operations.

A riddle noted by Prof. Zasbig Harvalik may be also explicable in bio-electric terms. His experiments showed that in a magnetic field produced by a DC current, the dowsing reaction succeeded only when the left side of the dowser was towards the electrode carrying the negative flow. When the dowser turned around and walked back towards the start of the route, the reaction ceased. When we consider that amongst the *mêlée* of natural current in the brain there is one which flows constantly, as DC current, from back to front, along the calcarine fissure (the middle of the brain, where the two halves meet), we can see that an equal but opposite current will negate the natural brain signal. The brains of dowsers do show higher than background delta and theta rhythms when dowsing.

The late Dr Bill Sutherland, who was working on the physics of the dowsing response prior to his death, discovered that areas of high energy, which Guy Underwood called 'blind springs', exit the Earth vertically, or near vertically at the end of a fault. (These blind springs are similar to the black or white spirals from subterranean sources which we will encounter shortly.) To visualize a fault, think of a line of trees running for perhaps a few thousand yards. Then, in your imagination, turn the line upside down and place it well below the surface of the earth. There is, then, a main trunk (the primary fault), the thick branches (the secondary order fault), the thinner branches (third order fault) and the twigs (fourth order fault). In addition, there will be dilation (expansion) or compression of the rock strata below the earth, and in the clay, chalk, or sandstone, etc., near the surface, depending upon the deep strata movements, so it is easy to see why the ends of such faults have powerful blind springs and higher energy levels.

SPIRALS OF INSECTS

Many insects and animals are drawn to Earth energy sources in the just same way as they are drawn by the energy emitted near electric cables (as distinct from the energy running inside them). Many people have observed how ants and termites like to crawl along such cables. In *Pattern of the Past* (Abacus, 1970), Guy Underwood noted that cattle tended to congregate on top of barrows (man-made mounds from the pre-Roman period) and that these are located over blind springs. Cows and deer like to sleep at these places, hares make their forms (nests) there and black-cocks (a type of grouse) have their ritual courting at such spots. Hares were considered to be sacred in the past. Could this be due to the fact that they unerringly made their way to areas of high, naturally healthy ener-gies? Also, as Underwood remarked, 'The nest hills of moles, "fortresses", where they give birth to their young, are always on "blind springs", as are badger sets.'

Underwood also relates an interesting story from an old book on the Peninsular Wars. Old campaigners, sleeping rough, would always choose a place where cows had lain down, due to the fact that if they slept there, they knew they could not get rheumatism. In classical literature Cadmus founded Thebes at the place where a sacred cow came to rest and Troy was reputedly selected for the same reason.

The Clerk of the Works at Salisbury cathedral told Guy Underwood that sometimes great swarms of gnats would arrive in a cloud. In 1736, 1952 and on other occasions, when the gnats circled the spire, the sight was mistaken for a fire and the fire alarm sounded. The clerk told Guy Underwood that these gnats or flying ants were 12 mm long and if a workman was bitten by one, the bite was very painful.[1]

We are all familiar with those irritating columns of flying insects in our summer gardens. These columns, comprised of hundreds of gnats or midges, will, if disturbed by someone walking by, or swatted away, return speedily to the same place, a vertical column of Earth energy. In my large garden in the Chilterns, three such columns were visible year after year, always in the same places. What is especially curious is that tulips planted in two identical dwarf wall beds on the terrace, each 17 yards (15 metres) long, grew prodigiously in the bed by the insect column. Indeed, the above ground part of the tulips was often measured at 3 feet (91 cm), whereas in the other bed, planted with the same bulbs at the same time, the height was a modest 18 inches (46 cm). Sunlight and watering were identical; the only variable, apart from energy sites, was the height of the plants.

REFERENCES

1   Guy Underwood, *The Pattern of the Past*, Abacus, 1970

3

WALKING THE ENERGY LEYS

Cup-Marks – the Key to Ancient Art and Science

Every body placed in the luminous air spreads out in circles
and fills the surrounding space with infinite likenesses of
itself and appears all in all and all in every part.

LEONARDO DA VINCI, *JOURNALS*

Cup-marks, sometimes called petroglyphs or rock art, have puzzled scientist and layman alike for over a century. They range from simple hollows about half an inch (12 mm) across, carved on rock, to large 'basins' 6 inches (15 cm) wide. Some are surrounded by a ring or rings which may be gapped or have a groove running through them. Others are joined together by a groove, usually running from the cup, suggesting to some people that the stones were once used for sacrificial purposes and the grooves let the blood run away, although there is no archaeological evidence for this.[1]

Since there is very little datable evidence associated with cup-marks, experts can only guess their age. In 1979, one eminent archaeologist, Ronald W. B. Morris, who spent the major part of his working life investigating them, suggested a date of approximately 3200 BC to AD 100. This vague dating has not been improved upon by other researchers.

Cup-marks can be found world-wide, usually in clusters. In Britain there are few north of Perthshire or south of Yorkshire,[2] although some can be found in Derbyshire.[3] They may be discovered on standing stones, in cists or Stone Age coffins, on earthfast boulders in fields, small movable boulders and horizontal rock faces, or hidden in caves, like Wemyss Cave,

33

Fife. They can also be found below ground in chambered mounds and souterrains (sometimes called weems, fogous or earth houses), like Pitcur near Dundee. Here a heavily cup-marked stone guards the interior chamber *(see plate section)*.

A few years ago, a remarkable discovery of rock carvings was made near the village of Mauchline, Ayrshire, where a cliff face with cup-marks, sun symbols and other carvings was uncovered, having lain unnoticed for years behind the thick vegetation which preserved the figures in the soft sandstone. At Ormaig, near Kilmartin in Argyllshire, another beautifully preserved series of carvings of over 300 cups, rosettes, keyholes and cup-and-rings has recently been discovered under a carpet of grass *(see plate section)*.

CUP-MARK THEORIES

R. Morris, in *The Prehistoric Rock Art of Galloway and the Isle of Man*, gives 104 different theories regarding cup-marks. These include a belief in magic, in the afterlife, use as a tuning device and as a plan for megalithic structures.

Figure 9: The cup-marked cliff face at Mauchline, Ayrshire.

As will be shown, each of these theories appears to have an element of truth in it.

Morris also provides some clues, which he thought might lead to the rediscovery of the reason behind this ancient art:

1 Cup-marks are nearly always carved where there is a fine open view, often within sight of the sea or estuary.
2 Carvings on outcrops of rocks are usually made on parts of the rock which are horizontal.
3 There is no evidence of any fortification of the site.
4 On standing stones, carvings appear on the principal stones on an astronomical alignment.
5 If they are on outcrops of natural rock, they are within 6 miles (10 kilometres) of a site where copper or gold ore has been worked.

Most petroglyphs are carved in such a position that the sun can shine on their surfaces, even those in some underground structures like Newgrange in Ireland. Here, Martin Brennan and researchers have discovered that the remarkable construction techniques of the builders allow thin shafts of light to penetrate the furthest recesses of the chambers to highlight specific carvings for a short period of time on important days of the year.[4]

This form of 'light-beam dialling' has been noticed in other countries, too. At Fajada Butte in Chaco Canyon, New Mexico, a similar form of light enhancement takes place on two spirals carved on a rock face. A sliver of light shining between two rocks moves vertically across the faces of one carving at noon on the summer solstice, while a narrow beam crosses the smaller spiral at the equinoxes, although some researchers, I have heard recently, are not entirely convinced that this is a genuine ancient artefact.

In Italy, some interesting discoveries were made under the leadership of Emmanuel Anati, who researched 130,000 carvings in an area north of Milan. He discovered that the ancient artists used a wide variety of colours to emphasize their carvings. One site he surveyed was the 'Map of Bedolina' at Valcamonica Lombardi, a flat outcrop of rock which had been carved with cup-marks surrounded by squares and rectangles and, rather more unusually, some reasonably straight lines which are thought to be a map showing buildings, fields, paths and streams.[5] This is likely to be closer to the truth than many of the theories proposed to date. The carvings are no ordinary map, but a pattern of telluric or Earth energies, with the petroglyphs transmitting telluric energy between standing stones, stone circles, burial-grounds and homesteads in an astonishingly highly evolved manner.

Many archaeologists regard these ancient marks inscribed on stone as of less interest than standing stones and circles. However, I am sure it will be found, in due course, that they are basic to them. This book argues that the carvings can be decoded to explain many of the mysteries behind the perplexing stone monuments. In Welsh folklore it is even claimed that they hold the key to all the knowledge of the arts and sciences of the ancient world.[6]

THE STONE AT CONNACHAN FARM

Following my initiation into the energies between the standing stone at Stonefield Farm and its nearby earthworks, I decided to spend a quiet hour or two mapping the energies around a recumbent cup-marked stone at Connachan Farm. This lies in the centre of a hollow in the hills near the entrance to the beautiful Sma' Glen, to the north-east of Crieff. Little did I realize that my 'quiet hour or two' would stretch into eight years' hard labour!

From this stone I found many waves of energy, but I picked one at random, intent on following it until I discovered its purpose. The summer and the autumn had slipped past, winter was approaching, and it was time to start walking the peaks in earnest.

Mile after mile I plodded along, quite unsure that I was going to find anything at all, but glad to be back walking the 2–3,000-foot hills covered with snow and ice. Every so often I would encounter something of interest on this energy ley, which I came to call a 'cup-mark ley' (all of the leys in this book are comprised of waves of energy, therefore from now on I may omit the word 'energy'). Sometimes it was a church, sometimes a burial-ground or castle, and even, on occasion, ancient tracks which had evolved into modern roads. Many of the old burial-grounds were unknown to me and were not marked on the 1:50,000 OS map, convincing me that I was following an ancient circuit. The cup-mark energy had been used and deliberately focused through the dead in these prehistoric burial-grounds. This area is wild, mountainous country and the telluric energies were still working through the burial-grounds and other ancient sites, much the same as they had done when they were constructed thousands of years ago.

Figure 10: The cup-marked stone at Connachan Farm, near Foulford Inn, in the Sma' Glen, Crieff. This is the centre piece of a whole system of Earth energies.

My research was beginning to take on the air of a major undertaking, judging by a large board which I had constructed, with several 1:50,000 OS maps pinned to it. I could watch my progress growing week by week, but unfortunately, the cup-mark ley I was now working on seemed to be going nowhere at all. It appeared to wander in a haphazard fashion across country, and at times I became dismayed and frustrated with the pattern which was beginning to emerge – it bore no resemblance to the cup-marks on the parent stone at Connachan Farm. Nevertheless, I obstinately followed the energy, which took me north to Loch Tay, further north to Loch Rannoch, round the northern shore, and at last, to my relief, back southward to Loch Tay, with an almost circular excursion around Loch Earn. Then, to complete the circuit, it returned to Gilmerton, a small village to the east of Crieff. Here there are some artificial mounds, which I later realized are part of the circuitry responsible for directing the cup-mark leys over a wide area of Scotland and northern England *(see Map 1)*.

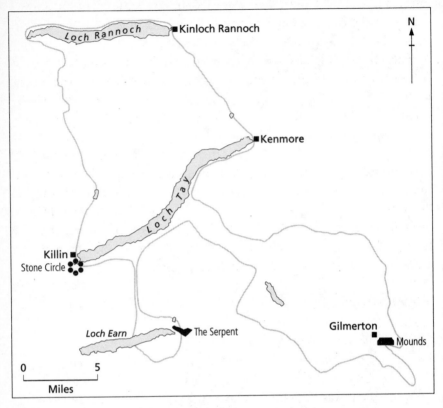

Map 1: The energy circuits at first made no sense. This was to come later.

THE CIRCUITS TAKE SHAPE

Many hundreds of miles of walking later, other patterns emerged inside the first, each becoming a little more like a dumb-bell in shape, until the basic dumb-bell circuit emerged, just like a very prominent cup-mark on the Connachan Farm stone *(see Figure 11)*. Yet even this cup-mark ley had another circuit inside it, a mere skeleton, which in turn was composed of other fields of energy building the pattern piece by piece.

It had become obvious that I had been blindly following the complicated dumb-bell shaped energy fields from the outside to the inside, rather like opening Pandora's box. Earth energy researchers are often accused of having 'belief systems', of forming a theory and subconsciously following their own 'thought patterns' to prove that it is correct, but most of the

38

research in this book cannot be dismissed in this manner. The energy systems were discovered by following them with divining rods; the theories came later.

The dumb-bell shaped ley closely resembled the cup-mark on the stone at Connachan, as already mentioned, and the circular detour around Loch Earn on the outer circuit neatly mirrored a smaller cup-mark nearby. Eventually, other roughly circular leys were found which could be associated with the patterns carved on the stone.

Through experimental work I had discovered that when a cup-mark ley encountered a stone circle, it was warped to a different area. So I went to the stone circle at Killin, west of Loch Tay, to pick up this warped energy, and in the depths of winter, followed it, sometimes floundering on my belly like a penguin on snow too soft to stand in. Three streams of energy were emitted through the six gaps of this stone circle, all travelling to the Balquhidder area, famous for the outlaw Rob Roy MacGregor.

Figure 11: This dumb-bell shaped petroglyph eventually revealed its secrets.

This pattern and the dumb-bell shape, together with the circuit from the stone circle, tallied with the dumb-bell cup-mark and one of its smaller satellite cup-marks on the stone. The mystery of the petroglyphs had at last been unravelled.

'STRAIGHT' LEYS

There was, however, much more to the energy system in this area than this. For some years I had realized that burial-grounds, churches and so on had streams of telluric energy passing through them, not only from cup-mark leys, but also from other directions. These were the traditional 'straight' leys. They intersected the terrestrial cup-mark energy system and at the crossing-points ancient sites had been placed. My evolving telluric map was slowly and painfully taking shape.

I also discovered another type of straight ley, with surprisingly few ancient sites upon it, that just touched the cup-mark leys, apparently moulding them into shape.

But to gain further insights into our ancestors' use of telluric energy, it was necessary to understand what it is attracted to and what repels it.

REFERENCES
1   Ronald W. B. Morris, *The Prehistoric Rock Art of Argyll*, Dolphin Press, 1977
2   Ronald W. B. Morris, *The Prehistoric Rock Art of Galloway and the Isle of Man*, Dolphin Press, 1979
3   Stan Beckensall, *Rock Carvings of Northern Britain*, Shire Publications Ltd
4   Martin Brennan, *The Stars and the Stones*, Thames & Hudson
5   P. and O. Stochan, *Ireland: A Journey into Lost Time*
6   Rodney Castleden, *The Stonehenge People*, Routledge & Kegan Paul

THE STRANGE
QUALiTiES OF
CUP-MARK ENERGY

An Intriguing Insight into the Earth Energy System

> He who has a professorship may be said to receive his food
> from the stall. But he who finds his food for himself at the
> hands of Nature is better off in the open field.
> SCHOPENHAUER, 1788–1860

Cup-marked stones emit energies of unusual qualities. The waves associated with the cup-marked stone at Connachan Farm, for instance, are quite
different from the straight leys which most people associate with Earth
energy or telluric energy. (We will have a closer look at these later.)

The energy emitted from the cup-marked stone in the Sma' Glen follows
the contours of hills and valleys. It does not travel over hills as straight leys
do. It has similarities with the Chinese energy *ch'i*, which flows along the
'dragon paths' the Chinese geomancers know so much about. In addition,
this site is located in a saucer-shaped depression amongst the hills, a
yin (female) power point. Examples of yang (male) power points are
Edinburgh and Stirling Castles, dominant rocks surrounded by plains.

Even though some of the standing stones and circles associated with the
Connachan Farm stone have been partly or completely destroyed, it is still
'working', and I was able to use it to uncover some of the properties of the
telluric energy.

FEATURES OF THE ENERGY

Taking the Easiest Path

As the circuits slowly came to light, it became apparent that apart from following the contours of the land, the energy also followed ancient tracks and modern roads. The roads simply evolved through time from the tracks along the original route. This seemed logical, since the weak type of cup-mark energy always follows the easiest path, free of obstacles. On occasion it would follow railway tracks for some distance, until it abruptly broke away from its modern route and went back to its prehistoric path. The rails, in most cases, had been removed long ago and the cup-mark ley simply followed the easiest route once again. On several occasions it followed sheep tracks across hillsides heavily overgrown with ferns or ran down 'tramlines' in cornfields, which may be of interest to researchers into the crop circle phenomenon.

The Attraction to Water

The cup-mark leys I followed are attracted to bodies of water including lochs, the smaller lochans and quite small puddles of water, even if they are covered in ice, but not if they are frozen solid.

That this type of energy was attracted to water and followed the contours of hills was easy enough to understand, but some months later there occurred a series of bizarre incidents which gave me a unique insight into the manner in which these circuits propagate, even thousands of years after their construction.

Tuning into Animal Carcasses

It was late spring in 1981 and I was hard at work following the almost circular cup-mark ley around Loch Earn (*see Map 1, p.38*). Near St Fillans on the shore of Loch Earn is a rock, some 33 feet (10 metres) in length, visible from the roadside, called 'the Crocodile', which I had discovered on my endless perambulations of this energy system to be part of the circuit. More correctly known as 'the Serpent', it is not a stone carved by nature in one of her capricious moods, but one carved by man and no doubt painted by him from its earliest inception *(see plate section)*. The tradition of painting this stone is still regularly carried out by a local resident. I followed the sinuous energy down a glen to this peculiar stone with some amusement, realizing that it was part of the age-old serpent cult. Stone Age man, unable to understand the propagation of wave energy as we do today, must have regarded any creature which moved in a sinuous fashion with great reverence. The wave led me to a narrow gorge a few hundred feet up the hillside.

The winter had been harsh, and nature had taken her toll of the unfortunate and weak of the wild animals, so I was not surprised when my divining rod led me over the carcass of a deer in that narrow ravine. There seemed, however, to be something more to this – the rod seemed to 'tune into' the remains of the beast. I recalled a similar incident on another hill a few years prior to this, when the rods had responded in a similar manner. As I mentioned earlier, this form of telluric energy is very lazy and takes the easiest path, picking out the weak points on a hill, the lowest point of a ridge for example. So it came as no surprise that the dead deer was on the path of energy in this ravine, which is possibly what Earth energy researchers call a 'hill notch', carved out of the hillside by human hands. This acts as a 'telluric flyover', with another ley crossing above at this point. My angle rod did seem, however, to pull me towards the carcass, moving accurately over the centre of the partially frozen animal.

There was no time to investigate further, however. A high wind and snow scudding horizontally across the hill forbade me to do anything else but walk on to keep warm. Several hundred feet higher I gave a grunt of disgust. The snow-covered 'boulder' I had just stood on was soft and mushy – a dead sheep this time. Slightly perplexed, I carried on once more, until a few hundred feet higher, on the summit of a small heather-covered mound swept bare of snow by the bitter, screaming wind, the ever-weaving wave led me to the remains of a racing pigeon caught in the heather, killed by a bird of prey, judging by the feathers scattered around.

Puzzled, I walked on, to be led to another dead bird, and another, and yet another, each time my divining rod tuning in with unerring accuracy.

As I jumped down from a high peat bog, something gleaming white caught the corner of my eye. There, in the lee of the mound, was the skeleton of a large gull, lying on its back, wings outspread. This, too, was on the outer edge of the cup-mark ley. At this height I could spare no time at all for a closer investigation, as the ground was frozen solid and the biting wind and scudding snow insisted that I keep going. In the distance I could see a small stream tumbling down the hillside. This, I thought, would slake my thirst and could also be used to mark the point at which I had left off, so that I could return the following weekend.

Pausing at the side of the foaming water, I drank copiously, then shrank back in amazement. There, indistinct in the rippling water, just beneath my cupped hands, was yet another dead bird! I stared at it for a few seconds in disbelief, then walked back down the glen and home.

HOMESTEADS ON THE CIRCUIT

The following weekend I returned to that little burn from the Loch Tay side. The previous week's storm had abated and it was a beautiful spring day with blue skies and a hint of warmth in the air. With some misgivings, remembering the strange – even sinister – events of the previous week, I started where I had left off following the cup-mark ley, this time down to Loch Tay.

On the way I occasionally tuned into the remains of some unfortunate animal or bird, until contouring the side of a hill, several hundred feet above Loch Tay, a ruined building came into view. As I drew closer it became obvious that this was no derelict farmhouse, but an old church with its attendant burial-ground. It was not marked on the map and was one ancient site I certainly did not know about: Cille-ma-Charmaig, the cell of St Carmaig.

The fact that this old site was unknown to me and on the circuit boosted my morale. I took a short break to investigate the old gravestones, while giving some reflection to their position, several hundred feet above the loch. The modern road was far below, near the loch, which was much more convenient, but there was no doubt that the ancient shielings, the little stone homesteads, were built higher up, alongside Cille-ma-Charmaig and in the closely spaced waves which were always a feature of the outer part of the cup-mark circuit. It was obvious that they were built to take advantage of the waves of energy which contoured the hill at this point.

In many years of hill-walking I had come across many puzzling features of our past in the landscape, such as these old homesteads. Many of them seemed to be situated strangely far from water, a basic necessity of life. Now the siting of these little shielings and churches was beginning to fit a pattern – a pattern of telluric energies.

Walking briskly now, over the grassy farmland, with my divining rod smoothly following the sinuous wave, I began to feel more comfortable since this recent discovery. Something, however, in the distance gleamed white, something I couldn't identify at that range. Nevertheless, the rod was turning towards it and, somewhat apprehensive again, I slowly followed it. A few score yards away, the object became clearer. It was a skull – a sheep's skull!

Bewildered, I decided to call it a day and walked back to my car. Driving home, my mind went back over recent events. Discovering the church and burial-ground was a bonus, but this energy seemed to possess the strangest qualities. It tuned into so many different and strange objects: skulls, dead deer, sheep and birds, caves and also, I reflected, a discarded oil drum and cattle troughs.

Then, as I drove along, the answer came in a flash – the objects were all *resonant cavities*. If you can imagine standing in a cave whistling and increasing the pitch until your whistling vibrates, you will get the idea of a resonant cavity. The sheep's skull was a perfect one. Whether clothed in tissue and flesh or the bare bone, apparently it made little or no difference. This was one of the most fascinating and important discoveries of my research.

CAVITY-SEEKING ENERGY

Later that spring it became obvious just how sensitive to cavities this type of energy is. On one occasion it warped from its normal path and round a hillock to focus on a pelvic girdle, all that remained of the skeleton of a deer, and a short time later it did the same with the scattered vertebrae of yet another animal. On another occasion it deviated to the body of a fox, lying with its head on its paws at the entrance to a rabbit warren and literally frozen solid.

Over the years I have made more discoveries about this curious effect. It has become obvious that the energy in a cup-mark ley responds to a number of objects besides bones and skulls. Cars, lorries and tractors parked near a circuit will immediately draw the energy into them. In Glen Almond I found a derelict house that attracted the energy into it. The energy passed neatly through the door and out of the fireplace. Later I found many such houses and noticed that chimneys and doors were usually the entrance or exit points of this particular type of energy. Windows, another weak point in a building, were also an attraction.

Curiously, although the outside 'working edge' of the cup-mark ley tuned into the centre of a deer stalker's one-roomed bothy near Schiehallion, multi-roomed houses (and burial-grounds, as I discovered later) are just on and within the outer circumference.

Near Killin, at the west end of Loch Tay, a concrete conduit underneath the road pulled a circuit well away from its original track and neatly gathered the energy into its mouth. On other occasions, a number of similar concrete and iron pipes stacked up awaiting the construction of a hydro-electric scheme were also powerful attractions.

Mounds of boulders had the same effect, as the interstices between the stones were sufficient to create a strong attraction. This was, presumably, one of the reasons why they were used in the construction of burial-chambers – to attract this energy into them.

This also helped to explain why I had so often come across old shielings on my journeys. Along with the prehistoric burial-cairns, our ancestors had built their little dwellings on cup-mark leys. It was also noticeable that the major cup-mark leys passed through these shielings along their lengths. I discovered the reason for this much later, when I stumbled upon another form of Earth energy which entered the broad side of the buildings and was responsible for their precise location.

New Graves Attract Energy

Other aspects of this phenomenon were found. At the burial-ground of Lawers, on the north side of Loch Tay, when some friends asked me to teach them to find this particular form of Earth energy. I showed them how to find the outside 'working edge', with other similar waves running parallel to it. (Burial-grounds, like castles, were always placed on these powerful points.) One person found that many of the waves were focused into a recent interment instead of flowing evenly across the burial-ground. This was another aspect of the cavity-seeking qualities of cup-mark energy. This time it was tuning into a cavity below ground (see Figure 12).

Figure 12: This old burial-ground has been placed at the outer edge of a cup-mark ley. For clarity, the wave effect is not shown. Notice that the waves are more concentrated at the outer edge (top of illustration) and that the recent interment attracts a number of waves.

Quarries

Sheep fanks (circular structures of drystone walling) and quarries also pulled this circuit in from some considerable distance. While doggedly following a cup-mark ley, I would sometimes be confronted with a yawning chasm directly in my path, through the centre of which the working edge of the cup-mark ley neatly passed.

Quarries, like any other resonant cavity, emit one wave which spirals out for some distance before eventually collapsing back to complete the circuit and another wave travelling in the opposite direction, which does likewise. When I walked out from the centre of the spiral in a quarry, the interval between each wave decreased until I found the outside 'working' wave. This is similar to the cup-mark leys, which have waves compacted close together at the outside edge, where burial-grounds are situated.

WAVELENGTH AND AMPLITUDE

The sinuous waves in both straight and cup-mark leys both have amplitude and wavelength. The wavelength is measured from two similar points on each wave, whilst the amplitude is from the central line to the crest of the wave. Straight leys have waves which do not move (standing waves) and cup-mark leys have just one wave which has a cycle – imagine tying a rope to a pole and shaking it slowly from side to side.

If you carefully follow such a wave on snow-covered ground, your footprints will indicate the wide sinuous energy. After a few minutes, stop and retrace your steps. Initially, you will retrace your footprints, but after a few seconds you will be out of phase, and it will take almost two minutes before you are completely back in phase again.

SHAPE WAVES

The discovery that cup-mark energy is attracted to cavities had been preying on my mind for some time that winter. I was still working the cup-mark leys when an opportunity for further research presented itself, after another series of winter storm casualties. This culminated in several sheep skeletons dotted along a cup-mark ley.

On my first encounter with the sheep's skull I had noticed that the outside wave I had been following had given a curious little circle directly above the skull, which made me suspect that the skull itself radiated energy. Now, when I tuned into one of the skulls, I found a 'shape wave' circling around it, similar to the stone at Connachan Farm, as well as to quarries and other resonant cavities. The wave spiralled out from the skull until it collapsed back to begin another circuit *ad infinitum*. It was emitted from one side of the skull, spiralled clockwise in an ever-increasing replica of the skull's shape, eventually collapsing back into it from the opposite side, no matter which way the skull was turned. The image formed by this shape wave from the skull was 354 feet (108 metres) taken across the width of the skull. There was also an identical shape wave, but in the opposite direction, anticlockwise. The waves were compressed together at the outer edge, just like the cup-mark ley *(see Figure 13)*.

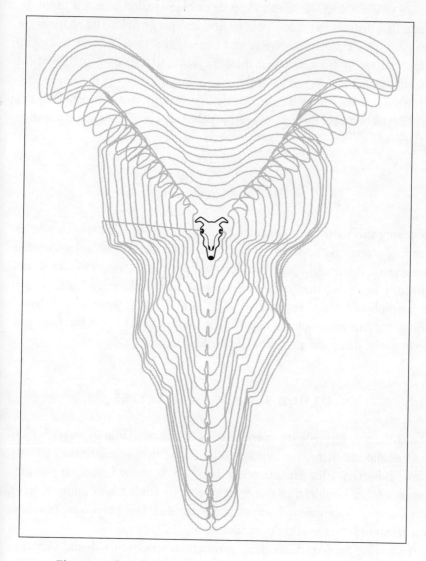

Figure 13: The telluric pattern of energy around a sheep's skull.

What had happened was now becoming clearer. The incoming cup-mark energy, as it chanced to touch the shape wave created by the skull, was directed towards the centre, passing through it and continuing on its way. There seems to be a law of physics which insists that the incoming cup-mark waves radiate inwards at right angles when they contact such a shape wave.

A similar type of shape wave is produced by any object standing on the surface of the planet – a telephone pole or high tension pole, for example. I tested an ordinary wooden pole to find its energy field. The shape wave around it was circular, as one would expect, and travelled out clockwise before collapsing back to begin the anticlockwise circuit again. This field extended as far as the shadow of the pole.

This shape wave may be induced by solar energy. The wavelength is 144 inches (366 cm) and the amplitude 24 inches (61 cm). The cycle is a standing one.

The Chieftain's Grave

Following this discovery, I decided to investigate 'the Chieftain's Grave', a standing stone on the shore of Loch Rannoch, to find its solar-induced shape wave. A wave of energy was emitted down the shadow of this stone, faithfully following the outline on the ground, wavelength 86 inches (218 cm), amplitude 8 inches (20 cm). This is a standing wave. It also has a strange 'mirror image' circuit copying the shadow of the stone, but falling in the opposite direction, into the sun (see Figure 15).

OTHER STRANGE QUALITIES

In open country, cup-mark energy travels in smooth, sinuous waves, which can be followed using the divining rod. I found that on a number of occasions, however, after encountering boulders, it would veer, apparently towards other boulders, as if it were selectively tuning into them. A wave was sometimes compressed, sometimes expanded. This perplexing problem was resolved by yet another coincidence.

Following the outside working wave across a steep hillside full of rocks, I found the wave suddenly turned at right angles and travelled uphill for

Figure 14: The Chieftain, Loch Rannoch. There is a tiny incised carving of an axe on the reverse. Schiehallion, the Faery Hill of the Caledonians, with its white quartzite speckled slopes, is at top left.

Figure 15: A wave of telluric energy flows down the shadow of the Chieftain standing stone, accurately following its contours. There is also a mirror image of energy into the sun.

some distance. This was quite unusual. As I walked slowly on, puzzled by this curious departure, I noticed that one of the boulders the wave had tuned into had the remains of an iron spike embedded into it. A short distance away, another similar boulder, also with a decaying iron spike, was the focal point. Then, as abruptly as it started, the wave swung back onto its original track, towards a loch, almost as if it had strayed too far from its original programmed route.

The iron-studded boulders had been part of a drystone wall and at one time had been strung with wire to form a boundary fence. An avalanche had destroyed it, leaving the boulders scattered in disarray. In effect, there were now a number of boulders, each with an iron core, randomly distributed.

With mounting curiosity, I retraced my steps. The cup-mark energy had, by chance, encountered the first iron-spiked boulder and then begun to seek out other similar boulders, before breaking off, back to its original route. These particular boulders had, apparently, a powerful attraction, which I was later to call 'sympathetic resonance'. Later still I was to encounter a similar effect with the stumps of trees in a cleared forest. It is probable that any objects in tandem, made of the same material, would exhibit this effect, providing the cup-mark ley had been programmed to find them.

Reflecting on my original theory of cavity-seeking energy, which had picked out the bodies of animals between Loch Tay and Loch Earn, I could see that sympathetic resonance of this type could also have been a factor in the attraction of the energy to these animal carcasses.

THE STRANGEST CHARACTERISTIC OF ALL

Some months later I was following a long sinuous cup-mark wave in Glen Lyon. With experience, I had no need to concentrate at all and my mind wandered as I walked along, enjoying the beautiful scenery and thinking of a host of trivialities.

Then, without warning, the wavelength began to decrease. From a measured 24 feet, 2 inches (7 metres, 32 cm), it suddenly decreased to less than a yard, while the amplitude remained the same (3 feet, 8 inches or 1 metre, 7 cm), making me weave sharply from side to side. Obviously, there had been an input of energy from some source, but where?

As I concentrated on this new quirk, the wavelength gradually increased, until it was back to its original length. 'Perhaps it was interference from a crossing ley,' I thought, so I followed the wave back the way I had come, only to find that it obstinately refused to repeat the occurrence, so I walked on and gradually forgot about the incident.

A few minutes later there was a repeat performance and I floundered around, bewildered by this sudden change in the energy's characteristics. Again, reversing direction and concentrating on trying to explain the anomaly failed miserably.

Puzzled, I stopped and took stock of the situation. After a little while, with growing trepidation, I realized that there *was* a link. On both occasions I had been thinking of the years a friend and I had roamed the hills together, before his early death. When I once more concentrated on these thoughts and followed the wave, the same effect took place!

When I cleared my mind of any thoughts, the wavelength eased out to its normal distance, but every time I concentrated on my deceased friend, or anyone else who had died, the wavelength decreased, although it did take a little while to take effect with some people I had known – the longer they had been dead, it seemed, the longer it took for this strange energy input to take effect. Thinking of ancient warriors, like Fingal for instance, also worked, but concentrating on someone still alive had no effect whatsoever.

Since then I have not taken this any further, and I leave it to others to investigate and explain this characteristic of cup-mark leys. Straight leys are not affected in this way. I doubt if this is a personal quirk, but it was with unease that I realized that this type of energy was one of the most important of the telluric energies connected with the ancient burial-grounds.

MODERN ATTRACTIONS

On several occasions the circuit would pointedly swing away from its normal route and tune into one of the high-tension suspension towers of the national grid, noticeably on the north shore of Loch Rannoch. It passed neatly between the legs of the pylons, one after the other, for some miles, until it abruptly veered back to its original course. A few other researchers had noticed this before and believed that the wave had simply attached itself to the electric or electromagnetic fields associated with HT cables. However, on several occasions, in open farmland, the wave I had been following had tuned into water derricks – windmills with a very similar construction to HT pylons – therefore the electric field theory could not be valid.

Closer inspection revealed that the legs of the pylons emit their own highly elliptical circuit, radiating away from each other. (The wooden two-legged pylons had similar telluric loops from their legs.) The energy induced by the feet of pylons, whether of wood or metal, forms a telluric 'net' which captures the roving cup-mark ley when it happens to be in the vicinity *(see Figure 16)*.

BARRIERS

Cup-mark energy avoids Forestry Commission plantations. The trees are so close together that they form an impenetrable barrier. Often, the energy will deviate some distance to pass by the edge, or travel down the firebreaks.

Wire fences are another noticeably awkward barrier. I noted that where a cup-mark ley crossed a field surrounded by a wire fence it would enter by a wooden gate, or an open metal gate, and exit by the distant corner post, almost as if it were leaving the unpleasant obstacle to the last possible moment. Other favourite entrance and exit points were via collapsed or partially collapsed drystone dykes.

Figure 16: The outside 'working' wave of this cup-mark energy ley passes through the tiny standing stone 'the Bhacain', bottom left, then tunes into a resonant cavity (oil drum) and through the weakest point in the wall. It is then attracted through the HT pylons to the horse trough containing water before passing down the line of HT pylons.

Now it is time to go back to the Connachan Farm stone and follow the shells of energy from its basic shape wave to its outer energy shell, remembering the qualities of cup-mark leys:

1 Their ability to follow the contours of hills.
2 Their cavity-seeking qualities.
3 Their sympathetic resonance to objects.
4 Their ability to tune into lochs and small bodies of water.
5 Their taking the easiest route, one devoid of obstacles if possible.
6 Their 'shell', comprised of a single wave of energy spiralling out from a powerful cup-marked stone. The outer working edge is where the waves are closest together.

THE CUP-MARK
SKELETON

A Portal into the Past

The great book of Nature can only be read by those who
know the language in which it was written.

GALILEO GALILEI, ITALIAN PHYSICIST

AND ASTRONOMER, 1564–1642

Near Connachan Farm, opposite Foulford Inn, at the entrance to the Sma'
Glen in Perthshire, is the recumbent megalith which has grudgingly yielded
many of its secrets. It is heavily adorned with cup-marks and serves an
entirely different and more powerful function than any of the standing
stones in the area. The reason for its particularly powerful nature may be an
underground aquifer several hundred feet down and several hundred feet
wide.

From this stone, a wave can be found spiralling out clockwise, until
it abruptly leaves at an acute angle and travels across country to a small
mound about 100 yards away, spirals around this in turn, then returns to the
stone, inside the original spiral (see Figure 17).

The spiral is formed by a secondary wave of energy pulsing from the
stone and interacting with the spiral. To understand this it is better to think
of the first or primary spiral as a series of dots, travelling outwards in ever-
increasing circles from the stone. The secondary pulsing energy travels
around every dot and back until, having reached its zenith, it collapses,
ready to begin the circuit afresh (see Figures 18 and 19).

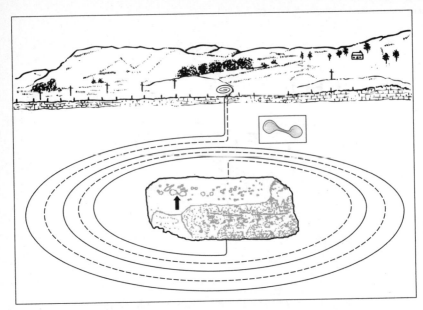

Figure 17: The primary spiral. A wave is emitted from the stone, spirals around it, then is ejected to the small mound at the top of the picture. The inset shows the dumb-bell shaped petroglyph.

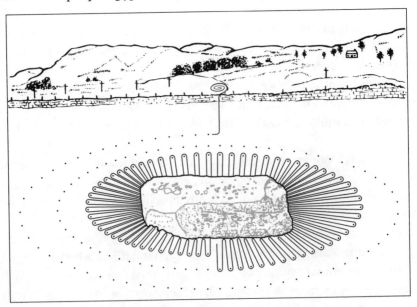

Figure 18: Imagine the spiral as a series of dots. A second wave is emitted from the stone around each dot and back...

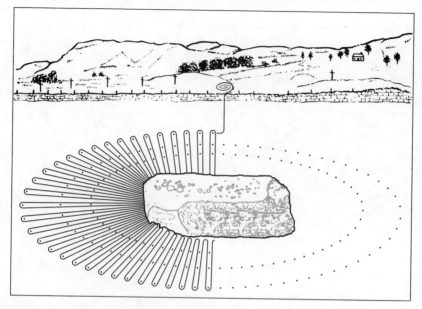

Figure 19: ...until it collapses back into the stone to begin the circuit afresh. The primary wave is now free to travel to the mound. Note that the area round this stone is concave in shape, like a modern TV satellite dish.

The primary spiral, held in place by this pulsing energy, collapses and is ejected to find an attractive location, in this case the low mound, which it spirals around a few times, before returning to the stone, inside the primary spiral, forming a dumb-bell shape very similar to a prominent cup-mark on the surface of the stone. Initially, I believed that this pattern was the secret of this particular cup-mark, but it turned out to be misleading.

THE SKELETON

This spiral is the initial building block of the energy circuits from the cup-marked stone and around it is formed a larger circuit, like the skeleton of a dumb-bell, which in turn has another shell of energy, this time strikingly like the dumb-bell shaped petroglyph.

Let us follow the skeleton circuit from the stone. For the sake of simplicity, assume that the energy is emitted from the stone and travels in a clockwise direction, although in practice it is very much more complicated than this, since there appears to be inputs of energy from other sources at various points.

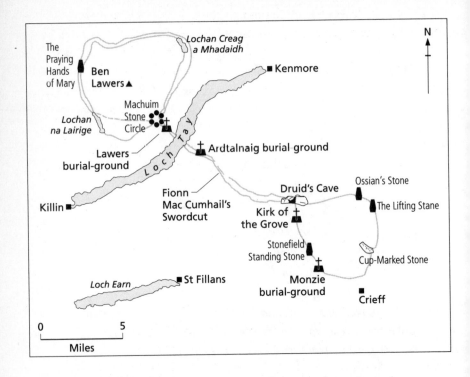

Map 2: Telluric energy from the cup-marked stone (bottom right) is attracted clockwise up to the concave cavity of the Druid's Cave, passes through interstices at the rear and then travels across the hills to Fionn Mac Cumhail's Swordcut and further north to the centre of Loch Tay. Passing across the water, it enters Machuim stone circle and is then warped into two circuits around Ben Lawers. Exiting from the stone circle it travels back to the Druid's Cave and on to the cup-marked stone.

This type of energy has several peculiarities: it normally contours hills, it is attracted to the centre of bodies of water, like lochs, and to resonating cavities, which attract it uphill.

There are four old communal burial-grounds and two individual cists on this circuit. The dashed line from Machuim stone circle to the north-west is the circuit's presumed original route, as the modern reservoir, Lochan na Lairige, deforms the original path.

The energy leaves the stone *(lower right of Map 2)* and travels along the road to Monzie, where it passes through the first of the churches and burial-grounds on this circuit. From here it contours round to the standing stone at Stonefield Farm mentioned earlier, before travelling in a north-easterly direction to the Druid's Cave, and, as it does so, through the site of another chapel, the Kirk of the Grove. Around this chapel, long ago, according to one source, there was a burial-ground, although there is nothing of it to be seen today.[1] (The word 'grove' at the focal point of this system would have delighted Alfred Watkins, since his studies led him to understand that any place so named was on a ley line.)[2]

THE DRUID'S CAVE

Figure 20: A portal into another world – the Druid's Cave from the remains of the Kirk of the Grove. This, the focal point of the cup-mark leys for a wide area, may explain why this type of ley tunes into cavities as it crosses the country.

Just a few hundred yards from the entrance to the Druid's Cave in this bleak inhospitable landscape is a lone battered and aged Scots pine tree. It has been left in peace for a long time, as there is a strange story attached to it. It is said that if any man cuts off a branch of this tree, the tree will survive, but the man will die. This is similar to the classical story of *The Golden Bough*, where the current Rex Nemorensis, the keeper of the tree, is challenged to mortal combat by any contender who wishes to fight to the death, simply by breaking off a branch of the sacred tree and offering it to the current king.

The Druid's Cave itself is an impressive man-made cave, built from several large boulders. The largest is a 16-foot (5-metre) square block, with another five large slabs placed against it to form a cavity slightly smaller than the average living-room. Not surprisingly this cavern attracts the cup-mark energy from a wide area and is the heart of the energy system for a large area of Scotland and northern England. The structure is primitive, the size impressive.

Since the cave is the nucleus of the system, with energy of different types associated with it, it is not surprising that there is at least one paranormal story connected with it. The shepherd who supervises this area told me that he climbed up to the cave one day with his collie at his heels to see if there were any dead sheep inside. He entered the cave and was startled to hear a moaning sound, as if a wind was soughing around the massive boulders. It was a hot day, however, hot enough for him to be in shirt sleeves, with not a breath of wind in the air. The collie, meantime, remained at the entrance, cowing with ears held back and refusing to go any further.

The slabs resting against the boulder have been placed in a concave shape, with interstices at the rear, to the north, and through one of these gaps the energy streams out, contouring high across the hills, the huge cave having already attracted the circuit to a height of 1,600 feet (487 metres).

THE FLOWER OF HIGHLAND MANHOOD

Some 3.5 miles (6 kilometres) to the north-east, the circuit tunes into another form of cavity – Fionn Mac Cumhail's Swordcut, a large ravine near the summit of the Sidh or Faery Hill of Ardtalnaig, to the south of Loch Tay. Fionn Mac Cumhail, better known as Fingal, was one of the mighty warriors of ancient times, who kept the peace in Ireland as well

Figure 21: This ravine was carved, according to legend, by the warrior Fionn Mac Cumhail using his magic sword. Snow still lies here on the first day of July 1997.

as Scotland. Thought by some historians to have been the captain of the warriors of King Cormack around AD 224–83, it was he who gave the ravine its name. Standing with one foot on a hill to the east of the Sidh of Ardtalnaig and one foot to the west, he is said to have stooped to drink out of Loch Tay. Then, with one swipe of his magic sword, Mac-an-Luin, every stroke of which was mortal, he carved out this chasm *(see Figure 21)*. He was indeed a mighty man of old, as the hills are several miles apart!

This is not the last we shall hear of Fionn, or of his band of warriors, the Fian, or his father Cumhail, for that matter. Even his son Ossian, the warrior who became blind in later life and who ended his days as one of the greatest bards, crops up again on the other side of this circuit.

The name Cumhail signifies a sky god (hence the word 'cumulus') and the warriors of this Celtic period, like their chief, were a magnificent breed of men. Proud and boastful with magical qualities, they wore colourful garments, had a highly developed artistic and musical culture, were careful of their personal hygiene, kept their word loyally and provided laws to govern their countries. On horse, chariot or foot, they were fierce adversaries for the Romans. In winter this peace-keeping army was quartered amongst the civilian population. In summer they roamed the country engaged in their favourite pastime of hunting deer and wild boar, while at the same time honing their strength and skills.

Early in this research I came to the conclusion that these ancient legends of warriors, who may well have existed as early heroes, poets and kings, were often allegorical tales of the qualities and location of the cup-mark circuits.

THE ENERGY TUNES INTO THE CENTRE OF LOCH TAY

From the ravine, where the stream of energy is focused to a few feet wide, it now descends rapidly, tuning into the centre of Loch Tay, which forms a very powerful attraction. It passes through the burial-ground at Ardtalnaig, the third burial-ground so far, down to the shore and into the loch.

Adept at following this form of energy by now, I picked it up on the north shore and followed it up to the church at Lawers, then further up some steep ground to the burial-ground there and higher still to the stone circle at Machuim. Entering this six-stone circle from the south, the energy was warped through the gap between two of the stones on the west side and up over the foothills of Ben Lawers, to Loch na Lairige, now a reservoir, perched near the top of the pass, and down into Glen Lyon, the Crooked Glen of the Stones.

'THE PRAYING HANDS OF MARY'

On a blistering hot day I followed the circuit until I was confronted with a huge rock, almost like an unusually large standing stone. It was immediately apparent that this was not natural. Some 13 feet (4 metres) high, its massive

Figure 22: The Praying Hands of Mary.

bulk overshadowed me. Sensing something unusual and important, I walked round it and was thrilled to see the broad face change into two narrow pillars *(see plate section)*. As I looked between the split stone, in the distance I knew, just out of sight, was Fortingall burial-ground, famed for its ancient yew tree, and beyond that, a cluster of four-stone circles.

From the other side, the summit of Creag nan Eildeag appeared to the west in accurate alignment between the two narrow tongues of rock. There could be no mistaking it: a straight ley it must be.

A glance at the map revealed that Meggernie Castle was the next in line to the west and a little further on was its tiny burial-ground, where I had found the tunnel.

The original size of the stone pillar must have been impressive, judging by the amount of debris scattered at its base. Its width is now less than half of what it must have been, and its height must have been appreciably higher.

A local farmer told me that this rock was well enough known to himself and his shepherds. They called it 'the Split Rock' or 'the Praying Hands of Mary', but few others could have seen it tucked away here, visible from the road only with difficulty.

THE GHOST OF A ROMAN

I followed the old hill track, as old as the circuit itself, down to the floor of the glen. This was as far north as the circuit travelled and I now followed it alongside the river, through the site of another old church at Roro Farm and on to another isolated farm, Roromore, where the intrigued shepherd asked me what I was doing. 'Can that explain the ghost in my upstairs corridor?' he asked brightly, after I had given him a rough outline of my research.

Apparently several years ago, a guest, a businessman from London, had had to go to the toilet early in the morning and had been aghast to see the figure of a Roman centurion materialize in the corridor, then fade away. As it happened, there had been a small Roman camp at Fortingall, 5 miles (8 kilometres) to the east, where Pontius Pilate was reputedly born.

I continued following the circuit and it became obvious that it was returning over the top of the hill, this time through a jumbled mass of debris from the scarred hillface above. Guessing that another loch was attracting the cup-mark ley, I wasn't in the least surprised to see Lochan Creag a' Mhadaidh (the Loch of the Rock of the Fox), in front of me at the summit of the east shoulder of the Ben Lawers range. Then the energy ran down into Machuim stone circle and through the gap between another two of the stones, before warping out to begin another circuit running roughly parallel to the first back to the stone circle.

From here, on its homeward journey, it passed through Lawers burial-ground for the second time, the old cemetery having one of its corners truncated, perhaps because of the curving nature of the cup-mark ley here, and back across Loch Tay, into Fingal's Swordcut. From here it crossed the hills back to the Druid's Cave, where it entered one of the gaps at the rear, then exited from the mouth and ran down the Auchnafree road to

Craignaver burial-ground, close to the road, down the Sma' Glen, under a bridge and on to Ossian's stone. This is a large square stone, which rested at one time, reputedly, on the remains of Ossian, the blind poet son of Fingal.

The last leg of this circuit, just a few miles, followed the old road up through this beautiful narrow glen to the Lifting Stane, part of the original circuit which was used as a test of strength for Covenanters, who had to lift the heavy boulder on top. Then it was back to the stone at Connachan Farm.

It is interesting to look at the complete circuit *(see Map 2)*. It bears a striking similarity to the dumb-bell shaped cup-mark, but almost like a skeleton. It shows the circuit designed to accept seven burial-grounds.

Figure 23: Plan view of the recumbent stone at Connachan Farm. The cup-marks, for some reason, are deeper at the far end.

CAVE ROOFS, DOMES AND SATELLITE DISHES

There are two important focal points of telluric power on this circuit: the concave cavity inside the Druid's Cave and the concave depression in the hills which houses the Connachan Farm cup-marked stone.

Down the millennia, from the Neolithic period through to the Bronze Age, the Etruscan, Greek, Roman, Christian, Islamic religions and the many others of today, there is a common denominator in sacred places – the physics of the dome. This continues quietly to work its magic upon us, from the earliest realization of its significance to the fainter echoes of its potential today. Renaissance architects believed that the classical domed temple had special associations with divinity, perfection and unity, while in Roman times, a *cella* was the underground central chamber in a temple. Over the centuries this was corrupted into the word 'cellar'.

A knowledge of the power of the dome can explain some types of paranormal phenomena. Both spherical and parabolic curves will focus energies, not only light, as in a mirror, but also sound, acoustics (as with radars and sonars), heat (as in the thermal cookers used now in the Third World) and energy.

For gardeners, a simple example of the power of curved surfaces to focus energy is a dome-shaped drop of water on a plant leaf. In bright sun this will focus heat from the sun and burn the leaf below. For car owners, a puddle of water on the roof and bonnet of some cars can have the same effect, leading to light patches of paintwork.

The principle of energy focusing by domes was described by Nikola Tesla in 1900 and in 1904 the German Hulsmeyer designed the *Telemobiloskop* (mobile telephonescope) as an anti-collision device for ships, based on this idea. The first patent for radar was credited to the Germans.[3]

In Sardinia there are 50 sophisticated sanctuaries dating from 1000 BC all with domes of stone, all built over sacred springs and wells, scattered all over the island. Some of these waters are still credited with healing powers.[4]

If you look around, you will probably see the same dome shape on the satellite TV dishes of your neighbours' houses, but you will also see, in the centre of the dish, a rod-like antenna which picks up the focused signal and transfers it down the cable to your television set. Similarly, at the beginning of the Second World War at least one cliff face on the English coast had a special concave alcove sculpted into its surface and, with other similarly shaped structures made of metal at other less geologically convenient locations, was used as a listening post, ready to pick up the first amplified hum of invading aircraft. Special listeners, some of them blind, since such people often have more acute hearing, manned these posts.[5]

An easy and practical demonstration of this focusing effect, which applies to light, sound and all electromagnetic signals, is the small magnifying mirror found in many bathrooms. Here again the signal input, in this case light, is amplified and focused to a point. Exactly the same effect is found with any energy, whether light waves or acoustic waves. It is relevant to note that Apollonius Rhodius, a Greek poet, is reported as writing: 'Stones placed at the apex of a Tumulus are so sensitive as to be movable by the mind.'[6]

Figure 24 shows some of the domes world-wide and also some very twentieth-century uses for (nearly) the same effect. In Holland, for instance, at Hune-bedden (Giant's Bed) on the northern outskirts of Borger, sitting beside an 80-foot (24-metre) dolmen is a fine trilithon where 'the capstones are rounded like tortoiseshells'.[7] This is dated to before the Bronze Age, around 3400 BC, and is similar to the many other dolmens or cromlechs scattered around the British Isles, like Chûn Quoit in Cornwall.

'Otherworldly Whistlings' in a Cave

In the 1990s, Sean Jones, a British traveller, was close to Zutrol Puk, on the sacred Mount Kailas in Tibet. Seeking shelter for the night, he entered a cave-like place. Under a concave slice of rock, to his great surprise, when he awoke he found himself serenaded by 'otherworldly whistlings, and what seemed to be bird calls mixed with the sound of rocks and water falling'. 'Am I really hearing this?' he asked himself. Then he realized that the naturally-shaped rock was a kind of acoustic dish that gathered all the sounds of the mountain and transferred them into a form of natural music, rather like the noise the shepherd had heard in the Druid's Cave. Like the shepherd, Sean Jones had been honoured by a practical demonstration of curved surfaces.[8]

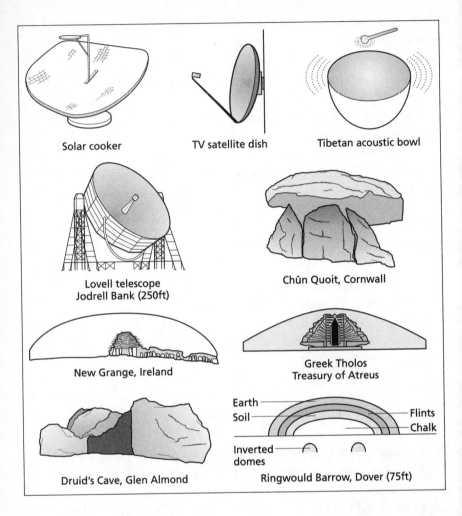

Figure 24: Different types of parabolic surfaces used to focus energies down through the ages.

Keeping Bad Spirits at Bay

Another indication of the reflective and refractive properties of concave surfaces is their appearance in both historical and mythical tradition.

A curious fact from Babylonia, for example, is that the citizens there were found to have made 'Devil Traps' by burying inverted bowls beneath the floor, concave side up. These were to keep bad spirits away. It is interesting to realize that 5,000 years ago, the fact that not all Earth energies were good was already known.[9]

The archaeologist and historian Dr Tom Lethbridge noted also that centuries ago in the UK bells were buried to ward off malignant forces. There is the legend that at Thetford Castle in Norfolk, when the priory was destroyed in the Dissolution, six silver bells were buried beneath the hill on which the castle now stands.[10]

On the other side of the world, in Japanese myth, Emm-O was the chief of the Jigokan, the underground hell. He would ride past lines of men to pass judgement upon them and the sentence would be reflected and amplified back to them by a great bronze mirror on his chest.

And what is the significance of the bowl of the Nig-Gil-ma of Babylon, made of silver and known as 'the Preserver of the Seeds of Mankind'?[11]

Greek Caves

The word 'Hypogeum' is derived from the Greek *Hypogeios*, meaning 'underground', and is used as a term to cover the cult centres of Chalcolithic Malta, built about 3500 BC. It is thought that this complex had its beginnings as a natural cave to the rear of a temple, and the cave was progressively enlarged and embellished in an exact imitation of a temple. An intriguing part of the Hypogeum is the Oracle Chamber, which has a strange acoustic property. In this chamber is a shallow hole in the wall, something like a niche. The voice of a man facing the hole will echo eerily, but there is no such effect with the higher pitched female voice.[12]

In *Unknown Greece* (Johnson, 1973) Pillemont describes the Tholos at the Tomb of Agamemnon, or Treasury of Atreus, as 'one of the most extraordinary monuments in the whole of Greece'.[13] It is reached by a deep trench whose sides are lined with carefully hewn stones. The Tholos is shaped like a beehive, 33 feet (13 metres) high and 48 feet (14.5 metres) in diameter. The cupola, or dome, is formed of 33 superimposed corbelled rings, surmounted by a round slab. Pausanias and other writers of antiquity called these *tholoi* 'treasure houses'. What was the treasure?

Dragons

Let us come forward to our own Anglo-Saxon history and the epic poem *Beowulf*. In the Gnomic verses is written *Draca sceal on Hlaewe, frod, fraetwum wlanc* (The dragon shall be in the tumulus, old, rich in treasures). As Margaret Gelling notes, in relation to placenames of tumuli, or domed man-made forms in the landscape, 'If not flying through the air, a dragon was most likely to be found in a barrow.' When this very visual remark is placed in the context of places in England with 'Draca' or 'Wyrm' in their name, dozens of them relate to tumuli, where dragons guard treasure. Gelling lists Drakelow, Dragley, Drechowe and Drakehowe. Drakestone, near Sudbury, is at the eastern end of a fault. Wormegay, south-east of King's Lynn in Norfolk, has a legendary dragon. Then there are the 'Shuck' placenames – Scucca was an early name for a demon – including Shugborough in Staffordshire, Shuckbugh in Warwickshire and Shucknall in Herefordshire. There are many others. Pucca, Puck and Pouke, meanwhile, mean 'goblin', as does Hob.

Field names as well as placenames can yield a rich haul of meaning, provided that the antiquity of the field name can be verified from old county records offices.

One has to ask, what phenomena did our ancestors experience in these places to lead them to give such names to sites? The many 'Grim' names, Gelling feels, are associated with Woden. Anne Silk has found a possible link with lightning-prone areas, with ironstone or basalt below ground. Further work has to be done on this theoretical aspect, but it should be noticed that once rocks have been struck by lightning, their magnetic properties change. As Professor Nagata writes in *Rock Magnetism*,

> *Generally speaking, the residual permanent magnetization possessed by a rock mass in its natural state in the field can be called its natural remanent magnetization. But a rock mass very near the earth's surface may have a rather intense residual magnetization as the result of the sudden occurrence of a strong magnetic field caused by a thunderbolt on or near the rock mass.*[14]

BEEHIVE STRUCTURES IN FRANCE

Most people have heard of Rennes-le-Château in south-west France and the strange story of its former priest, Father Saunière, who reputedly stumbled upon a great secret and then came into great wealth. But the historian Henry Lincoln has found another feature of the region which has so far received little attention. In the area known as Capitelles, high in the hills above Coustaussa, there are hundreds of stone-built cells thought to be of great antiquity. As Lincoln states, 'Little has been written about the early history of this part of France.'[15] These beehive-shaped structures are 'scattered across the countryside as far as the eye [can] see'. Each contains one small room with a doorway and a narrow window. Some are square, some are rectangular, some ovoid and some circular. All had 'beautifully and skilfully constructed dry-stone domed roofs'. A historian who examined Lincoln's photographs described them as reminiscent of neolithic chambers. Roy Davies, then the editor of the BBC *Timewatch* programme, found the whole site similar to Mycenae in Greece.

Rennes-le-Château is only half a mile (800 metres) away from Capitelles. However, if we consider Earth energy sources, there are some surprises. Equidistant from Rennes-le-Château and Coustaussa is Roque Fumade (Smoking Rock), which Lincoln says, in a letter to the author in 1992, 'Certainly still smokes.' Four miles (6.5 kilometres) to the east is Fôret de l'Orme Mort (Forest of the Dead Worm) and at Rennes-les-Bains, a mile (1.6 kilometres) away, there are geothermal hot water baths.

THE PHYSICS OF CONCAVE SURFACES

Concave surfaces, then, such as those on saucer-like satellite dishes, had a special significance for peoples of old, as well as for many religions nowadays. They also have great importance in current communications technology. Why should this be so?

As we have seen, such surfaces have a special property by virtue of their concave shape. This is the ability to focus many types of radiation into a very small area, due to the fact that the angle of incidence for incident light, sound and radiation equals the angle of reflection (*see Figure 25*).

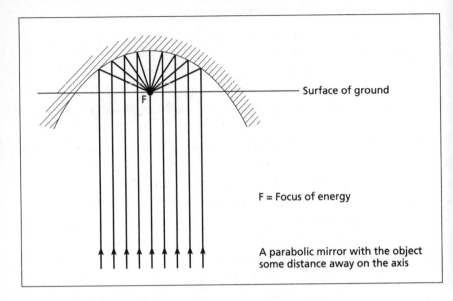

Figure 25: Energy focus in concave surfaces.

Ultrasonic energy for therapeutic and military use is normally focused by means of either a curved transducer or an acoustic lens. For the former the energy is brought to a focus at its centre of curvature. Quartz is also used for ultrasonic propagation, the lower frequencies being produced when the crystal is cut across its width.[16]

Many writers have observed the layering of alternate and inorganic matter in the roofs of tumuli. There is an interesting parallel in physics known as giant magnetoresistance. In this, the resistivity of a layered structure of alternate magnetic and non-magnetic materials dramatically changes when a sufficiently high magnetic field is applied. The effect seems to be due to the fact that the magnetizations in the alternate layers are anti-parallel. At zero field the resistivity is at a maximum, but in high fields the magnetizations become parallel to the applied field and resistance drops sharply.[17]

REFERENCES

1   Oliphant, Anderson and Ferrier, *Historic Scenes in Perthshire*, 1880

2   Alfred Watkins, *Early British Trackways*, Simpkin Marshall, 1922

3   P. S. Hall, *Battlehead Weapons Systems*, Brassey, 1991

4   D. Mackenzie, *Crete in Myth and Legend*, Senate, 1996

5   Robert Buderi, *The Invention That Changed the World*, Little, Brown and Company, 1996

6   Apollonius Rhodius, quoted in M. A. Thalbourne, 'Apollonius of Tyana', *Journal of the Society for Psychical Research*, 60:837 (1995) 240–8

7   Aubrey Burl, *Prehistoric Stone Circles*, Shire, 1977

8   J. Snelling, *The Sacred Mountain: Tibet's Mt Kailas*, East–West Press, 1990

9   *Electronics World*, January 1995

10 P. Howat, *Norfolk Ghosts and Legends*, Countryside Books, 1993

11 D. A. McKenzie, *China and Japan: Myths and Legends*, Senate, 1995

12 J. Bradbury and A. Service, *The Standing Stones of Europe*, J. M. Dent, 1993

13 Pillemont, *Unknown Greece, Athens, The Peloponnesus*, Johnson, London, 1973

14 T. Nagata, *Rock Magnetism*, Maruzca, Tokyo, 1953

15 H. Lincoln, *The Holy Place*, Jonathan Cape, 1991

16 M. Wilson, *Energy*, TimeLife, 1965

17 J. Blitz, *Ultrasonics*, Butterworth, 1962

6

THE SECRET OF THE PETROGLYPHS

*A Mass Murder, an Unknown Cup-Marked
Stone and the Bubonic Plague*

> If the doors of perception were cleansed, everything would
> appear to Man as it is – infinite.
> WILLIAM BLAKE, 1757–1827,
> *THE MARRIAGE OF HEAVEN AND HELL*

When working on the circuit from Connachan Farm, I had often noticed that there were many ancient sites running roughly parallel to it. Burial-grounds, churches, stone circles and standing stones were all tantalizingly close, but appeared to belong to another circuit running alongside. When I eventually followed the leys through these sacred sites I found a circuit whose shape mirrors the dumb-bell petroglyph on the Connachan Farm stone.

For clarity, it is best to follow this circuit in a clockwise direction from some mounds near the village of Gilmerton, bottom right of Map 3. There is another connection here with the ancient warriors. According to local legend, Fingal's father, Cumhail, was defeated here by the Romans. Significantly, this site is where the circuit terminates, reflecting, perhaps, the death of the warrior.

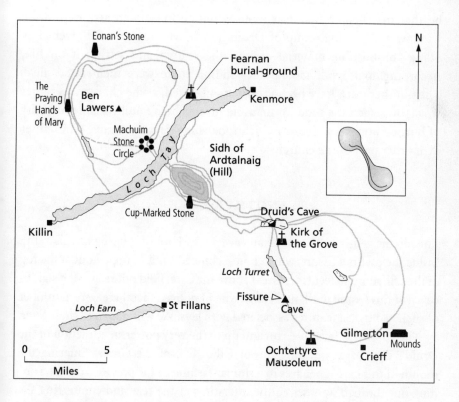

Map 3: This circuit mirrors the dumb-bell shaped petroglyph on the Connachan Farm stone (inset, top right). From several mounds at Gilmerton (bottom right), it curves round clockwise to the Druid's Cave and north to Loch Tay. The previous circuit tuned into the centre of the loch and this circuit now 'sees' the loch as two separate halves and crosses one quarter of its width to the west over to Glen Lyon and back across Loch Tay to the Druid's Cave and further on to Gilmerton. There are three communal burial-grounds on this circuit: Ochtertyre Mausoleum, Kirk of the Grove and Fearnan.

There are numerous legends of the burial-places of these warriors in Scotland and Ireland, with different localities claiming similar stories. Possibly these places have a similar association – the death of Cumhail at Gilmerton has similarities to the terminal points of a similar cup-mark system of telluric energies in Ireland.

The next site on this ley is Ochtertyre Mausoleum and burial-ground, on the site of a church destroyed in 1490 by two feuding clans, the Murrays and the Drummonds. One of the Murray archers, hiding in the old heather-thatched church, was foolish enough to send an arrow from the window at a passing group of Drummonds, who took fearful revenge by piling combustible material around the church and setting it on fire. According to legend, 120 families hiding there were incinerated alive. The number must have been grossly exaggerated, as the church was rather small, but when the modern mausoleum was being built, a large quantity of burned bones was found, which took some days to remove and reinter in another part of the churchyard.[1]

ANOTHER CAVE

The circuit gently rises to a small cave at the base of a perpendicular cliff. Inside the cave is a fissure, which I once climbed until I popped out at the top of the hill, some 50 feet (15 metres) above the cave. I did not realize the significance of this fissure until much later, when I noticed that there were a number of such geological features associated with leys. We will return to these later.

The cup-mark ley travels on and up to the very powerful attraction of the Druid's Cave, again passing through the Kirk of the Grove. Entering the mouth of this cave it behaves in a similar fashion to the previous circuit, running out through another of the interstices at the rear and contouring the hills to the Sidh of Ardtalnaig again, but this time much lower down, to another split stone, this time heavily cup-marked. Whether this stone has been carved by man or nature I have yet to find out, but the circuit goes on, through a nearby shieling and down towards Loch Tay, to an old road, which it follows, until about half a mile (a kilometre) from the shoreline, both the road and cup-mark ley turn sharply to follow the loch. Intrigued at the energy turning so abruptly, I retraced my steps to the bend in the road, to find that the road had been carved into the living rock. This 'peat road', as it is called, may well have been used for carrying fuel, but it is more likely to have been part of the construction of the cup-mark ley.

THE BUBONIC PLAGUE

The previous circuit centred itself on Loch Tay and this one now 'sees' the loch as two separate halves and contours the shore, bisecting the western half, before going up again to Lochan na Lairige and through the Praying Hands

Figure 26: St Adamnan's stone. Note the cross facing the camera.

of Mary to Glen Lyon, where I waded across the river waist-deep on a pleasant summer's day to continue the circuit on the far bank. I could see the next site as I waded – St Adamnan's or St Eonan's stone, a Christianized standing stone dedicated to the scribe of St Columba.

It was at this place, called A' Chreag Fhiannaidh, the Rock of Safety, that Eonan is said to have banished the plague in about AD 664. The people of the glen, terrified at the approach of the plague, here beseeched him, saying, 'Eonan of the ruddy cheeks, rise and check the plague of thy people. Save us from the death and let it not come upon us, east or west.' It is said that Eonan put his knowledge (of Earth energies?) to the test by raising his arm

79

Figure 27: The Rock of Safety in Glen Lyon, where St Eonan banished the plague.

and, with the people kneeling around him, he exhorted the devil body of the pestilence to come to him – almost too late, for a child was already dying just a stone's throw away. The plague, however, is said to have vanished into a nearby boulder, making in its passage a deep, round hole, almost as if it had been carved.

This fascinated me. Is it possible that plagues can follow telluric energies? It is well known that fleas from rats can carry bubonic plague, but I agree with other investigators that there are 'black streams' of natural Earth energies which are associated with illness in the population. Perhaps this cup-mark ley had turned 'black', attacking the immune system of those living upon it until they were at risk of infection.

Figure 28: This cup-marked stone is on the circuit to the west of the Sidh of Ardtalnaig.

The plague could hardly have bored a hole in the stone. It is more likely that Eonan did. In effect he may have short-circuited the cup-mark ley, stopping the plague in its tracks. He also took the very sensible precaution of sending the remaining healthy people up to their shielings in the hills, well away from the disease.

The most northerly point of the circuit now travels eastwards, following the road for some distance, but occasionally wandering off into nearby fields, then turns south, through the burial-ground at Fearnan and across the loch to the little village of Ardtalnaig, just touching its burial-ground. Along by the foot of the Sidh of Ardtalnaig it passes through a line of old shielings, down the long axes as usual, then back to the Druid's Cave. Here it enters one of the remaining gaps at the rear and circles down to the nest of mounds at Gilmerton.

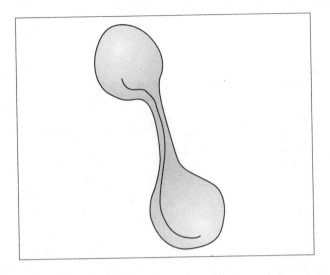

Figure 29: The dumb-bell shape. Note the 'S' shape inside.

Comparing Map 3 to the close-up picture of the dumb-bell cup-mark on the stone at Connachan Farm *(Figure 29)*, it can be seen that this circuit now shows a definite similarity to the cup-mark. Note also the weathered and incised line inside, which indicates the inner skeleton.

REFERENCES

1   John Hunter, *Chronicles of Strathearn*, W. B. MacDougall, 1886

7

THE ROAD TO RANNOCH

Walking the Serpent

Great things are done when men and mountains meet.
WILLIAM BLAKE, 1757–1827, *GNOMIC VERSES*

Flanking the previous cup-mark system is another shell of energy. It is very similar in character, but a look at Map 4 will show that it has been constructed in a slightly different manner.

This cup-mark ley also has the ability to tune into lochs and lochans, but, surprisingly, it also contours the edges of some lochs. I suspect that a special type of straight ley moulds it into shape. We will investigate this shortly.

Again, for the sake of clarity, let us assume that the circuit travels clockwise from the mounds at Gilmerton at the bottom right of Map 4. This circuit is emitted from these mounds as before, then follows a straight road for several miles to Drummond Pond.

Looking at the circuit on the map was at first very disconcerting, as there is a very obvious kink on its route. All the lochs in the past had helped mould the outline, but this one appeared as an anomaly, warping the system extensively. A little research, however, revealed the cause. Drummond Pond is a very recent addition to the topography of the area and has provided the cup-mark ley with a new and powerful attraction. In 1762, on the orders of the Countess of Perth, this area was flooded in order to cover the houses and land of the families who had taken part in the 1745 rebellion and had, in consequence, been granted land in this area. The countess was determined that their loyal service would be forgotten as quickly as possible.

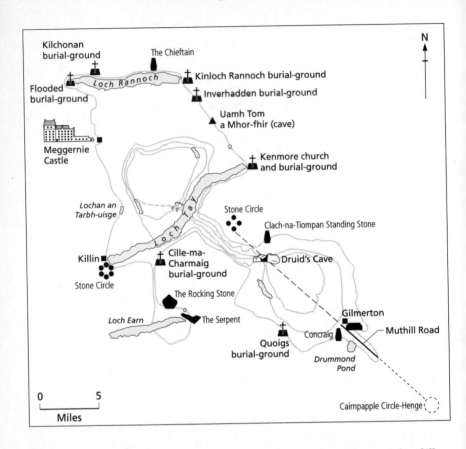

Map 4: Another shell of energy from the Gilmerton mounds (bottom right of illustration). Again travelling clockwise, it moves up to Loch Tay, contouring the hills to run back southwards to tune into the centre of Loch Earn, then north to Killin stone circle, further north to Loch Rannoch and south to Loch Tay, Clach-na-Tiompan standing stone and Gilmerton. There are seven burial-grounds on this circuit. Notice how it has been badly warped by tuning into Drummond Pond, a recently built loch (bottom right), and also the deliberate alignment from Cairnpapple, 54 miles (87 kilometres) to the south-east, to an 'old straight track' between Crieff and Muthill, now a modern road, through Ochtertyre burial-ground (not shown for clarity) and the Druid's Cave to the four-stone circle near Clach-na-Tiompan.

This is a good example of a comparatively modern construction altering the pattern of telluric energy. It can also be seen that a major long-distance ley from one of the most important sites in Scotland, the circle-henge of Cairnpapple, 33 miles (54 kilometres) to the south-east, runs accurately along the Muthill–Crieff road, originally an 'old straight track,' then through Ochtertyre Mausoleum to the Druid's Cave, terminating at the four-stone circle near Clach-na-Tiompan.

THE ROCKING STONE OF GLEN TARKEN

The circuit runs clockwise to a standing stone at Concraig Farm and then to a monument occupying a prominent position on a hill, once dominated by a wooden castle, then travels round to Quoigs burial-ground, across the hills to the Sidh of Ardtalnaig and Loch Tay, to the burial-ground of Cille-ma-Charmaig. Still contouring the hill, it starts to turn in a southerly direction, down Glen Beith. Following this section, I was dismayed, as this route was not my idea of how the circuit should look. It was leading me across a desolate 5-mile (8-kilometre) stretch of high moorland towards Loch Earn, and there was little I could do but follow it or abandon the project entirely.

Eventually, however, my persistence paid off handsomely. A huge boulder came into view and my divining rod led me unerringly towards it. This was the Glen Tarken Rocking Stone, the size of a small bungalow and poised like a faceted diamond on its point. It is estimated that at a height of 10 feet (3 metres) its circumference is 110 feet (34 metres) and it is about 25,000 cubic feet in mass. Sixty men can shelter under its overhang. At one time this huge boulder could rock to and fro at a push, but now it stands motionless, as solid as the hills themselves.

The effort and skill which went into the construction of this stone left me in awe – megalithic engineering at its finest. Years later I was to see it as a key part of the Earth energy system, with its faceted faces receiving and transmitting streams of telluric energy. Possibly, when it was working, its oscillations altered the wavelengths of the energy system.

As I left this strange monster I cast many a long wondering look at it as it gradually faded from my view and was lost in the corner of the glen. It was not to be the last time we would meet, as my research brought me back again and again to this spot.

THE SERPENT OF ST FILLANS

Across the hills in the direction of St Fillans the circuit led me to another small loch, Loch Boltachan, and down a few miles towards St Fillans. It was a day of thick fog and walking slowly along I was startled to hear a car a short distance away. Now aware that I had come much further than I had intended, I knelt down and peered through the mist over the edge of the strangely familiar rock I was walking along. A huge eye and garishly coloured teeth stared back at me! I had walked down the spine of the Serpent and onto its head. If the car had not passed I would have walked off its nose into thin air.

AN ANCIENT HEALING WELL

Continuing southward, I walked on, to the summit of Dundurn, a prominent cone-shaped hill overlooking Loch Earn. St Fillan once prayed on the flat rock on its summit, perched high above the glen. Two round depressions on this natural pulpit with its curious lipped edge marked the spot where he knelt, with the breathtaking scenery spread below.

There was, I knew, a well just below the summit. For centuries, people with rheumatism would drink the water and then be pulled several hundred feet to the bottom by their ankles – a sure cure for their ailment!

I fully expected the circuit to tune into this well, but it was not to be. Pointedly refusing to touch the well, it passed just a few yards away. I walked on, rather irritated by this refusal to add such an obvious power point to my map.

In *The Sun and the Serpent* (Pendragon Press, 1989) Hamish Miller and Paul Broadhurst consider wells to be on particular energy systems. Cup-mark leys have some similarities to these. Most of these wells were used to cure specific illnesses. The mineral content of the water, and the telluric energy focused into them, appears to have curative properties, at least when the system was working properly. Some wells were at their most powerful on certain days of the year.

WORMS ACROSS THE WORLD

Anne Silk has looked at place- and 'worm' names in many cultures.

Evidence of the sinuous nature of Earth energy can be found at certain healing wells, giving rise to legends about 'wurrams' as guardians, or a fish, such as a trout, as the personification of wave energy. In ancient Gaelic stories we hear of the venomous serpent, the Buarach Bhaoibh. This has its origins in fact, as it is actually a lamprey, a type of eel which frequents rivers and lochs and was thought at one time to possess magical properties.

The legends and myths which have come down to us over thousands of years are of special interest to Earth energy researchers. The many tales of 'waves and lines', together with the prodigious feats of 'giants' who, in the long ago, threw rocks at one another, bear a striking resemblance to geophysics and known Earth movements. Magma explosions, such as are now happening on the Hawaiian island chain, at Mount Etna and in Alaska on the Kamchatka Peninsula, send out molten magma in great volumes. Whether it flows down to the sea or is explosively erupted into the air depends on the depth from which it has come. Sometimes it creeps up through fissures and dykes are formed. There are hundreds of such dykes in the UK.

Worms, by definition, move on and under the earth. They can vary in size from the small compost heap worms and glow worms to large worms maybe 10 inches (25 cm) in length. Although they do a great job of aerating the soil and making compost, they most certainly do not have the power to throw rocks. So why do they figure so strongly in myths and legends from all over the world?

Placenames, as already mentioned, give us the pointer to interesting facts. The word 'worm' in Anglo Saxon was *Wyrm*, in German *Würm*, in Icelandic *Orm*, in Greek *rhomos*, Latin *vermis* and French *orme*.

The worms of legend, like the giants, achieved prodigious feats, far beyond those of the fattest and best-fed earthworms of today. For example, in Hebrew legend the Shamir was a magic worm, able to cut through stone. As no axe or metal tool could be used to cut the stones to build an altar, the ability of the Shamir was reputedly used by Solomon to aid him in the building of the Temple in Jerusalem.

Snakes, serpents, dragons and worms were all considered protectors of hidden treasure. In our material world, we equate 'treasure' with gold, wealth and gems, but what greater treasure in the world is there than good health, serenity and fertility?

There are some remarkable parallels in the legends of serpents, wouivres, dragons and other wavy creatures as they wandered across the Earth millennia ago. Some are listed below:

Kuei (Chinese): This spirit could only travel in straight lines and disliked iron and steel.
Echidna (Greek): This wormlike spirit lived in caves, moved only at night and shunned the light of day.
Orme (Gaelic): A worm which shunned daylight.
Tiamat (Mesopotamian): A dragon which lived below the water and was evil-natured.
Omniont (Native American): A giant snake god and powerful deity who, when angry, made thunder and lightning, hail and rain.
Whowie (Aboriginal): A wormlike spirit which lived in caves and travelled at night.
Bunyip (Aboriginal): A similar spirit which lived in damp sand.
Uroo (Aboriginal): A giant water serpent which twisted and turned below the surface of the Earth.

In the world-wide tales of sinuous forms which have phenomenal properties for both good and ill, there are remarkable parallels with sinuous natural waves. The great number of locally considered 'centre of the world' or omphalos (navel) sites, such as Delphi in Greece, Arbor Low in the UK and Nan Madol in the Pacific, among others, may indicate areas of standing waves due to intersections of multiply sourced energies.

BACK TO THE CIRCUIT

In the weeks that followed, I continued on the serpent's path, contouring gently up and over Glen Ghoinean and down to the centre of Loch Earn. I picked up the circuit on its north shore and walked back to Loch Tay, to stand in the narrow glen just a few metres away from the spot where I had reluctantly turned south a few weeks before. The energy had, in fact, followed the contours of that narrow glen to tune into the centre of Loch Earn, going round in a rough circle and back to the other side of the glen. On the map it looked very like one of the cup-marks next to the dumb-bell shaped cup-mark on the stone at Connachan Farm *(see*

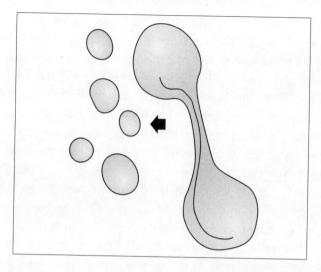

Figure 30: The cup-mark (arrowed) bears a remarkable resemblance to the circuit around Loch Earn.

Figure 30) – well worth investigating further, but I would have to leave that to a later date.

Heading at last to Killin, the cell or burial-place of Fingal, the circuit approaches a six-stone circle which I had been eagerly anticipating. However, it contoured around the circle, keeping close to the loch, in very boggy ground. Disgusted, I squelched, sometimes knee deep in mud and water, past all the historic sites only a few hundred tempting yards away, into a culvert under the road, where the cavity-seeking energy naturally focused, before heading northwards into the 3,000-foot (900-metre) hills of the Ben Lawers group.

THE LOCH OF THE WATER BULL

The circuit climbed ever higher, to the west of Loch na Lairige, with the black clouds lowering threateningly over the hills. 'There must surely be another loch here to pull the energy to this height,' I muttered to myself. Sheltering from the screaming wind, a quick look at the map revealed that there certainly was a loch, only a short distance ahead: Lochan an Tarbh-uisge. My elementary Gaelic recognized the words immediately – the Loch of the Water Bull.

This was the second occasion I had come across the site of this fabled creature, which is sometimes a water bull, sometimes a horse, sometimes the terrifying water kelpie, with hair of rushes and sedges, mussels for eyes, huge fins for arms and a scaly, shell-covered tail. In Highland folklore such creatures are said to inhabit specific lochs, to appear in the guise of a horse or bull and tempt any passer-by to sit on their back. Once seated there is usually no turning back, as the rider is firmly stuck to the seat. Sometimes these creatures appeared on the Sabbath, when all the good people really should be in the kirk!

Water bulls are sometimes helpful and let themselves be used for ploughing or stud, as in the case at Lochan an Tarbh-uisge, where a local farmer is said to have used one to sire cattle which had crumpled horns and coats like black velvet. On the other hand, the water horse, though a magnificent animal, was invariably evil. If you happened across a horse at the side of one of these Highland lochs, you had to inspect it carefully – if there was sand or seaweed caught in its mane, it was time to make a sharp exit!

On this occasion the elements and the very loch itself seemed to resent my intrusion. The screaming wind sent curtains of spray high into the air and the troubled waters heaved, flecked with foam. I could imagine our ancestors fearfully scanning the loch for the fabled water spirits.

Only their Livers Survived

Among the many tales of the water creatures there is one from Perthshire, in which 10 children climbed on the back of a water horse. When the beast plunged into the watery depths only one boy survived.

In other, similar stories, one child notices something amiss, as at Aberfeldy. Here six girls and a boy chanced upon a beautiful pony on the shore of a loch. The girls jumped on the beast's back, while the boy stood in growing trepidation as it slowly grew in length to accommodate each small addition!

Realizing what was about to happen, he hid himself amongst some rocks and watched helplessly as the water horse plunged into the depths of the loch to devour the unfortunate girls. Strangely, the viscera of the victims often remain untouched, and here six small livers were washed ashore.

Bridges

Lochan an Tarbh-uisge, like its neighbour, Lochan na Lairige, 7 miles (11 kilometres) away, is a high point on this circuit, which now carries on down to Glen Lyon.

Four miles (6 kilometres) away from the loch, my divining rod led me towards Meggernie Castle, virgin white against its green lawns, brown hills and blue skies. Once again I was impressed by the sensitivity of this form of energy, which tuned into the little wooden bridge spanning the River Lyon. I had observed this on a number of occasions. No matter if a bridge was constructed of steel, stone or wood, the foundations on the banks emitted an elongated spiral pattern, just like the HT pylons mentioned earlier.

There have been a number of stories handed down to us concerning bridges. Witches would place wax effigies of clay or lead under a bridge in the belief that as they dissolved, so did the health of the victim.

Cup-mark leys seek water, generally in the form of lochs, but what happens when the working outside wave encounters a river? The answer is quite simple – it tunes into the widest and deepest pool in the vicinity. Pools such as these have long been associated with kelpies, a type of spirit similar to the water horse and water bull which inhabits lochs. This applies particularly to pools under bridges, 'the bridge over which the dead and the living shall pass'. Cup-mark leys tune into the centre of such pools. They also tune into the centre of bridges. Robert Burns tells how Tam o' Shanter, pursued by demons, fled to the safety of the centre of a bridge, for past the keystone no demon could venture.

SIXTEENTH-CENTURY JUSTICE

Let us retrace our steps to Meggernie Castle. This place has had a wild and colourful history. Built about 1585 by 'Mad' Colin Campbell, it was originally a square tower house. Some years prior to building Meggernie, Colin had received a violent blow to his head, which reputedly made him unpredictable. *Gorach* (foolish) was the term the Highlanders used.

Once a band of cattle thieves raided Colin's land and left two of his Campbells dead. Mad Colin and his followers took their weapons and followed them, returning with three dozen of the raiders and the leader. The little dungeon was quite incapable of holding them and so they were temporarily imprisoned in another part of the castle, until Colin's son went to Edinburgh to seek justice from the Privy Council. When he returned, however, he found that 'Gorach' Colin had meted out his own brand of justice – 36 bodies were swinging from 36 trees leading to the castle. Their leader was treated with respect and Highland chivalry, as befitted his position: he was shot by Mad Colin himself and buried.

Meggernie Castle was still in private hands, so I sought permission from the factor before walking round the perimeter of the building, where the outside wave of the circuit passed just wide of the cornerstone in a similar manner to its skirting the edges of old burial-grounds. The other waves, about a yard apart, went through the remainder of the castle, which is a peculiarity of cup-mark leys (see Figure 12, p.47).

A FLOODED BURIAL-GROUND

Continuing northwards, over the hills and down to Loch Rannoch, something unusual happened to the circuit. Instead of contouring the loch neatly, as it had done at Loch Tay, the cup-mark ley went down to the loch, to enter it some little distance from the western end. The circuit obstinately refused to run round the loch as it had done with other lochs and I had to walk around and pick it up on the other side.

I was puzzled as to why this ley had such unusual characteristics. The loch had been dammed at one end and the water raised by some 13 feet (4 metres), but the cup-mark ley still travelled along its original path and into the loch. Some research revealed part of the answer.

An old burial-ground at this end had been flooded when the dam had been built. The cup-mark ley could still travel to that site, even though it had been submerged. It was not, therefore, only the lochs which were shaping the circuit. Some other agency was at work. It was some years later that I discovered what it was – a form of straight ley from stone circles. It appeared these were used to build the circuits, forming them and moulding them into complex shapes. We shall leave this for the moment.

Ploughing waist deep in ferns, I walked on to another burial-ground at Kilchonan. I tuned into the ley again here and followed it around the north shore of Loch Rannoch, the most northerly point of this circuit. It continued to the Chieftain standing stone and then went back to the loch near the eastern end of Kinloch Rannoch.

Another healing well, Clach na h'Tobairte (Stone of the Sacrifice) is close to this circuit. However, the circuit avoids it and passes through another old burial-ground at Kinloch Rannoch, then turns southward into the hills.

As I plodded determinedly along, with Schiehallion's symmetrical cone rearing to my left, I got another surprise. Deep in a wood I stumbled upon a tiny burial-ground at Inverhadden. Some distance from the road and hidden by trees, this neglected little cemetery lay decaying on Schiehallion's foothills, the outside 'working wave' taking me accurately to one corner *(see Figure 12, p.47)*.

THE CAVE ON THE HILL OF THE BIG MEN

There was a long walk ahead, up over the shoulder of Schiehallion and down into Glen Mhor, where the cup-mark energy unerringly found Uamh Tom a Mhor-fhir (the Cave on the Hill of the Big Men), tucked away from the prying eyes of the casual sightseer. Years ago I had set out to find this cave, without success, as I had no idea that it was so tiny. There is a story that a piper had once walked into it, the sound of his pipes becoming fainter and fainter as he followed it deep underground. He was never to be seen again. Despite the story, here was the cave, barely a foot (30 cm) high!

Continuing on, up and over to Fortingall I walked, to Drummond Hill, sometimes called Fingal's Ridge, into a tiny lochan at its summit and down to Kenmore, through the neat white church and burial-ground, and round Loch Tay, close to the shore to Ardtalnaig. Turning south here, the circuit follows close to the previous one, over Auchnafree Hill to another standing stone, Clach-na-Tiompan, down the old road, veering off to a stone ring in a nearby glen. The stone ring, I might add, is close to the remains of an old wooden shooting bothy and can barely be recognized. If this circuit, and the next, had not deviated so obviously into it I would never have noticed it.

Figure 31: Clach-na-Tiompan in Glen Almond.

The circuit then goes down to the Sma' Glen and is captured by a large slate quarry on its way back to the mounds at Gilmerton.

8

THE FINAL
CIRCUIT

Cup-Mark Maps across Scotland and Northern England

When a scientist states that something is possible, he is
almost certainly right; when he states that something is
impossible, he is very probably wrong.

ARTHUR C. CLARKE

The next circuit once again behaves in a very similar manner to the previous one. It travels from the mounds at Gilmerton *(bottom right of Map 5)* to the outer edge of Drummond Pond, then on to Strowan burial-ground and the standing stone at Lawers, the same stone which initiated this research.

A short distance to the north the circuit encounters the old priory mentioned earlier, then runs parallel to the previous circuit to Loch Tay, returning to the burial-ground at Dundurn, St Fillans, before making another circuit around Loch Earn and returning to Loch Tay and Killin.

Several hundred yards from the previous circuit, running parallel to it, I walked on, aware that on this occasion the circuit was at last heading directly to the stone circle at Killin, having previously missed it by a few yards, as related in the previous chapter. This was the second major stone circle I had encountered on this project. I was not quite sure what to expect, so I slowed down to concentrate on following my divining rod.

The wave led me directly between two of the stones, then warped to the west, towards Glen Ogle (Terrible Glen). The streams of energy here are so confusing, however, that for the moment it is best to by-pass the circle and leave it until later in the chapter.

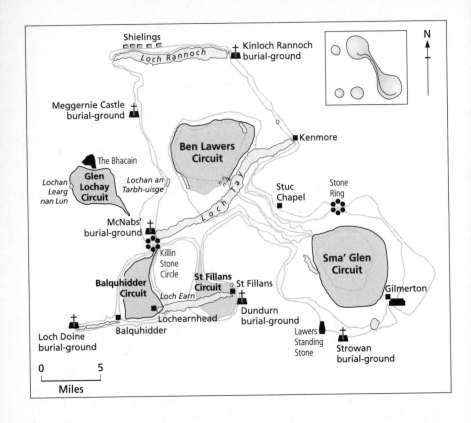

Map 5: The outer shell, from the Gilmerton mounds, travels clockwise to Strowan burial-ground and north-east to Loch Tay, back to St Fillans and round to tune into the centre of Loch Earn. From there it travels to Killin stone circle, where it makes three circuits around Balquhidder. The five circuits (shaded in this illustration), plus the dumb-bell shape, are similar to a group of petroglyphs on the Connachan cup-marked stone (inset). There are seven burial-grounds on this circuit.

I carried on a short distance to the little burial-ground of the McNabs on Inchbuie (the Yellow Island) below the picturesque Falls of Dochart in Killin. This is the tiniest of burial-grounds on the tiniest of islands, with the thundering river foaming on either side. Originally it contained only McNabs, now others are buried there too. It has an ancient story: the spirit of the last person to die must keep vigil over the resting-place of the McNabs until another dies to take over.[1] This has telluric similarities to Lawers burial-ground, where the circuit is strongly drawn to the most

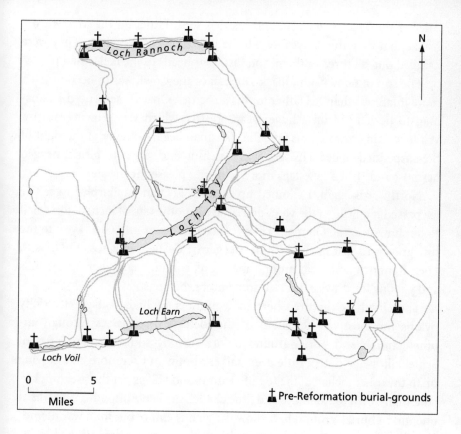

Map 6: Pre-Reformation burial-grounds situated on the cup-mark energy systems.

recent burial, since that is the most attractive cavity. Perhaps this is the reasoning behind the stories of graveyard guardians.

On the other side of the river I passed through the old village burial-ground and on to yet another, this time a very modern one. The ever-searching energy was encompassing it, presumably attracted to the many underground cavities.

THE BEHEADING PIT

A short distance away were the ruins of Finlarig Castle. The remains of this decaying pile include the grim beheading pit at the foot of the castle windows, where 'Grey' Colin Campbell held out the hand of friendship to the chief of the MacGregor clan and his two sons. Little did the MacGregors realize that they themselves were to be the climax of festivities. They were dragged out, all three of them, and lost their heads to the beheading pit.[2]

The son of Grey Colin, Black Duncan of the Cowl, was to become even more infamous than his father for his atrocities. Once he sentenced a clansman to be hanged on a huge sycamore tree which was growing nearby. While walking towards his fate, the clansman began to falter at the sight of the suspended noose. His wife was watching and, eager to please, begged her husband, 'Just a few steps more, Colin, to please the maister!'

Northwards again, I climbed up towards Lochan na Tairbh-uisge. The ley passed it a little to the west, diverting to another small lochan, too small to be shown on the OS map. Then it travelled down into Glen Lyon to the tiny graveyard just to the west of Meggernie Castle, ran across the hills to Loch Rannoch and went around the shore, contouring higher up the hills and passing lengthwise through some more shielings.

The circuit is captured here by a number of high voltage electricity pylons for most of the length of the loch. It then passes through another church and burial-ground before turning south to the slopes of Schiehallion again, to a little deer stalker's bothy in Glenmore and moving on to the other lochan at the top of Drummond Hill as per the previous circuit, then down to Kenmore and Stuc chapel, in Glen Almond. There was at one time a burial-ground here; now the glen is empty but for a war memorial. The circuit then pays another visit to the stone ring mentioned in the previous chapter before it turns in a wide sweep back to Gilmerton.

A WORKING STONE CIRCLE

The most interesting part of this circuit is the stone circle at Killin. This circle is still intact and gives an excellent working energy circuit, probably much the same as the original. There are actually three circuits involved here (see Figure 32).

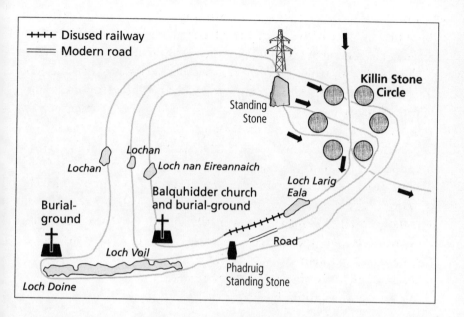

Figure 32: This is a stylized map of the ley circuits from Killin stone circle. Note the outlying standing stone, which acts as one of the original crossing-points. The three small lochs to the left are situated on the summits of hills to attract the cup-mark ley up and over the top.

Most of the stones in the circle have a wide 'V' shape in their plan view, one part facing inwards and one facing outwards. From the flat face of each stone a wave of energy can be found, spiralling out clockwise for seven circuits around the circle, then back into the stone on the opposite side. In the same way, another wave spirals out anti-clockwise.

From the north, the cup-mark ley enters between two of the stones and, since the circle is actually oval, its point of exit is between the two adjacent stones on the opposite side, which are closest and most attractive to it.

Now clear of the circle and the energy pattern around it, it finds another more distant attraction, this time Lochan Larig Cheile or Eala, at the top of the pass leading down to Glen Ogle.

There are three circuits from the stone circle, tuning into two churches (not shown) and also two burial-grounds: the important Balquhidder church with its burial-ground, Loch Doine burial-ground *(far left)* and the MacGregor Mausoleum on the road to the east of the Phadruig standing stone *(see Figure 33)*. Another three lochs at the summit of hill passes *(to the*

Figure 33: Mourners journeying to the distant burial-grounds of Loch Doine and Balquhidder would place the coffin on the flat top of Phadruig. The working edge of the cup-mark ley is most powerful at this point.

left of the illustration) pull the energy up the hills and help the circuits on their way.

There are also two standing stones: Phadruig, on the flat top of which funeral parties would leave the coffin, and a standing stone on the Killin road which acts as a cross-over point. I had often wondered why some stone circles had outlying standing stones and this neatly explains the puzzle. Presumably the HT pylon in the illustration is a modern attraction, taking over another crossing-point for that circuit.

There is only one remaining gap in the circle which the energy can use, and it passes through this and out of the circle back to its original route.

Notice that the outside circuit circumnavigates Lochs Doine and Voil.

Figure 34: This outlying standing stone near Killin is the crossing-point of a ley stream to the stone circle. The hill behind is Ben Lawers.

A GHASTLY BEHEADING

The church at Balquhidder has two cup-mark leys running through it. This is where the famous outlaw Rob Roy MacGregor lived. The beauty of the area is breathtaking, the cruelty of past generations frightening. One of the cruelest stories in the Highlands is connected with this picturesque little church.

One day the McDonalds were poaching in Glenartney, when they were caught by the 'keeper, Drummond of Drummondernoch. He cut off their ears. Some time later the McDonalds took a fearful revenge when they ambushed Drummond and beheaded him. Then they carried the head in a plaid to the home of his sister at the side of Loch Earn.

Upon entering they demanded the traditional Highland hospitality, which was duly given to them. Mrs Stewart, heavy with child, laid bread and cheese on the table before them, then withdrew to obtain more substantial fare.

When she had gone, the McDonalds took out the head of her brother, laid it, still dripping with blood, on the table and stuffed some bread and cheese into its mouth. When Mrs Stewart returned and beheld the atrocity, she fled screaming into the hills, quite insane. It was some days before she could be pacified and brought home, where she had her child, a boy, who was destined to have a notorious reputation. He made many enemies when he lived and when he died the mourners carried his body along the road towards the burial-ground at Dundurn. During a severe snowstorm they buried it temporarily by the roadside, fearful lest his enemies get hold of it. A stone to mark this burial still stands at this spot.

THE GLEN LYON CIRCUIT

To complete the map of telluric energy it was necessary to discover one more circuit which would coincide with a cluster of cup-marks on the Connachan stone. Since the other cup-marks featured standing stones, I went to a tiny standing stone in Glen Lyon and picked up the circuit there.

Figure 35: The tiny Bhacain in Glen Lyon.

This, the most charming of standing stones, only 18 inches (45 cm) high and shaped like a dog's head, is called 'the Bhacain'. It is said to have tethered the hounds of the Fian, and no doubt Fingal's own hunting dogs, Bran and Sgeolan, both jet black, with yellow paws and collars and chains of pure gold.[3]

The circuit passes through this stone and as it progresses up the glen, it picks up Fingal's 'castles' one by one. They are rather curious and have been recognized by archaeologists as homesteads, often taking commanding positions at the entrances to glens. There is little remaining of these ancient positions now, but it appears that they were built and placed with telluric energy very much in mind.

The circuit follows an old track, now metalled, and reaches the pass via a cairn which marks the point used as a respite by funeral processions not so long ago. It was the custom to place a stone on the cairn when they left for the remainder of the journey.

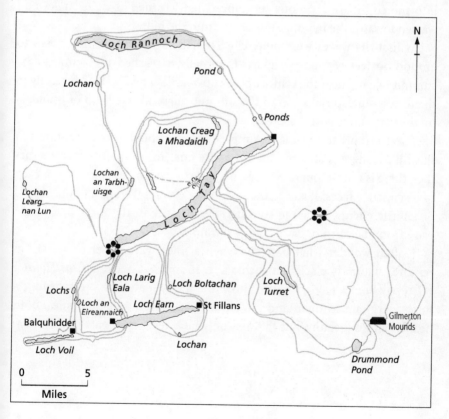

Map 7: Lochs, large and small, help form the telluric pattern around Perthshire.

At the highest point of this circuit is yet another loch, Lochan Learg nan Lun, which, like the other summit lochs, attracts the cup-mark ley to the top of the hill and down into Glen Lochay, where it is once again captured by HT pylons, this time the wooden two-poled type, which the circuit follows down towards Killin, passing under a modern bridge.

From the Bhacain eastwards, there is little of interest. It passes under yet another bridge, then contours down towards Killin.

THE TELLURIC CENTRE

Now that the four cup-marks had been mapped, it seemed that there must be some focal point within each cup-mark ley. I went back to the Balquhidder circuit and the standing stone Phadruig, and once again tuned into the cup-mark ley along its spine. Then I turned at right angles and walked towards the hypothetical centre, into the hills.

At first the waves were quite close together, but they settled down to around 20 feet (6 metres) apart. Eventually, I reached the centre – the summit of a hill near the centre of the cup-mark shape. I walked carefully to the focal point, spiralling in to the summit cairn, a loose heap of boulders on the very summit of the Creag.

There is more to this than a simple clockwise spiral from the summit of this hill, as there is also an anti-clockwise one. To complicate matters further, there is now a square survey cairn nearby, which has spirals from each of its concrete faces! Possibly, the summit of every hill emits a double spiral of telluric energy for some considerable distance in the form of a shape wave from the cairn or cairns on its summit.

I often wonder what happens when a microwave tower or television repeater station is placed on such a site. In my first book, *Safe as Houses?* (Gateway Books, 1996), I showed how they attract natural subterranean telluric energy up to them and radiate it out in enormous quantities, both healthy and unhealthy, but this can only be a very small part of the story.

THE COMPLETE PATTERN

The basic dumb-bell cup-mark with its satellite cups on the Connachan Farm stone can now be compared to the circuits I have followed on foot. Using these as a guide, the complete pattern across mainland Scotland, Rum, Skye and other smaller islands can be established, as well as other circuits as far away as Northumberland and Durham in the north of England. There is, perhaps because of weathering, a wide gap between the cup-mark just to the west of Edinburgh and the Duns (Borders) area and a cluster around Newcastle-upon-Tyne.

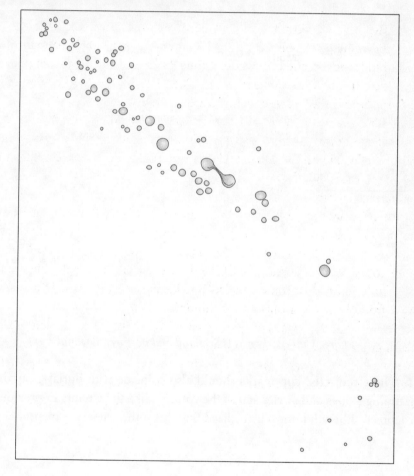

Figure 36: The cup-marks on the Connachan Farm stone can now be compared with Map 8.

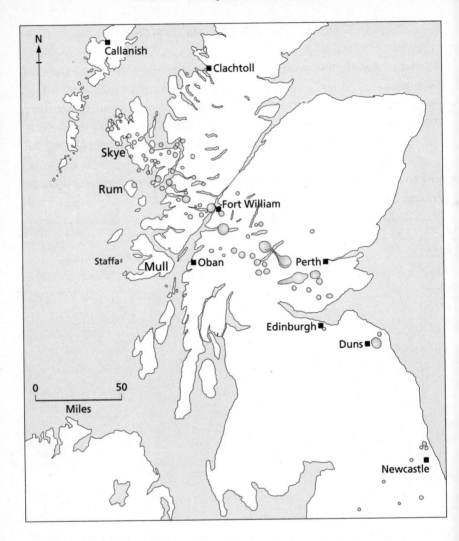

Map 8: Cup-marks across Scotland and northern England.

These projected cup-marks should also coincide with burial-grounds, standing stones and circles across the country, like the circuits in previous chapters, although it must be realized that this is the crudest of maps.

A DIFFERENT TYPE OF CIRCUIT

I have mentioned on several occasions that the cup-mark leys pass through the longitudinal axes of old shielings. One day, following a cup-mark ley up a remote glen, I stopped and sat on a boulder, exhausted. As I recovered, I noticed that the boulder was part of an old shieling and decided that this was a good opportunity to find the crossing energy which must surely be focused through the dwelling.

The pattern, however, was totally unexpected. The cup-mark ley passed through the long axis of the little building, but this crossing wave turned to my right, running around the building and back to the nearby burn. Another wave turned in the opposite direction, across to the other bank of the burn, forming a bifurcated bubble of energy which completely surrounded the shieling. I traced the energy downstream, following the high banks which the dashing waters had carved for themselves, down onto the floor of Glen Lyon. Here the tributary entered the River Lyon and the energy waves continued along both banks of the river for some distance, hugging the banks all the time.

Leaving Glen Lyon, I found a local cup-marked stone more suitable for my purpose, close to the Connachan Farm stone in the Sma' Glen. This had been carved with nine cup-marks, one surrounded with a ring *(see Figure 37)*. I picked up a stream of telluric energy from this stone and followed it across the hills to the Falls of Turret, a geological fault where the ground to the north has risen about 100 feet (30 metres) in relation to the ground of the south.

Surprisingly, instead of passing straight across, the waves turned and followed the River Turret up past the modern reservoir, again hugging the banks. Near the source of the river, a small lochan nestling beneath a 3,000-foot (900-metre) hill, the ley followed a tributary for a short distance. Further on it turned unexpectedly at right angles, across the rough heathery moor to encircle the remains of one of a group of shielings.

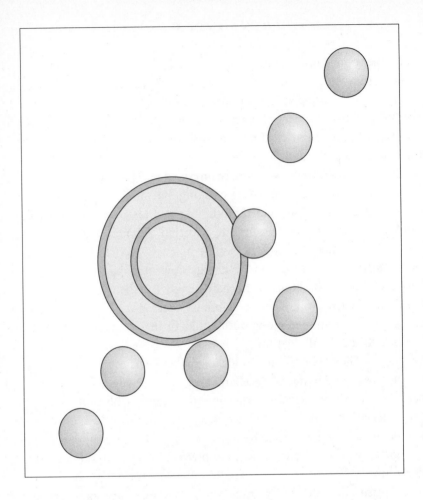

Figure 37: Plan view of the cup-marks on the stone (see Figure 38).

The local cup-marked stone, in essence, appeared to throw its telluric pattern across country, using a subterranean stream beneath it as a wave carrier initially to take it into the hills and around the group of shielings *(see Figure 39)*. Subterranean streams beneath cup-marked stones are not unknown – at Petroglyph Park, near Ontario, Canada, there is a rock inscribed with animal and other designs by the Ojibway tribe as recently as 500–1,000 years ago.

Figure 38: This is the local cup-marked stone which has also yielded its secrets.

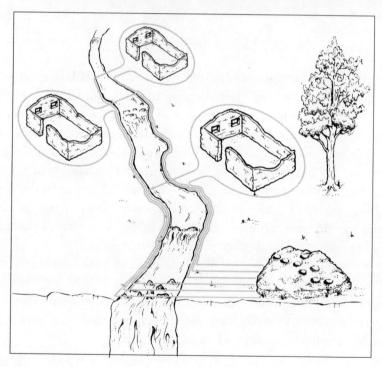

Figure 39: A stream of telluric energy is emitted from this stone to surround ancient shielings.

Figure 40: A typical shieling near Schiehallion.

Why go to all the trouble of encasing shielings in a bubble of energy? On an impulse I took out my black divining rod and tuned into 'unhealthy energies'. (With a little practice a biolocator can use coloured rods to tune their mind into looking for different things: black for unhealthy energies, white for healthy energies, blue for underground water. The colours may differ from one biolocator to another.) There were four heading to one side of the shieling (this was in the late 1970s, when unhealthy energies were not nearly so common). The unhealthy energies were abruptly warped away around the old home. The energy from that local cup-marked stone appeared to protect the house from these unpleasant influences.

It is possible that this bubble of energy could give the inhabitants good health and a feeling of well-being by projecting healthy negative ions through their homes. These would be carried by the energy waves from the cup-marked stone. Probably, they pick up the ions from the burn as its waters dash and foam down the bed of the stream.

Another mystery was the energized cup-marked stones. How were the varied shapes, pecked into stones, transmitted across country as a magnified telluric replica of a cup-mark?

The answer came when I went to the island of Mull to do more research. Flooded out of my tent during the night, I put my sodden clothing on a nearby fence to dry. One of the iron stanchions had been inserted into a large earthfast stone and I tried my divining rod here to see what I could find. Incredibly, there was a little ellipse of energy which extended for a few yards before returning to the stone. Apparently, drilling a hole in a stone causes it to emit a form of energy.

Later that day, waiting for the ferry to Iona, I sat and read a tourist's guide to the islands, and discovered that a nearby quarry had exported its beautiful pink granite world-wide. It was only a few hundred yards away and a short time later I was walking among some of the large blocks of stone quarried from the rock face. The first gave four waves – narrow ellipses again – travelling a few feet out from the stone. Puzzled, I walked round the other side to find four holes about 1 inch (2.5 cm) and 8 inches (20 cm) deep, which corresponded with the four waves from the opposite face. Mystified, I discovered another large boulder the size of a small bungalow with over 20 holes bored on its edge. There was one wave of energy for every hole. To split these rocks, the quarrymen had drilled these holes, then inserted wedges to split them roughly into shape. The holes apparently had the ability to project highly elliptical waves on the opposite side of the stone.

The quarry-keeper's hut, built of hand-carved and faced granite, stood nearby. Every few inches I could detect waves of energy which reacted only to my white divining rod – healthy waves only. The wavelength was 66 inches (168 cm).

A nearby burial-ground was surrounded with the same faced granite stone, which gave me an intriguing new theory – could the ley from nearby Staffa, passing down and through the length of this burial-ground as healthy energy, be changed to black energy as it crossed the decaying interments and then be 'cleaned up' by the faced granite walls on the downstream side? This seemed to be the case, as my black divining rod worked only on the waves inside the graveyard, but not on the upstream or downstream side.

Since I knew that healthy energy waves could pass through glass easily, while unhealthy ones avoided it, I obtained a sheet of glass from a nearby rubbish dump and tried again. Outside the cemetery the waves passed through the glass. Inside they were warped around, which appeared to demonstrate their polarity.

A MUSEUM ON IONA

One of the museums on Iona had a number of carved cist covers of nuns and abbots, centuries old. They had been laboriously carved by hand and each of these engravings emitted a surprising amount of energy which could not be interpreted as individual waves but was more like an aura. It takes no great stretch of the imagination to see the carvings surrounded by invisible energy, the same shape as the images themselves.

The next step was to carve my own cup-mark on a loose boulder and find out what pattern emerged. With a heavy hammer and cold chisel I pecked out a nice deep depression on a boulder in a field. My divining rod showed me that the stone now emitted a narrow beam of energy which widened out after several yards to form a telluric circle on the ground. Why in that particular direction? I eventually discovered that the energy from the stone was transmitted into the sun at the time of carving. When I completed carving the stone, I turned it. The cup-mark energy obligingly followed. Using my black divining rod I found that all the unhealthy waves in that area were diverted around the pattern on the ground.

Placing the stone above an underground pipe filled with running water, I discovered that the energy turned and followed the pipe downhill, using it as a carrier wave.

Locating such a carved stone outside my house caused the bubble of energy to expand until it encompassed the entire building. I was to use this later as an extremely effective method of eliminating unhealthy Earth energies, especially 'black spirals' in the houses of people suffering from the many illnesses related to geopathic stress. Having worked in this field for a number of years, it is obvious to me that most illnesses, from minor to major, are at least exacerbated, and possibly even initiated, by black Earth energies.

For anyone wishing to experiment with this, please use a good pair of goggles when you carve the stones. How to protect houses and other buildings using this technique from the ever-increasing problem of unhealthy Earth energies will be found in my previous book. The most important points are that when you carve a cup-marked stone you must not move it until you have completed the carving. Then you must carve a line from the cup-mark directly into the sun. Now place the stone close to your house (within a foot), with the carved line pointing exactly at the wall.

REFERENCES

1   Duncan Frazer, *Highland Perthshire*, Montrose Press, 1969
2   *Fair Perthshire*, 1930
3   John Matthews and R. J. Stewart, *Celtic Battle Heroes*, Firebird Books, 1988

9

STRAIGHT
LEYS

And How They Work

Many roads hast thou fashioned and all of them lead to the light.

RUDYARD KIPLING, *SONG TO MITHRAS THE SUN GOD*

Map 9: Some of these straight leys were followed on foot. Since they appeared to be just touching the cup-marked leys, this map has been compiled from leys from stone circles and the three rocking stones in the area. It seems that there is at least one type of straight ley which helps to form the cup-mark leys.

Three long-distance leys have been included, one from the Callanish stone ring on Lewis and also the primary ley from St Kilda to Balfarg stone circle. Only a few standing stones on this complex have been shown for clarity.

The inset shows the ley from the Giant's Causeway in Ireland to Callanish, which may act as a telluric 'block' for the cup-mark energy ley across mainland Scotland. The east arm of Callanish may emit another ley across the north coast of Scotland, blocking yet another cup-mark ley complex.

As my map of the cup-mark leys progressed, I was often struck by the peculiar and unexpected shapes which had evolved. Some of the circuits had been altered by roads and pylons pirating the energy, but that by no means explained all of them. Some had been moulded by straight leys – corridors of telluric energy comprised of individual waves which cross the country in straight lines, oblivious of hills and valleys (the cup-mark leys which we

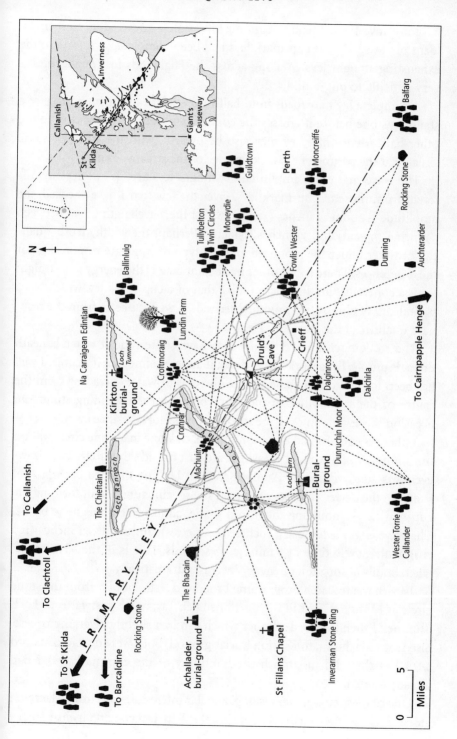

have just investigated tend to contour hills, unless attracted up to them by lochs or caves). As the cup-mark leys had been completed, I turned to the exhausting straight leys. Walking across the Highlands in straight lines is very difficult, to put it mildly.

A complete ley may focus in to half of the width of the broad face of a standing stone before it crosses the country and returns to focus in to the other half. A cup-mark ley may also be present, with the standing stone situated at the perimeter or working edge of the stream of energy.

The wavelength and amplitude of straight leys are also noticeably different from those of cup-mark leys. Over the few that I have checked, the amplitude is about 12 inches (31 cm), whilst the wavelength varies between 39 inches (99 cm) and 59 inches (150 cm). Perhaps the width, depth, quantity of water under the monolith and the type of stone are responsible for the differences. There is one other important factor: the energy in a straight ley is a coherent standing wave, unlike that of a cup-mark ley, which has a periodicity of almost two minutes, derived, as we have seen, from the resonant qualities of the Druid's Cave.

The stone circles in Perthshire also have subterranean water beneath them. From the little work I have done, it appears almost as if a capped well has been formed under these sites, with veins of water spreading from the centre of the stone circle to the space between each standing stone. On occasion the water comes to the surface only a short distance away.

Other researchers had also found that each stone in a stone circle was on the boundary of a straight ley which ran just outside the circle. This, however, was subtly different. Another straight ley just touched each *pair* of stones in the circle. These seem to have the specific function of forming the cup-mark leys, moulding them into shape, almost like a magnetic bottle. The wavelength is 24 feet, 3 inches (9.4 metres), amplitude 42 inches (107 cm), with a cycle time of 1 minute, 53 seconds. This is in the VHF range, when bodily absorption of energy increases dramatically.

Late in the research programme I followed a straight ley from the stone circle at Machuim, just to the north of Loch Tay, north-eastwards to Loch Tummel. I then followed another which ran in a slightly diverging course, also from Machuim, to Kirkton burial-ground. Both were devoid of sacred sites, but they did just touch the boundary of the cup-mark leys I had already plotted.

One of these straight leys is of particular interest. It runs from Machuim stone circle to the north-west, inside the Ben Lawers circuit, just to the north of Loch Tay *(see Map 9)*. The cup-mark ley which it forms is shown as a dotted line, since this is the presumed original path of the cup-mark shape, as the modern reservoir has warped it out of its original shape. But the straight ley, following its presumed original path, carries on to the little 'Bhacain' standing stone, then runs westwards through several of the Fingalian 'castles', and in doing so, forms the upper part of the Glen Lochay circuit.

Following this line, it passes through one of the strangest of all the ancient sites in the area, Taigh-nam-Bodach (the House of the Old Man), on its way to Achallader burial-ground.

A STRANGE FAMILY

The first time I visited the little old Bodach's house, long before my interest in Earth energies had begun, it was simply to see the curious little structure. That visit had taken place during one of the most violent gales I have ever encountered, powerful enough to blow a ram into a tree, where it hung helplessly, its hooves clear of the ground. On this occasion, however, it was early summer, good walking and comfortable weather.

As I approached the Bodach's house, a feeling of being swept back hundreds, even thousands of years, came over me. Here, time had stood still, the hills unchanging.

The Bodach and his wife, the Cailleach, were standing at the entrance of their little home to welcome me, as they had welcomed so many travellers over the centuries. They are not mortals, like you or I, but little waterworn stones, 18 inches (45 cm) high and surprisingly heavy, if you are foolish enough to pick one up. I did, unaware of the bad luck that follows with anyone who tampers with the family. The stones themselves came from one particular spot in the nearby tumultuous burn, which gave them their curious shape. Now this timeless couple have five children, but they are not nearly so well formed as their parents.

Figure 40a: The Cailleach, her husband the Bodach and family. These little water-worn stones have greeted generations of our ancestors taking cattle up to their summer pastures. (© R. Money)

At one time this small shrine was thatched. When the people down in the glen, mainly MacGregors, took their cattle and possessions from the lower wintering pastures to the high ground here in the summer, the first thing they did was to take out the old couple, arrange them carefully around the little house and thatch it.

Nowadays, early every May, the 'keeper takes his boat up to the mouth of Gleann Cailleach and walks the remaining few miles to this house. He then opens it and arranges the family outside the entrance to welcome the spirits of the people who lived in this remote glen. In late September he returns to replace them in their little stone house, tucked safely away from the winter storms.

STRAIGHT LEYS AS FORMERS FOR CUP-MARK LEYS

Using my knowledge of straight leys as shapers of cup-mark leys, I constructed Map 9. The cup-mark leys, of course, have all been followed on foot, although I have adjusted the ley near Drummond Pond to mark its original presumed route. Many of the straight leys have also been followed on foot, but now that the bones of the cup-mark system have been laid bare, it is quite easy to draw the straight leys between stones and circles which form the cup-mark leys, such as the Clach-na-Tiompan stone to Dalchirla stone circle ley, which nudges a short stretch of the cup-mark ley out of the mouth of the Druid's Cave. This ley travels on to a four-stone circle near Clach-na-Tiompan, Auchnafree, and further on to another four-poster at Lundin Farm *(see Map 10)*. Some leys between single standing stones are involved in Map 9, but are not included, as it would complicate the map enormously.

The cup-mark leys to the east and west of Loch Tay and Loch Rannoch must also be formed by straight leys from Croft Moraig and Killin stone circles respectively, but there is a dearth of stone circles to the north-west of Perthshire.

Projecting a straight line from Killin north-north-east to form the cup-mark ley around the western side of Loch Rannoch leads eventually to a recently discovered stone circle 40 foot (12 metres) across with a huge central stone by the sea at Clachtoll, near Ullapool.

From Croft Moraig, another line can be drawn to Kinloch Rannoch, forming the cup-mark ley at the eastern side of Loch Tay/Rannoch. Extending this, there is nothing of note until the remarkable stone complex of Callanish on the island of Lewis *(inset, Map 9)*, where the ley enters (or exits) its south-eastern flank.

These two long-distance leys are purely hypothetical, though based on experience, of course, but there must be many other long-distance leys spread across the country which are part of this cup-mark ley system in Perthshire, which in turn is only a small part of the overall picture country-wide, or even world-wide.

The one major problem I cannot resolve at the moment is that straight leys sometimes pass through the cup-mark leys, occasionally using a standing stone as a cross-over point, and sometimes help form them.

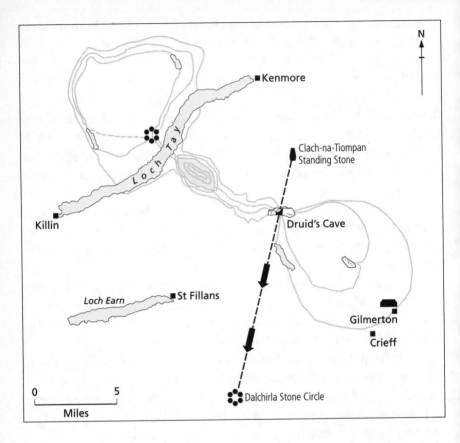

Map 10: The ley from Clach-na-Tiompan to the Druid's Cave.

THE POWERFUL PRIMARY LEY

Shortly after this, I found the main energy ley powering the entire system. It runs between two stone circles with centre stones *(see Map 11)*.

Until now I had explored the leys using some six 1:50,000 OS maps pasted on a large board, but it was not until I extended this with a further two maps that I discovered the fuller extent of this ley. From Balfarg stone circle *(bottom right of Map 11)*, I plotted it through the nearby Balbirnie henge, on to two stone circles with standing stones at Fowlis Wester and on again to the main target – the cup-marked stone at Connachan Farm. From there it travels north-west, passing neatly through the Druid's Cave on to Loch Tay and Machuim stone circle and then north-west off the map.

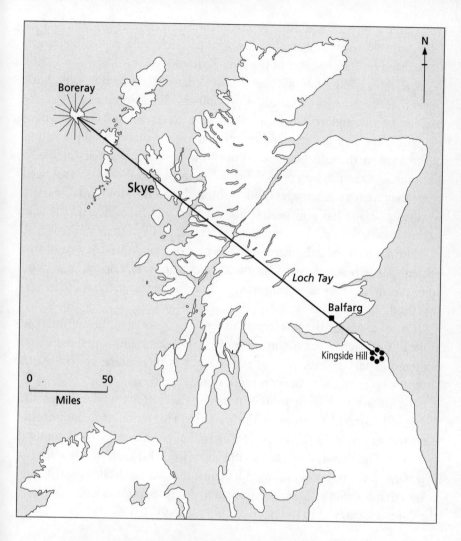

Map 11: The ley is initiated on the volcanic caldera of Boreray.

Projecting this line to the south-east as far as I can, it goes to Balfarg, north of the Firth of Forth, and possibly further on to the 30 stones of Kingside Hill, near Duns in the Borders.

Back to the north-east this line carries on to Skye, probably passing through a stone circle there, and continues across the Little Minch to North Uist, close to or through the massive standing stone Clach an t'Sagairt, the Stone of the Priest, before, initially very disappointingly, disappearing into the vastness of the Atlantic.

Later, reading through Aubrey Burl's *The Stone Circles of the British Isles* (Yale, 1976), I was astonished to see a stone circle with a possible centre stone listed on Boreray, part of the island complex of St Kilda.

Boreray is a tiny volcanic speck of an island some 50 miles (80 kilometres) from the nearest land. Its precipitous cliffs prohibit any but the hardiest of men and women from living there. Nevertheless it did once have a small village near the tiny landing site, but even at that a metal pin had to be inserted in the cliff face sometimes to make landing easier for the St Kildeans, who had to leap onto the cliff face from a 30-foot (9-metre) swell when they went to collect eggs (and the birds themselves) for food. This bare windswept island has now been left to the mercy of the wind and the wild Atlantic swell, with nothing but the largest colony of gannets in the world.

Yet even here, megalithic man has left a stone circle, on the rim of this ancient partially submerged volcano. Extinct volcanoes, caldera, plugs, and so on, seem to be the most important source of telluric energies our ancestors used.

It would appear that this ley, when working, resonated the cup-marked stone at Connachan Farm, throwing its cup-mark circuits across mainland Scotland as far as Skye. Why as far as Skye? Is there some system which determines the distance the cup-mark system can travel?

The answer may lie in another powerful energy ley to Callanish on the island of Lewis which acts as a telluric barrier. This remarkable but uncompleted stone circle, in the shape of a cross, has several stone rows running from it. A line drawn down the southern avenue of stones, which is almost precisely on the north–south meridian, just touches the western-most cup-mark circuit on Skye. Projecting it further, it arrives at the possible source – the Giant's Causeway in Ireland *(see inset, Map 9).*

SPLITTING STONE

Following a hunch which had bothered me for some years, I returned to the fissure above the tiny cave near Loch Turret *(see Map 12)* and found, as I suspected, that there was an energy ley running straight down the fissure roughly east–west. To the west it flows from the standing stone/circle near Braefordie and to the east I followed it part way to a standing stone at Monzie Castle, just touching the foot of the dumb-bell shape, and to the two standing stones at Crofthead mentioned in Chapter 14 *(see page 160).*

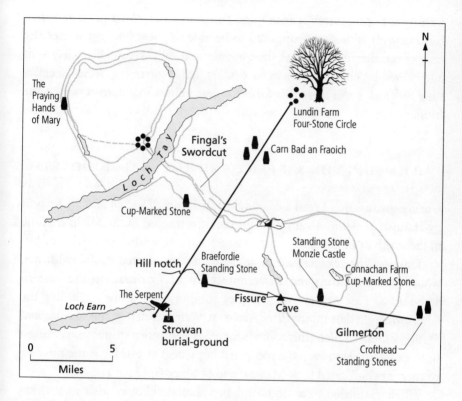

Map 12: *The ley from the standing stones at Crofthead to Braefordie passes through a fissure behind a cave near Loch Turret. This fissure is similar to Fingal's Swordcut and there is a cup-marked stone, also split, at the foot of the Sidh of Ardtalnaig. Are they natural, man-made or part of the phenomenon of energy leys? Other possible examples are the Praying Hands of Mary and a 'hill notch' on the ley which passes from Lundin Farm down to the Serpent at St Fillans.*

I was now forced to contemplate the unusual number of geological fissures and split stones on the circuits: the Praying Hands of Mary, with signs of an impending split at a joint on its broad face, Fingal's Swordcut on the summit of the Sidh of Ardtalnaig and the split cup-marked stone at its foot, the ravine forming the 'hill notch' at St Fillans, where I had found the dead deer, several other boulders, the locations of which I have long forgotten, and now the Loch Turret fissure.

Were the stones split by lightning and weather, were the fissures geological faults or is it possible that the telluric energies had enough power in the past to literally split large stones and even hillsides, especially if they had a weak point or fracture? Bear in mind that the Hebrew Shamir was a worm (ley energy?) which was supposed to be able to chew through stone. The only other alternative is that these stones and hills were deliberately split and carved by our ancestors as part of ley line engineering, which seems a little illogical. I will leave this for other researchers to enlarge upon in the future.

THE SUN, THE SERPENT AND THE FIRE GODDESS

During my research I read a roughly parallel work, *The Sun and the Serpent* by Hamish Miller and Paul Broadhurst, who tracked the St Michael's Line in the south of England.

This is a remarkable line of ancient sites, discovered by John Michel, which stretches from the westernmost tip of Cornwall to the eastern seaboard of East Anglia. Ancient sites abound on this line, including the Cheesewring, Glastonbury Tor, Avebury, West Kennett stone avenue and Trethevy Quoit, a Neolithic tomb built of six enormous stones supporting a huge capstone. However, the most striking aspect of this ley is the number of churches dedicated to St Michael and St Mary *(see Map 13)*.

When Hamish Miller and Paul Broadhurst followed this line, using divining rods, they made the fascinating discovery that it was not one line of energy, but two intertwining streams intersecting at nodal points where the more important sites were situated.

The St Michael Line is composed of a stream of energy about 20 paces wide, with the most powerful part in the centre, and tends to meander snake-like across the country, tuning not only into ancient sites, but also modern quarries, buildings, the centre of bridges, ravines, caves and castles.

The St Mary Line is slightly different: it meanders more and tends to tune into healing wells and church fonts – something which, if you remember, the cup-mark energies pointedly refused to do. I always knew there must be some other form of energy ley which prevented the cup-mark leys from tuning into the once powerful healing wells in Perthshire.

Recently, Anne Silk has discovered that the St Michael/Mary Line follows a line of earthquake epicentres *(see Map 14)*. This is verified by the fact that the churches on Glastonbury Tor and St Michael's Mount were destroyed by an earthquake in 1275. Clearly, these ancient structures were built in order to use natural energies for healing and ceremonial purposes.

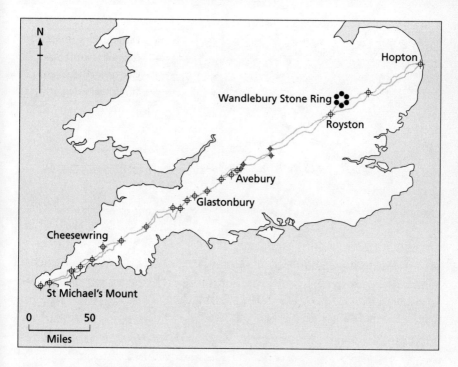

Map 13: The St Michael/Mary Line across southern England — not a straight ley, but two intertwining leys. The places where they cross were marked by sacred sites.

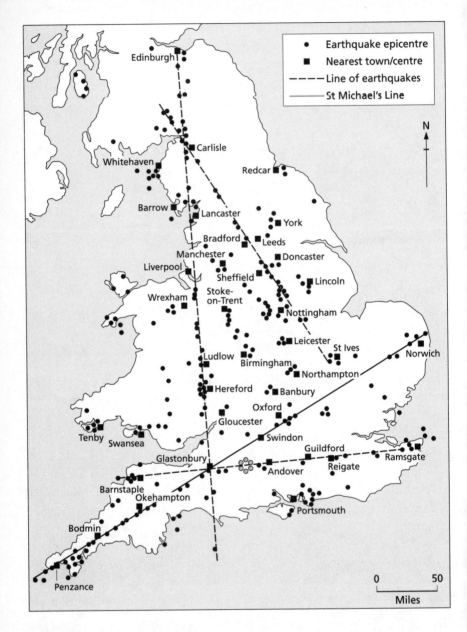

Map 14: The St Michael/Mary line (from bottom left of illustration) can be seen as one of several lines of earthquake epicentres across the country. These have been plotted from 1992 to 1996. (Composite map from many sources.)

10

EARTH ACUPUNCTURE

*Volcanic Plugs, Burial-Grounds,
'Spirit Paths' and 'the Electric Brae'*

Man also possesses a power by which he may see
his friends and the circumstances by which they
are surrounded, although such persons may be
a thousand miles from him at that time.

PARACELSUS, 1493–1541

Several straight leys gave me yet another insight into ancient legends and knowledge. I followed one from the east end of Loch Rannoch to Clach Ossian and the Lifting Stone, then to a standing stone at Dunning. Another, from St Michael's burial-ground at the west of Loch Rannoch, gave a difficult walk to St Adamnan's stone in Glen Lyon and on to Ardtalnaig burial-ground, south of Loch Tay, and yet another burial-ground in Crieff.

A similar line is to be found on the slopes of the extinct crater of Latium, Italy, where the Shrine of Diana and the Temple of the Queen of Heaven are in a straight line from the Temple of Jupiter on the summit.[1]

Back in Scotland, it took several years to follow the straight leys, until my maps were covered with sets of parallel lines, running in three directions through ancient burial-grounds and some standing stones.

Observing, eventually, that the lines were not quite parallel, I projected them, to find that some converged on Edinburgh Castle, some on Stirling Castle and, years later, others on the island of Ailsa Craig. These are all volcanic plugs. They are not the target, but the origin of the telluric energies.

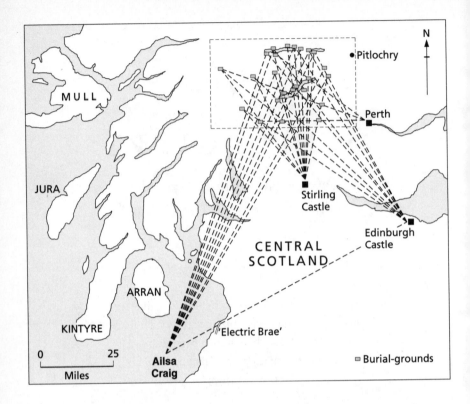

Map 15: A simplified diagram of burial-grounds across central Scotland (a few are shown as black rectangles). The dotted rectangle shows the mapped leys before they were projected to the volcanic plugs.

All of these volcanic plugs transmit straight leys through lines of burial-grounds (they probably return on the same ley to complete the circuit) and the cup-mark ley from Connachan Farm also transmits its own peculiar energies through them, with the dead accurately situated on the planet's pulse. Figure 41 is an idealized illustration of such a working burial-ground.

Ancient burial-grounds were also sometimes placed where the energies cross. As the map grew, it even became possible for me to predict the sites of burial-grounds unknown to me. Another volcanic sill, at Kinnoull Hill, near Perth, may also emit streams of energies through burial-grounds.

The waves emitted by volcanic plugs are the usual standing waves, 85 inches (216 cm) wavelength and 12 inches (30 cm) amplitude, not dissimilar to those emitted by standing stones and are in the VHF waveband.

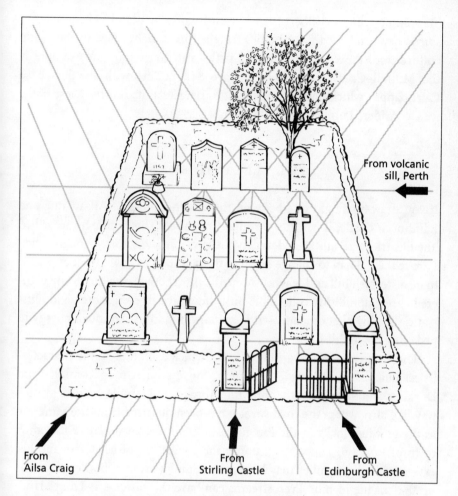

Figure 41: Leys from distant volcanic plugs cross through this burial-ground.

At the centre of these radial leys castles were sometimes built. These, of course, were the seats of the reigning monarchs or rulers (hence the term 'as straight as a ruler', as Paul Devereux points out). What the reigning monarchs of the past, sitting in the centre of these strange energies with a crown of precious stones on their heads, used this energy for, is an interesting question.

These straight leys are not unlike 'spirit paths', roads which lead to cemeteries. Medieval straight trackways called *Doodwegen*, which run from villages to cemeteries (hence the term 'dead straight'!) still survive in Holland. In several countries it was illegal to take the dead in anything but a straight line. Similarly in the Gilbert Islands, west Pacific, the islanders believed that spirits newly released from bodies travelled in straight lines. In the Celtic culture, too, the concept of 'faery paths' can be found. An example is the Muthill–Crieff road *(Map 4, page 84)*, in line with the henge of Cairnpapple, which had an important burial site at its centre. These paths were considered unlucky to build upon.

'THE ELECTRIC BRAE'

If you draw a straight line between the volcanic plugs of Ailsa Craig and Edinburgh Castle, it will run through Croy Brae. This is sometimes called 'the Electric Brae' and is said to defy the laws of gravity. Sure enough, when I drove there, I had to change down to third gear to go down what appeared to be a steepish hill and when I stopped halfway down, the car slowly gathered speed 'uphill'. My collapsible push-bike gave an even more vivid illustration of this phenomenon – it is quite galling to use so much energy in pedalling down this hill!

There are other places around the UK which exhibit the same characteristics. One is on Ranmore Common, Surrey, on a road coming from Dorking, and there is another on Mull. Abroad, an example is a new motorway in Cairo, where the road surface has been quarried from the same site as the granite blocks of the Pyramids. In Italy, meanwhile, near the small town of Rocca di Pappa, high up on the conical tip of Mt Cavo, another extinct volcano, families may be seen on Sundays rolling bottles and cans up the 'magnetic' hill.[2] Even streams can have this effect – at Long Mynd, Shropshire, and near the B797 in Ayrshire, for instance.

When any track or road is cut through virgin ground it forms its own energy ley, consisting of a series of vertical waves running parallel with it and following its twists and turns. They are usually 1 metre apart and the ley has a wavelength of 16 feet, 8 inches (508 cm), an amplitude 23 inches (58 cm) and is a standing wave. But here on the Electric Brae the wavelength is amplified to 1 foot (30 cm) and is only apparent on this part of the road. There is a small lay-by here, which has the same effect. The peaks of the waves are very close together on the tarmac, but ease out to the normal wavelength on the grass verge, both above and below the lay-by. When I tried the fields on both sides of the road, they showed no amplification at all. It was only on the tarmacadamed road that the compressed pattern of waves occurred.

Unfortunately, surveyors have confirmed that there is no gravitational anomaly – it is an optical illusion – but that does not fully explain this strange effect, which I have heard was unknown until the road was metalled.

REFERENCES

1 Margaret Stenhouse, *The Goddess of the Lake*, Press Time, Rome, 1997
2 Ibid.

11

THE LEYS FROM PILLAR ISLAND

The Glen Lyon Ley

The Earth hath bubbles, as the water has,
and these are of them.

WILLIAM SHAKESPEARE, *MACBETH*, I iii

One of the most interesting straight leys must be the one which runs through Glen Lyon to the west of Scotland, and I was determined to find both its source and destination.

The destination was in fact easily discovered. A little to the east of Fortingall there are three stone circles close together. These are the terminal points of three streams of leys which sweep across the country. Moreover, being circuits, they run in both directions, giving six streams of energy spread across the floor of this beautiful glen.

Walking westwards, the first element is Fortingall burial-ground, in line with the Praying Hands of Mary, the peculiar split stone which I had encountered years ago and had initiated my interest in this particular ley. Then there is another burial-ground at Bridge of Balgie, rectangular in shape like the others, and pointing down the glen.

Next is Meggernie Castle, which offers one of the better authenticated stories of a haunting in this country.

Figure 42: The volcanic island of Staffa (top) radiates telluric energy in all directions, like the spokes of a bicycle wheel. Here, a ley runs through a line of burial-grounds, an ancient shrine and some castles to Fortingall stone circles.

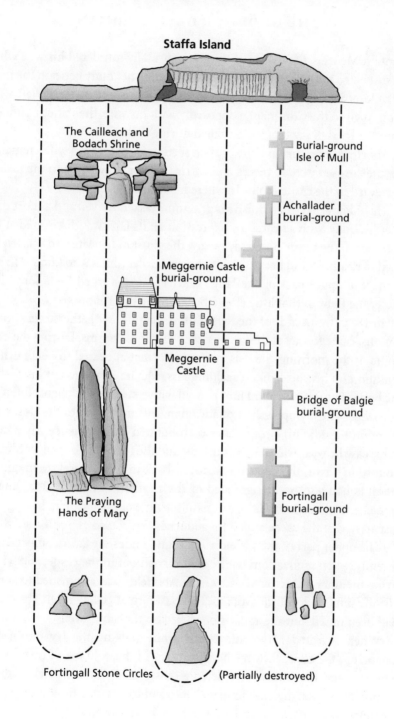

Staffa Island

The Cailleach and
Bodach Shrine

Burial-ground
Isle of Mull

Achallader
burial-ground

Meggernie Castle
burial-ground

Meggernie
Castle

Bridge of Balgie
burial-ground

The Praying
Hands of Mary

Fortingall
burial-ground

Fortingall Stone Circles   (Partially destroyed)

THE GHOST OF HALF A WOMAN

Captain Menzies, the owner of the castle, brutally murdered his wife when he suspected her of having an affair. After hiding her body beneath the floor of a closet in a space between two of the rooms in the castle, he left Glen Lyon to go to the Continent, supposedly with his wife, then after a suitable time returned to say that she had died during their visit.

Shortly after returning, the captain secretly recovered his wife's remains, cut the corpse into two pieces and carried the legs and torso to the nearby graveyard in the castle grounds, where he buried them.

He did not survive to finish his gruesome task, however, and a short time later his body, with a gruesome expression on its face, was discovered at the entrance to the tower. Some say he saw the ghost of his wife and was frightened to death. Or did her suspicious lover murder him – who knows? In any event, the upper part of the lady's body lay undisturbed for a long time under the floor of that little closet, between the two rooms.

In 1882, two friends of the tenant of Meggernie, Mr Fetherstone and Mr Simons, came to stay at the castle, occupying these rooms. During the early hours of the morning, Simons awoke with what appeared to be a burning sensation on his cheek, like a scalding kiss, which seemed to cut his flesh to the bone. The room around him glowed with a strange pink light. Terrified, he saw the ghostly upper half of a woman drifting away into the closet. His friend in the adjoining room later corroborated his experience, saying that in his case he was awakened by the light and the figure bending over him. As he rose in terror, the apparition moved back into the closet. Many of the servants had also been frightened of the ghastly figure, although the two gentlemen had no knowledge of this at the time of the incident, having only just arrived at the castle after a long journey.

The upper part of the skeleton was found under the floor comparatively recently, when renovations were being carried out in the castle, and within living memory a Doctor MacKay from Aberfeldy was astonished to see the ghostly upper part of the woman float past him at ceiling level. The ceiling had been raised, but the apparition stayed on the same level.[1]

When I visited Meggernie Castle while walking the ley outlined in Chapter 7, the estate factor, who accompanied me, told me of one evening when he and his family were driving down the private road close to the empty castle. As the building was unoccupied at the time and he was responsible for it, he looked up to check it. He noticed a pink light in a bedroom, one floor up. He had the keys in his pocket, so he walked across to the castle, watching the pink light grow brighter. Now alarmed that the castle might be on fire, he opened the door, ran up the stairs and burst into the bedroom. The pink light had vanished and it was with a chill of horror that he realized what it must have been – the ghost of Lady Menzies.

The third burial-ground on the trail of this ley is the castle graveyard itself, where Captain Menzies buried half of his wife. One young local, trying to keep a straight face, told me that one dark night he passed this eerie spot, to be confronted with a ghostly pair of legs, dangling over one of the gravestones!

FOLLOWING THE LEY

There was little more in the way of ancient sites as I followed the ley up Gleann Cailleach to the old Bodach's shrine. His family was still there, as usual, in a neat semi-circle outside their house, so I paid homage to them in passing, placing the small offering of a white quartzite stone on the roof. After so many years of research into this strange world I was becoming wary of the unseen and in any case the word *cailleach*, according to *Dwelly's Gaelic Dictionary*, means not only 'old wife' but also 'a supernatural or malign influence dwelling in dark caves, woods and corries'. Better to be safe, I thought, as I placed the offering and walked on, up to the ridge, over and down to the burial-ground near the farm of Achallader.

A short distance away is another castle, built by Black Duncan of the Cowl, which may have been on this wide ley. I ignored it as I had a long hard slog to Barcaldine Castle and further west to the coast, where I hoped to find the standing stone or stone circle which, I presumed, started this multiple energy ley.

To my disappointment, there was no stone circle, no standing stone, nothing. After an exhausting walk over rough bogland, I found myself standing on the seashore, quite exasperated, with my divining rod pointing across the sea to Lismore Island and beyond that the mystic island of Mull.

The ley was long enough to give me an accurate projection on my map, however. Lismore Island held nothing of interest, so I projected the line further to Mull, where it passed through a burial-ground.

A few weeks later I arrived on Mull and picked the ley up at this burial-ground, to discover that it, like all of the other burial-grounds on that ley, was predominantly Campbell. Perhaps the Campbells had the 'understanding' – they were certainly a very powerful clan in their day.

During the next few days I tracked across the island, until I once again found myself on a sandy shore, looking out to sea, more exasperated than ever. Where on Earth did this ley come from?

THE SOURCE

Again I projected the ley westwards on the map and this time the source was revealed – as obvious as Stirling and Edinburgh Castle rocks, and made from similar material! It was the island of Staffa, a few miles away across the sea.

Stafr ey (Pillar Island), as the early Norse in their long ships called it, is a geologically fascinating island 7 miles (11 kilometres) west of Mull, off the west coast of Scotland. It has unique basalt columns, the basalt having been poured from a volcano during the Tertiary period and contracted into hexagonal columns, which have been further sculpted by the pounding Atlantic breakers. The island shakes so much during violent storms that one

Figure 43: The island of Staffa. Note the boat sheltering in the cave.

Figure 44: Fingal's Cave.

family occupying a tiny clachan near the centre of the island in the late 1790s was forced to leave.[2]

Fingal's Cave is a prominent feature of the island. Fingal and his giants are common in ancient Celtic mythology, as one might expect. Apparently he built Staffa to avoid getting his feet wet when he walked across the sea from the Giant's Causeway in Ireland to Scotland to 'lift' cattle. 'The Wishing Chair' inside also has his name appended to it, although it was originally called 'the Priest's Chair', and the cave was at one time called the Gaelic equivalent of 'the musical cave'. 'The Herdsman', a group of basalt columns a short distance away, reputedly had a pedestal for each of Fingal's warriors, the Fian.

Unfortunately, it was some years after my visit that I realized that the caves are even more powerful than the island itself. I have read that a light at the back of Fingal's Cave can be seen on the nearby island of Mull, the Sacred Isle, and of course, if a light can cross that distance, so can a ley. It must be an unusually powerful one – the famous Iona Abbey is situated on it.

REFERENCES

1 Archie McKerracher, *Perthshire in History and Legend*, John Donald Publishers, Edinburgh, 1988

2 Donald R. McCulloch, *Staffa*, David & Charles

12

CIRCULAR
BURIAL-GROUNDS

Four-Poster Leys

Where plants perish and animals are absent,
there you also should not live.
The place is unhealthy.
MICHEL NOSTRADAMUS, 1503–66

Four-stone circles (four posters) work in a different manner from other circles. After several weekends following a ley from a four-stone circle at Lundin Farm near Aberfeldy, I was becoming a little disillusioned, having encountered nothing in the way of sacred sites. Now, after 7 miles (12 kilometres) plodding through deep snow in a blizzard, something appeared briefly in the distance. This was a group of three cairns at the head of Glen Sharvie. I took my map out in the howling wind and found that it was actually marked – Carn Bad an Fraoich, the Cairn of the Clusters of Heather. On closer inspection I found a pile of stones in a heap below the cairns, possibly the remains of an earlier and larger structure.

As I followed the ley through the cairns and, 9 miles (14 kilometres) further on, approached the east end of Loch Earn, I discovered that it was behaving in an unusual manner. There was no indication of it attempting to tune into the loch as I had expected. Nevertheless, I plodded doggedly along, down to St Fillans and, for the second time, along the tail and nose of the Serpent. The ley ran on across the river and the golf course, continuing perfectly straight until it began to turn towards the burial-ground of St Fillan himself.

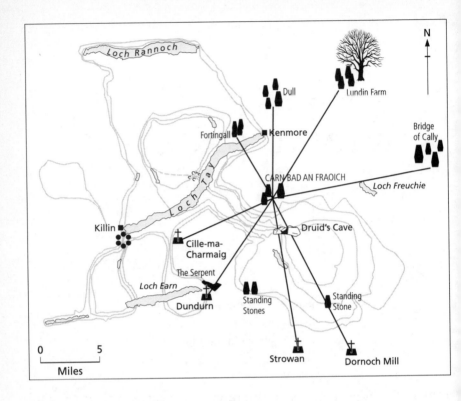

Map 16: Carn Bad an Fraoich (centre) is the focus of leys from four-stone circles (four posters), which transmit ley streams through the cairn and on to circular burial-grounds. The ley from Fortingall is the only one which was not followed on foot to verify it. Note how the standing stone at Stonefield and the Druid's Cave act as cross-over points on the cup-mark ley system. Another ley from two standing stones to the east of Dundurn may act as a 'stop' for this type of ley, turning it on its reciprocal (see Figure 48, p.144). Cille-ma-Charmaig and Dundurn burial-grounds are positioned on cup-mark leys as well as the leys from four-stone circles. Strowan and Dornoch Mill are, in all probability, also on cup-mark leys which have not yet been mapped.

Figure 45 (opposite): Carn Bad an Fraoich, the centre of the ley system connecting round burial-grounds to four-stone circles.

Figure 46 (opposite): The four-poster at Lundin Farm, near Aberfeldy. This is the beginning of the ley to St Fillans burial-ground.

Figure 47: Dundurn church and burial-ground, St Fillans. The stone in the fore-ground warps telluric energy around and into the church.

AN UNUSUAL HOLED STONE

The last resting-place of St Fillan the leper is circular, not rectangular like most of the other burial-grounds in the area. Here, the outer wave of the ley curves around the burial-ground. It then runs back parallel to the incoming energy, presumably returning to the four-poster whence it came.

Initially I thought that the ley collapsed naturally at the burial-ground, or possibly the burial-ground itself turned the ley on its reciprocal, but many years later, more in touch with Earth energies, I realized that the mechanism for this unique feature may be another ley, this time from a pair of standing stones just a few miles away from the burial-ground. These stones are nicely lined up with the burial-ground and the ley which they produce may act as a 'stop' for the four-poster ley, turning it completely around *(see Figure 48)*.

Circular graveyards are of considerable antiquity and in the grounds of this ancient cemetery is a peculiar gnarled stone, set upright among the gravestones. Many years ago a friend and I had noticed this stone, which has two holes pierced deep into its side. Inevitably, we tried to see if there was anything of interest in the cavities. Some old tarnished sixpenny and three-penny pieces came to light. We replaced them carefully and added some of our own coins to the collection. I had never heard or read anything about this stone or the votive collection of offerings inside it and even to this day it seems to have been ignored by local historians.

Now, after years of research, I thought this old stone must surely be part of the Earth energy network. I followed one of the curving waves from the outer edge of the cup-mark ley into the stone, through it and out of the opposite side.

A more careful examination revealed that one side of the stone had been flattened. This made it rather similar to some standing stones which emit waves from their flat faces. Intuitively, I tried to find a wave from the flat carved face of this stone. One wave from it went towards the nearby church, passed round it neatly and back. Another wave, a much thinner loop, trav-elled towards the centre of the church and went into the corner, over St Fillan's grave, before coming back through a little window (see Figure 48).

The two holes in the stone were of different shape and size. One was wide, which amplified the incoming telluric wave around the church, and the other was deep and narrow, which projected the second narrow wave into St Fillan's grave. In effect, the two circuits from that stone tuned the church and the remains of the saint into the telluric system.

Curiously, according to Dr J. Schneck of Bideford, Devon, there is a remarkably similar stone outside Lech church, in Graz, Austria. This, according to a plaque, was placed (or relocated) there in 1621. Nearby is the Herz Jesu church, which has a chapel used by the Knights of the Holy Grave. This has three freshly made cup-marked stones outside it, affording protec-tion. Someone in Austria has access to the ancient knowledge or has redis-covered it for himself or has read my first book!

Now it was simply a matter of following other similar leys from four-posters through Carn Bad an Fraoich to other burial-grounds to complete the picture. There is one anomaly: these leys are not straight, they have been warped by the cairn at the centre, although there is one which should satisfy the purist – from Fortingall to Carn Bad an Fraoich, the Druid's Cave, the standing stone at Stonefield and Dornoch burial-ground. I have not yet walked this one to verify it. The standing stone at Stonefield may have been used as a crossover point on this particular circuit (see Map 17, page 158).

Figure 48: The ley from a four-poster travels across the hills, through the Serpent (top right) and is warped around the old burial-ground by another ley from a pair of standing stones 2.5 miles (4 kilometres) away. Notice the hill notch at the top left of the illustration.

THE 'DEATH' OF ANOTHER ANCIENT WARRIOR

As I mentioned earlier, I was surprised to find that this particular type of ley was intentionally vectored away from lochs. There was one, however, the Dull to Strowan Ley, which passed through the southern edge of Loch Turret, now a reservoir, with its raised waters encroaching on the ley.

When following this particular circuit, I noticed a barely discernible change in its character after it had crossed the loch. It had been snowing,

Figure 49: A close-up of the holed stone in the graveyard.

and the only thing I could think of was to turn and follow the wave back the way I had come.

On the other circuits I had been following up until then, including this one, the sinuous waves of energy had moved gently out of phase until they were at full-scale deflection, then moved back into phase again. What was quite new and unexpected was that this wave was static. In other words, it was a standing wave like some of the straight leys, which resemble the caduceus.

Folklore can give many insights into the operation of telluric energies and one book by J. F. Campbell and George Henderson, *The Celtic Dragon Myth* (Newcastle Publishing Co. Inc., 1981), gave me some knowledge of the ancient story behind this particular circuit:

There was a warrior contemporary with Fingal. His name was Fraoch.

*[Could the hero's name have been replaced with the word fraoich (heather)
  as the ancient knowledge died, I wonder?]*

There is a loch called Freuchie, originally Fraoch's Loch.

[This loch is a few miles east of the cairns.]

Fraoch was healed at the hands of the Sidh [the faery people].

*[The ley from Carn Bad an Fraoich to Cille-ma-Charmaig burial-ground
  crosses the Sidh or Faery Hill of Ardtalnaig.]*

Fraoch was killed by a serpent.

*[The Serpent or Crocodile at St Fillans is where the Lundin Farm/Dundurn
  burial-ground ley ends, or dies.]*

*Fraoch must not go near water, otherwise there will be a conflict which will
  issue [sic] in his death.*

*[This explains the sinuous wave changing to a static wave after passing
  through Loch Turret.]*

Fraoch is associated with energy.

[Telluric energy, surely?]

Finally, consider the ley which runs from the four-poster at Lundin Farm
across the hills to the Serpent of St Fillans. In local folklore there is a story
that only the Serpent's head can be seen – its body lies buried under the
hills, with the tail sticking out in Loch Tayside!

13

SACRED GEOMETRY

A Town Based on the Earth Energy System and Feng Shui

Science at its best should leave room for poetry.
RICHARD DAWKINS, *UNWEAVING THE RAINBOW* (1998)

My home town of Crieff, situated in the heart of Perthshire, has two long straight streets which converge to the south of the town, rather like the bottom arm of a star, which prompted me to search for a telluric pattern.

King Street, running north–south, has a church and a stone circle visibly in line with it, and it was this straight ley which I followed on foot to the north-east. It passed through the stone circle to Gilmerton church and continued eventually to a pair of stone circles at Tullybelton, near Perth.

To the south, I ploughed my way, in deep snow, to a standing stone at Dalchirla Farm, set like a playing card with its edge lined up – almost – with King Street. Plotting this ley on the map gave a disappointing mis-match of about 330 feet (100 metres), but there is one type of ley, I knew, whose edge just touches standing stones in this manner.

The other major street is Burrell Street, whose ley I followed, first north-west towards the Sma' Glen through several hill summit cairns. By now I was almost crippled by this demanding research, so I had to resort to projecting this ley on my map. It continued to a standing stone at Ballinluig. To the south-east, after only three-quarters of a mile (1.6 kilometres), Concraig Farm standing stone came into view, neatly in line.

So here were two of the main streets of Crieff, in line with the megaliths, quietly chattering away to each other in their own code, century after

Figure 50: Dalchirla standing stone, roughly lined up with King Street, Crieff.

century. It seemed extraordinary. It is an ancient town, certainly, but how could standing stones have anything to do with relatively modern town planning? Yet there was no denying that two churches had been built on these two leys. Had the knowledge been passed on until comparatively recent times or was it a coincidence?

RECONSTRUCTING THE PATTERN

The most obvious next choice of street was the High Street. There was a ley here too, which I followed, passing through a parish church and burial-ground, the town hall, town clock and stocks, and out of the village in the direction of Killin stone circle. Faced with a difficult 19-mile (30-kilometre) walk over 2,000-foot (600-metre) hills, I was more than relieved when I

Figure 51: Braefordie standing stone, lined up with West High Street, Crieff.

suddenly came face-to-face with a standing stone on the summit of a hill at Braefordie, near Comrie, only 5.5 miles (9 kilometres) away. There was nothing on my map to indicate its presence at all, although later maps refer to it as a stone circle.

I projected this line to the east of the town and followed it to a standing stone near Aberuthven, then further to another standing stone in the centre of Dunning. Whatever anyone might think, there could be no denying it now. The town did have a structured layout.

What kind of pattern could have been used? It must surely have been a meaningful and powerful symbol. I found a clue in the street layout – King Street and Burrell Street meet at a point, as already mentioned. On a large-scale map this has a curious similarity to the point of a pentagram, an ancient and powerful symbol, but this pattern just did not fit.

Coincidentally, a letter arrived from a friend who had been to a talk by the late Wing Commander Beadon. The wing commander had discovered that in open countryside, unspoilt by human hand, a natural, complicated,

Figure 52: The star-shaped network discovered by Wing Commander Beadon.

interlocking series of star-shaped patterns could be found *(see Figure 52)*. When I copied the star onto acetate and laid it over the map of the town, the whole layout immediately sprang into shape. There were the standing stones, sending ley after ley through the old roads in a complex pattern.

One ley at the bottom of the hexagram caught my attention. Open country to the south-west of the town enabled me to pursue it to a small burial-ground about 5 miles (8 kilometres) away, near Comrie. In the opposite direction I followed the ley on foot to a standing stone near Scone. This took care of the lower arm of the hexagram.

To the east were two standing stones very close together, neatly lined up in tandem at Crofthead Farm.

THE SPIDER IN THE WEB

For the pattern to be of significance, I reasoned, there must be a powerful site in the centre. Indeed there was – in this system the omphalos is St Michael's church. In fact, this church was built on the site of a very much

Figure 53: The standing stone at Scone.

older church and graveyard, so old it had a heather-thatched roof and a wooden idol, now long since lost or destroyed.

St Michael and St George were the dragon-slaying (or dragon-manipulating) saints. The dragons, of course, were the telluric energy. St George's sword and St Michael's lance are symbolic of the weapons which pierced the dragon's head, to fix it as the focal point of the Earth energy system.[1]

The Crieff Masonic Lodge, no. 38, is a very old one and is also called St Michael's. The Freemasons do crop up occasionally in this line of research. Most people are aware of their symbol, a compass with its points facing down, intertwined with a set-square with its points facing up, but few realize that part of the symbol is hidden. If you draw a line across the open points of the compass and another across the set-square you have a six-pointed star. The knowledge of this sacred geometry must have been

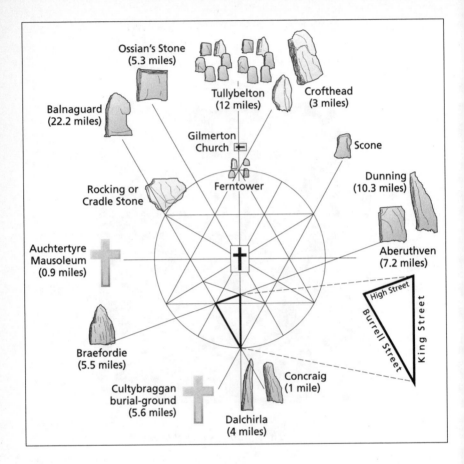

Figure 54: The star of Crieff, with standing stones forming the pattern.

handed down through the years to the practising Knights Templar and Freemasons, only to be lost comparatively recently, because of the powerful vows of secrecy kept by these lodges.

The angle between Burrell Street and King Street is 28.5°. Ideally the correct angle ought to be 30°, half of an equilateral triangle. The correct angle, however, would have been an immediate giveaway of the true nature of the symbol. Another possibility is that the symbol on the ground is not theoretically perfect, but an energy pattern, capable of being warped by various factors. A map of 1822 shows newly built houses along Burrell Street and a square at a nodal point of leys called 'the Octagon' which is not shown on a map of 1783.

THE SPIDER'S WEB OF GLASGOW

In the 1920s Ludovic Kennedy Mann discovered that Glasgow had been laid out like a clockface or a gigantic spider's web:

> *His (Neolithic philosopher and astronomer) radii, usually set out in a 19 divisional system (subdivided at times into 38ths and 76ths) dictated the positions, and ran through loci of prehistoric importance.*[2]

Glasgow might, of course, have had a similar pattern to the Crieff one. It may not be a coincidence that the symbol of the thirty-third and final degree of Freemasonry is a spider with three heads. It may be simply the telluric likeness to the web some old towns were constructed on. It is interesting to note, however, that Glasgow cathedral, the omphalos (though some say the nearby Necropolis is the centre), was constructed over a sacred healing well, which radiates out its pattern of energies. Faint vestiges of knowledge have come down to us over the centuries, in very individual form.

The Dying Remnants of Knowledge

As a teenager in Glasgow, visiting relatives in the Gorbals, I was sometimes intrigued, when walking up a dark and dingy close, to find beautiful and intricate patterns drawn in white chalk around the front doormats of some homes. These were step charms, sometimes called 'devil's patterns', and were handed down from mother to daughter. They were originally executed in white chalk, flour or sand and later in coloured crayon, all with an intricate weaved pattern as a basic part of the design. In all probability they were to be found in any city in the United Kingdom, but gradually vanished about the 1950s. They have been revived in India, where they are called *kolams*. The idea was that the lady of the house would spend some time, early in the morning, drawing the pattern, so that when her husband went to work through the front door, he would be entering the benevolent energy field she had created. During the afternoon she would redraw the pattern so that her husband would gain the benefits of the energy when returning home.

The problem of towns built on star patterns remains, however. Why should towns be built to a pattern at all?

Wing Commander Beadon pointed out that the star pattern was natural until buildings containing glass (windows, for example) were erected, then it collapsed. If our ancestors wished to remain in harmony with the natural energy, then they had to rebuild the energy system by using standing stones and circles.

FENG SHUI

Other countries have known about and used the beneficial aspects of Earth energies for millennia. In China and the Far East, the art of *feng shui* is practised to promote peace and harmony with the land. Providing one lives and works in a good *feng shui* site, good fortune and a long life will ensue.

China has the ancient concept of *ch'i*, or 'dragon lines', as the Chinese call them, which is comprised of two types of energy currents which traverse the country, one being yin, the tiger, the weaker female element, and the other yang, the dragon, the stronger male aspect. Both follow the contours of the land, in a similar way to the cup-mark leys outlined throughout this book. They travel along streams and watercourses, above and below the ground, and originate in the mountains. It is thought that the point where yin and yang meet is the best place to situate a burial-ground.

Multiple Souls

The location of burial-grounds was very important to the Chinese, since they believed that every person had three souls. One stayed with the body after death (Po), and of the other two (collectively called Hun), the first migrated to a shrine or tablet in the ancestral home and the second went on to Purgatory, or possibly Paradise as the case may be, out of reach of *feng shui* influences, evolving in its own manner. It was the first soul that the ancient Chinese were particularly interested in, as they believed that if this animal soul could be kept happy and comfortable, then it would smile benevolently on its descendants, bringing prosperity, happiness, good health and good luck.

After a bereavement, it was not uncommon for sons to be unable to agree as to who was to bury their father. Each son wanted the best possible *feng shui* site so that he and his family could reap the benefits of his parent's 'good luck'. Unfortunately the dead parent could remain unburied for some time while the site was agreed upon! In Amoy, not so long ago, missionaries were appalled to see large earthenware jars dotted around the hillside. Inside were the remains of Chinamen awaiting burial at a more propitious time. 'Potted Chinamen', they were called!

Even the time of burial was crucial, since if it was done correctly, the grave would accept beneficial energy from a particular vein of *ch'i* and keep it all year round, instead of for just a few days if the interment was haphazard.

The preservation of the body and its bones in as good a condition as possible was also of vital importance. If the entire body decayed, then the animal spirit would leave, since it was bound to its remains, so hard loamy soil, well drained, was considered best for the burial. Rock was not good, as it could not breathe the vital energy.

The position of the body in the grave also had to be precise and the professor of *feng shui* sometimes took an hour to correctly position it. He placed a red thread along the precise axis of the coffin, lined up with a similar thread held by the mourners above the grave, together with a geomancer's compass to assess the best alignment. This has similarities with other cultures, as mentioned earlier, like the Celtic 'faery paths', the Dutch *Doodwegen* (death roads) and also the 'ghost paths' of medieval Germany. These straight paths all either start or end at a cemetery.[3] Likewise the paths of energy from the megalithic culture pass through burial-grounds, individual tombs and cists in which the dead have been laid to rest.

Straight roads and streets (called 'secret arrows') are very bad *feng shui* to the Chinese, as are railways, tramways, lines of electric pylons and telephone poles.

It is easy for our culture to dismiss these concepts out of hand as superstitious nonsense, but most religions had a very similar understanding. The ancient Egyptians, for instance, believed that on death the individual would separate into three souls: the Ka, the Ba and the reanimated mummy. They were experts in the art of embalming, which they believed enabled the animal spirit to stay with the mortal remains as long as possible. The Huna tradition of the Polynesian Islands encompasses three spirits: the lower (animal), middle (conscious) and the higher (superconscious). The Native Americans had a similar belief, which was personified by their totem poles. These were composed of three figures: the lower being an animal, the animal spirit, the middle being the figure related to the middle self and the top being the guardian angel or Higher Self, occasionally depicted with out-spread wings.[4]

In the Scots Gaelic tradition, meanwhile, the remains of the person in the grave were distinguished by a type of shade, which travelled around the person's usual haunts or over the grave itself. On the island of Inchbuie, Killin, one of the McNab family's stone coffins was pierced with a hole 'so that the spirit can wander across the country it once knew so well'.

This is similar to stories from Ireland and elsewhere of spirits or faeries travelling along straight lines, or 'faery paths', those routes which we now call leys. The modern concept of a faery is the tiny impish or ephemeral figure waving a wand, but the Celts believed that such beings were very real and were to be treated with the greatest respect.

What can we make of the strange cocktail of energies which our ancestors used, moulded and focused through their houses and burial-grounds? They seemed not only to know about life after death and the benefits which could be gained by keeping the animal spirits of their forefathers happy, but they also used this knowledge in a similar manner to the Chinese tradition of *feng shui*.

Ancestor worship, an obvious link to ensure prosperity, is still practised in some countries. In the past, the system may have been used to promote health with the use of healing wells and a form of benevolent witchcraft and to install the psyche of individuals into the energy leys via the interment of their remains at power points.

The basic energy used for the construction of such a highly sophisticated system is entirely natural, coming basically from the Earth herself.

REFERENCES

1 Nigel Pennick, *The Ancient Science of Geomancy*, Thames & Hudson, 1979
2 Ludovic Kennedy Mann, Institute of Geomantic Research, Paper No. 7, ISSN: 0308–1996
3 Paul Devereux, *The New Ley Hunter's Guide*, Gothic Image Publications, 1994
4 Max Long, *The Secret Science at Work*, Devorss and Company, 1953

14

REBUILDING THE ANCIENT MAGIC

A Hypothetical Reconstruction of the Ley System

The fairest order in the world is a heap of random sweepings.

HERACLITUS, 535–475 BC

Now we know enough about the energy leys to rebuild a theoretical system from the basic standing stones and circles, burial-grounds and homesteads on the ley circuits to the sophisticated cup-mark complex, much the same as our ancestors did some 3,000–4,000 years ago.

The area, of course, will be the one which has been the focus of this book, from Skye to Newcastle, although I have used the henge of Balfarg, near the Forth Estuary, as the most southerly point as part of this long ley runs off my maps and I am uncertain of the henges and stone circles around Newcastle (*see Map 17*).

First, we must understand that Loch Tay is the key point of this corridor of energy leys as the basic cup-mark ley we are building will automatically seek out the centre of this loch, so a starting-point will be midway along its length.

Secondly, this primary ley we are about to rebuild should extend at roughly right angles to Loch Tay. Projecting this line to the north-west from Machuim, the stone circle at the centre of the north bank of Loch Tay, we find that our planned ley passes neatly across the island of Skye.

Next we must find a starting-point for our ley, one of great natural telluric power, and there is really only one, far out in the Atlantic, the group of islands forming the volcanic caldera of St Kilda.

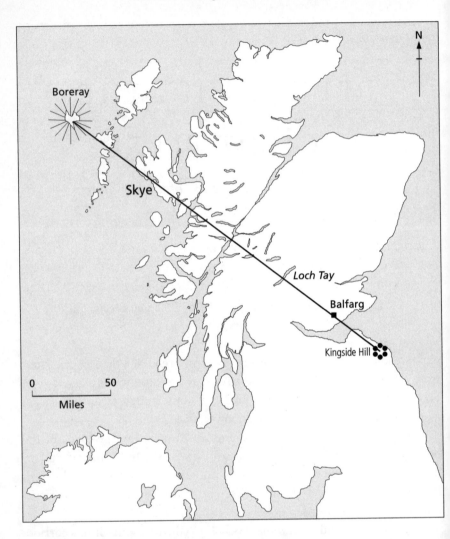

Map 17: Using the island of Boreray, an extinct volcano near St Kilda, as the source of telluric energy, a primary ley can be built across the country through the centre of Loch Tay. Balfarg stone circle can now be built on a natural power point on this hypothetical line. Once built, the power ley will be established.

Projecting this line to the south-east, Kingside stone circle also seems to be on this ley. Extending it further across Europe may give further clues – a volcano, perhaps, may be another source.

Every volcanic plug, caldera, etc., as we have seen, radiates out energy like the spokes of a bicycle wheel. We must now find the segment of the caldera which emits the radiating waves to the centre of Loch Tay and build a stone circle just at that point. This will be on the island of Boreray.

Project the line from Loch Tay to the south-east and find a power point as near the coast as you can – Balfarg, near the Forth Estuary, as it happens. This power point may simply be a place where underground streams cross. Plan your second stone circle there, but do not build it yet.

A MAJOR SITE

The next stage is to find a site for your major cup-marked stone. The place we shall choose is in the Sma' Glen. Since this is a major site and will be responsible for the initial shaping of the telluric image, we must landscape the area into an amphitheatre with a level floor – the amphitheatre will shape the initial spirals which will eventually be a vital part in the structure of the cup-mark ley *(see Figure 55)*.

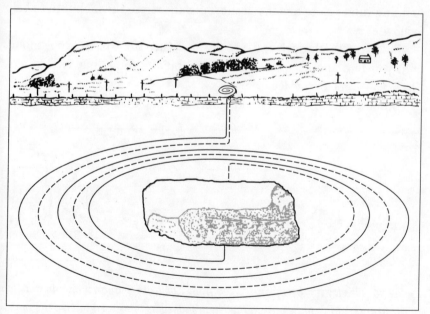

Figure 55: The stone, now energized, emits a spiral around itself which is projected to the low mound in the distance. This is the basic building-block of the entire cup-mark system.

For the sake of simplicity, we shall make this stone a recumbent one, although we shall shortly come to another similar cup-marked stone which is upright. Place a very large stone in the centre of the amphitheatre. It must be heavy enough not to be moved by any normal means.

Since the system has to be built up layer upon layer, the next step is to build a small mound a few hundred yards away to act like the positive pole of a battery, the potential cup-marked stone itself being the negative one. The mound may be composed of alternate layers of clay and earth, much in the same manner as Silbury Hill, or simply be a site of natural energy.

Energize the stone by percussing it until you initiate the shape wave which will find the nearest most attractive target – the small cairn we have just built.

Now we have to input another energy ley to further increase the main stone's power. At Crofthead Farm, carve a large monolith, giving it a flat face, and place it above two crossing underground streams. Since the ley will be projected from the broad flat face of the monolith, you will have to turn it gradually, until the ley is projected across the country to the blank cup-marked stone at Connachan Farm. You can also put two standing stones close together a short distance from the monolith to help focus the ley.

Now project it through and past the Sma' Glen stone into Glen Almond, until you find another power point, and build a four-stone circle there, Clach-na-Tiompan (*see Figure 56*).

You now have your first working ley focused on the cup-marked stone.

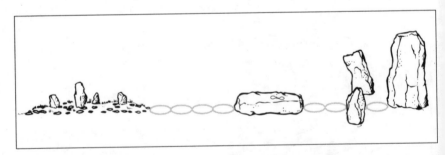

Figure 56: This ley has been constructed from Clach-na-Tiompan four-poster (left of illustration) to Crofthead standing stones and has been used to give the initial power to the stone which will be the cup-marked stone at Connachan Farm.

This underground souterrain or earth house at Pitcur, near Dundee, has this strange cup-marked stone guarding its inner recesses.

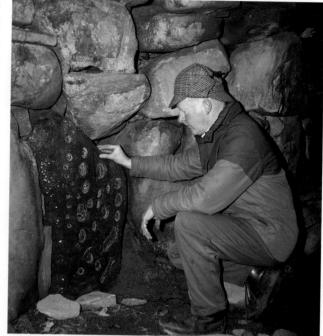

BELOW: The Rocking Stone of Glen Tarken, St Fillans, Perthshire. This rocking stone or Logan Stone at one time was so delicately balanced it would sway in a high wind.

The Serpent, or Crocodile, of St Fillans is placed at the crossing of energy leys.

This inhospitable island of Boreray, St Kilda (left), far out in the Atlantic, has a stone circle on it. The world's greatest gannetry, Stac an Armin, is at centre, Stac Lee to the right.
(© Colin Baxter)

A beautiful set of petroglyphs at Ormaig, near Kilmartin, Argyllshire.

The Praying Hands of Mary in Glen Lyon, Perthshire, is just one element of a long energy ley stretching across mainland Scotland to the islands.

This cliff face at Mauchline, Ayrshire, shows innumerable cup-marks and some cup-and-rings.

A nuclear submarine surfaces at Faslane, Holy Loch, western Scotland, after a long patrol. (© *The Glasgow Herald*)

Ball of light over Banbury at 19.50 hrs on 4 February 1995. (© Brian James Creail, Oxon.)

'WARP' by Michael Brown. Computer generated image exactly captures the multi-images present on every part of the earth. (© Michael Brown)

Crop circle. (© Lucy Pringle)

MAKING THE FIRST CUP-MARK

It is time to make your first cup-mark to initiate the cup-mark system. Peck out a small depression on the Connachan Farm stone and, carefully checking at intervals, find the perimeter of telluric energy which will be emitted from the stone. When the cup-mark energy is large enough to contour around the hills, find where it crosses the primary ley, still to be activated, and build a large cave from boulders, making sure that there are interstices at the rear for the cup-mark ley to flow out of when the cup-mark ley is started and also that the interior of the cave is dome-shaped.

Now that the cave is in position, you can adjust the shape of the southern circular cup-mark ley by making other minor leys, just touching the sides – Lundin Farm four-stone circle to Dunruchin Moor, the stone circle at Braefordie linking with Crofthead, etc. (see Map 9).

Finish building Balfarg stone circle near Glenrothes. This will start the main primary ley across the country to resonate with the energy from the stone circle on Boreray. (It is probable that Balfarg is not the ultimate power point on the south-east part of this ley. More likely it is another volcano or volcanic plug somewhere in Europe, or an ancient and major artificial construction, but until software capable of projecting this line accurately enough across the Continent is available, I will leave this open.)

Back at the cup-marked stone in the Sma' Glen, carve the arm of the dumb-bell shaped petroglyph, ensuring that it is pointing towards the centre of Loch Tay. The embryonic cup-mark ley should now leave the Druid's Cave and cross the hills towards the loch, and may be helped by carving out Fingal's Swordcut, leading the ley over the hills, down and across the centre of Loch Tay.

BUILDING A STONE CIRCLE

Find the energy exiting the north side of the loch and at the nearest power point on that line, build a six-stone circle. The circuit is now warped eastwards, contouring the hills, and is drawn up to Loch Creag a Mhadaidh, down into Glen Lyon, then back up to the hills to another powerful attraction, Loch na Lairaige, before contouring the hills to the stone circle at Machuim. Entering the circle, it is expelled for another circuit outside the first and back to the stone circle again.

Stone circles, incidentally, are built in a number of geometric shapes – pure circles, flattened circles, egg-shapes, ellipses, compound rings, etc., and there has been much speculation as to why. It may be that they conform to the natural patterns presented on the Earth's surface by underground fissures and streams. As we have seen, a theoretical underground stream, running perfectly horizontally beneath the surface, emits energy vertically upwards, giving spirals whose outer edge is almost circular. If the stream is running slightly downhill, the spirals will be naturally elongated on the down side, and if there is another stream crossing below, giving a power point, this will give a much more complicated pattern on the surface, though one entirely natural, obeying the laws of physics. It may be that our ancestors simply built their circles on top of this complicated geometric pattern, without necessarily knowing anything about the geometry involved.

Leaving the circle for the last time, the ley tunes into the centre of Loch Tay and naturally flows back up to Fingal's Swordcut and further on to the rear of the Druid's Cave. This form of telluric energy has a tendency to attach itself to similar energies, and flows parallel to them, but since we don't want it to follow the ley entering the mouth of the cave from the east, we nudge the energy out of the cave to the west by constructing another straight ley from the standing stone at Clach-na-Tiompan to Dalchirla stone circle and adjust it so that it passes close to the mouth of the Druid's Cave. The cup-mark ley is now warped to the south-west, contouring the hills, before running back to the cup-marked stone in the Sma' Glen (*see Map 18*).

Now that the circuit has been established, the resonating effect of the Druid's Cave at its focus will bring the original wavelength of the cup-mark ley to its working attitude – wavelength 24 feet, 2 inches (7.2 metres), amplitude 3 feet, 8 inches (1 metre) – and also give it the vital cavity-seeking quality which I discussed in Chapter 4.

The two outer shells can be taken together, since they are so similar. Construct the mounds at Gilmerton and shape them so that the ley will attach itself outside the circuits we have just constructed. The basic ley to power this may come from Cairnpapple henge to the south. As you can see from Map 19 the ley (*bottom right*) seems to push the outer shell straight to the Gilmerton mounds, so we must presume that this is the ley which powers the outer shell.

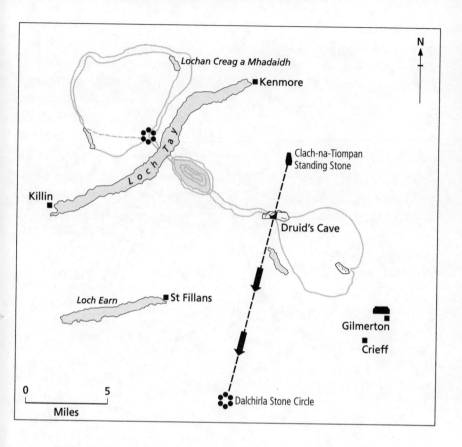

Map 18: The ley from Clach-na-Tiompan to Dalchirla has been constructed to force the cup-mark ley from the mouth of the Druid's Cave to the south-west.

This cup-mark ley contours clockwise, to the north-east, following the previous leys at a distance, past Loch Tay, round Loch Rannoch and back to Loch Tay again.

KILLIN STONE CIRCLE

Now we wish to warp the energy to Balquhidder, so build Killin stone circle at a power point on this line and warp the energy over Glen Ogle to Loch Larig Eala and down the hill to the Balquhidder area, constructing lochs where necessary to complete the three circuits around Loch Voil (*see Map 19, bottom left, and Figure 32, p.99*).

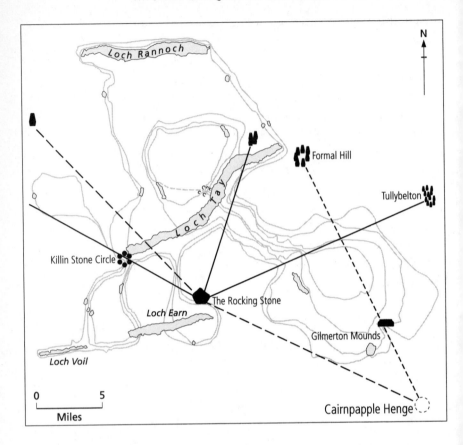

Map 19: The Gilmerton mounds (bottom right) have been constructed and a ley from Cairnpapple Hill to Formal Hill near Loch Tay has been passed through it to construct the two outer shells. The Rocking Stone has been put roughly in place. Its rocking motion may alter the wavelength/amplitude of the straight leys.

Now percuss this satellite cup-mark into the Connachan Farm cup-marked stone to coincide with this circuit.

Follow the energy from Killin stone circle, which naturally contours round the hills to centre on Loch Earn and run back northwards to Loch Tay through the Serpent stone, and finally place the Rocking Stone at an appropriate point. This has to be at a site where it will form as many straight leys as possible.

Construct another satellite cup-mark on the Connachan Farm stone to augment the energy on this, the Loch Earn circuit. The other cup-marks can now be pecked out on the cup-marked stone to conform to the circuits required across the mainland of Scotland and the island of Skye.

Since the island of Skye is the northern limit of our intended cup-mark system, we must build another 'blocking' ley from Callanish on Lewis down to the remarkable geological feature in Northern Ireland, the Giant's Causeway. These basalt rocks, so similar to the island of Staffa, are only a part of this volcanic intrusion and it is probable that the hidden focal point of this site is several miles south of the well-trodden visitors' sight-seeing area.

Build the remarkable circle complex at Callanish with its southern arm picking up the energies from the Giant's Causeway, well to the south. This boxes in the cup-mark ley on the mainland and another ley from the eastern arm of Callanish runs neatly along the north coast of Scotland, likewise containing yet another cup-mark system, still to be built, running through the Inverness area (*see Map 9, inset*).

Map 9 (inset): *Callanish stone circle sends out a ley south to the Giant's Causeway to contain the cup-marked leys.*

A CROSSING PRIMARY LEY

We can also use the natural energies from the Giant's Causeway and the Loch Laidon fault line to build another cup-mark ley crossing the original Connachan Farm one.

Back at the Giant's Causeway, use the powerful energies running from here up the Loch Laidon/Ericht fault on the Scottish mainland, part of the Great Glen fault complex, which runs north-east–south-west. On this powerful line, find another spot, this time as close to the west coast as possible, where sightings of the moon running down the slopes of the backdrop of hills can be found, and erect another cup-marked stone there – in this case the unique lunar observatory of Kilmartin *(see Map 20)*.

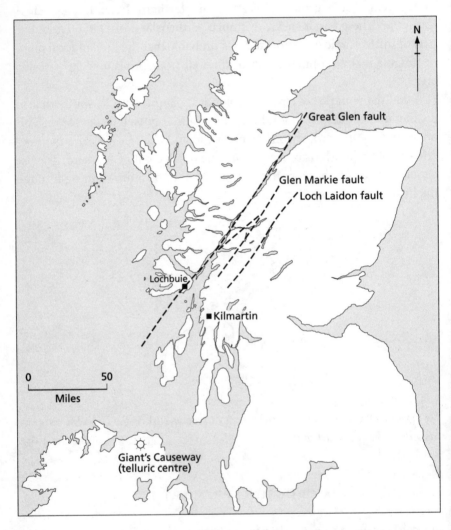

Map 20: The Great Glen fault lines. A ley can be constructed from the end of the Loch Laidon fault to the Giant's Causeway (bottom left), with the lunar observatory standing stone at Kilmartin now in place.

Figure 57: The standing stone at Kilmartin is part of the twin lunar standstill observatory.

On this primary ley, a short distance from the cup-marked stone, find the spot where the moon, at its northern major standstill, can just be seen behind, in this case, a hill notch. Erect two standing stones, straddling the centre of the primary ley and far enough apart that the full disk of the moon can be seen just touching the top of Bellanoch Hill, to the south, at the southern major standstill. This gives a precise timing for ceremonial practices, observes the maximum and minimum cyclic perturbations of the moon, and also gives an input of lunar light.

This ley, now working, will project the percussed cup-marks on the Kilmartin stone across country. Obviously, the cup-marks will be carved precisely to throw their telluric shadow across the country as before, bearing in mind that they are required to travel around the valleys and glens, where the majority of people live, farm and worship.

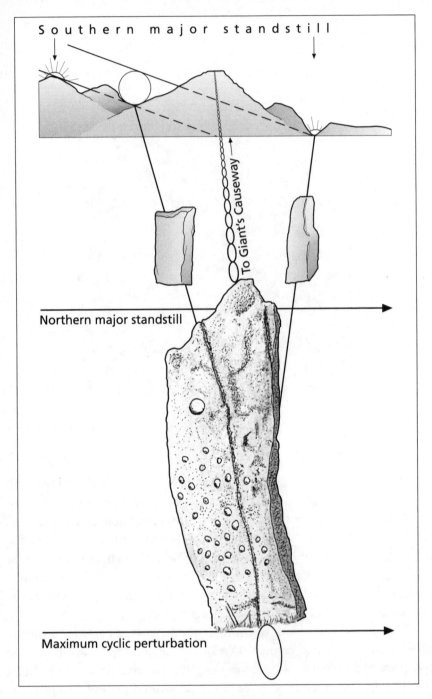

Figure 58: Kilmartin lunar observatory.

SITING HOMESTEADS

You can also construct your little homesteads, which must have their long axes on the cup-mark leys and circuits from smaller local cup-mark circuits running through their short axes.

Burial-grounds are also based on the major cup-mark circuits, but must also be placed where leys from volcanic plugs cross.

Villages can be planned using standing stones, flat face in line with the cup-mark ley, also with their burial-grounds and churches located at power points. These geometric shapes must be the same as the underlying natural star pattern of Earth energy.

Large stones hollowed by hammering into fonts and placed at the correct point inside a church can be used for baptisms, since the water they contain will pick up telluric energies readily, and small hand-held rubbing stones can be used for the treatment of various diseases and ailments. Springs and pools in rivers which are on the energy circuits can also be used for healing. Drinking the waters, of course, is one way of benefiting, and leaving an offering in the shape of a garment is another method, but as the health of the sufferer is supposed to improve as the garment decays, so nylon and other long-lasting modern materials are definitely out! Some standing stones have holes carved through them, sometimes for healing, sometimes to ensure fertility, like the peculiar and aesthetically satisfying standing stone at Onich, Argyll (see Figure 59).

SPIRIT GUARDIANS

The remains of venerated individuals in your society – saints, bards, chiefs and warriors can be patched into the system by making a cup-marked stone focus its energy around a church and through their graves, as at Dundurn, St Fillans. (To gain acceptance and benevolence from the spirits, what better than to donate a little personal gift – a coin, perhaps, placed as a votive offering into one of the holes in the stone?)

Returning to infusing the system with spiritual energy, Balbirnie stone circle, near Balfarg henge (both major points on the primary ley), has a stone-lined grave with a heavily cup-marked stone at the head of the cist, presumably to allow the spirit access to the telluric system.

Another method, of course, is burial or cremation at burial-grounds

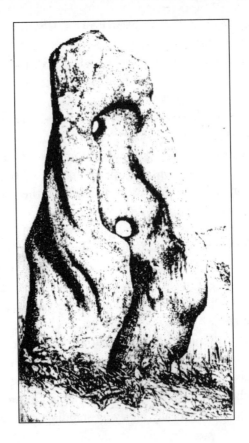

Figure 59: The holed standing stone at Onich, Argyll. (Engraving from The Proceedings of the Society of Antiquaries of Scotland 1864–66*)*

carefully situated on power points. This allows the dead to be carried to their final resting-place in straight lines down 'faery paths' or on circuitous routes on purpose-built roads on cup-mark leys, and even, on occasion, allows the coffin to be rested on the powerful outer working edge of a cup-mark ley, as in the case of the standing stone Phadruig, near Balquhidder.

THE PURPOSE OF EARTH-HOUSES?

If the energy from cup-marked stones can, indeed, allow access to the system for the spirits of the dead, then it must also do the same for the living, so building an underground chamber or souterrain with a powerful cup-marked capstone in the roof and below it, in the passage, another upright inside the entrance so that initiates, wizards or shamans could meditate and perhaps retrieve knowledge would be an important part of the ceremonies of the ancients. The Native Americans had a similar procedure, building subterranean kiva (magnetic chambers), where they could achieve lucid dreaming and imagery, helped by hallucinogenic plants.

For the inauguration of a king, footprints or a single footprint incised in the living rock, overlooking the land about to be ruled over, could be used, as at Glen Lyon and Dunadd in Argyll. This ancient and tellurically powerful hill-fort overlooks 14 of Argyllshire's hill-forts. No king, surely, could rule with authority if he had not undergone the correct ceremony at the correct time and place, linking, as Paul Devereux puts it in his book *Shamanism and the Mystery Lines* (Quantum, 1992), the spiritual life of the people and the maintenance of the health of the land to himself. There are other 'kingstones' across the United Kingdom, including that of the Saxons at Kingston-upon-Thames and the double footprint on the St Magnus stone in Orkney. Ireland, as one would expect, has several stones: the 7-foot (2-metre) square stone of the kings of O'Doherty in Derry (Londonderry), the Lia Fal at the Mound of Hostages, which is said to cry out when the correct king sits upon it, and at Tullahoge a stone fashioned into a throne by the placement of three slabs around it.

A more mobile stone may also be used, one of great antiquity and veneration, like the black meteoritic stone 'carved with symbols and hollows' (cup-marks?) which was intended to be built into the coronation chair for the crowning of royalty at a major power point like Westminster Abbey. This, corruptly called the Stone of Destiny, has long since been lost or secreted away, leaving a number of copies and fakes in its wake to mystify, amuse and titillate the general public and historians alike.

There we have a rough picture of how to construct and use the quite extraordinary ley system, using primitive tools and natural energy from the planet to power it. It was extremely difficult to recover this knowledge, even with the aid of accurate OS maps, but of course 3,000–4,000 years ago this must have been an immense undertaking, reflecting its importance to the communities it served.

STRANGE HAPPENINGS ⊙N THE EARTH ENERGY SYSTEM

Black Spirals, Ill-Health and Apparitions

> The lodestone causes mental disorders, makes people
> melancholic and is often fatal. With a sort of fumes
> it can greatly affect the mind.
>
> WILLIAM GILBERT, *DE MAGNETE*, 1600

Earth energies play a part in phenomena of various types. The apparitions, poltergeists and strange phenomena with which I have been involved seem to be broadly divided into three categories:

1 Holograms, where the image of a person or object is captured in crossing energy leys.
2 Earth energy spirals (blind springs), where spirits appear to be trapped.
3 Hallucinatory experiences caused by telluric spirals, 'hot spots' from modern electrical sources, natural Earth and seismic energies (including outgassing (the releasing of gas) from the planet).

The first, the hologram, is an automatic repeat performance of an event. The second is where an apparition sometimes shows awareness. The third, the hallucinatory experience, may be caused by an input of external extremely low frequency (ELF), radio frequency or microwave energy into the brain, causing the temporal lobes to produce powerful hallucinatory images. These, and seismic energies and outgassing, will be discussed in more detail in later chapters.

Earlier I explained how leys were formed from standing stones situated on 'hot spots' directly above at least two veins of water crossing underground at different depths. Energy from a vein, fissure or pipe, is emitted vertically to the surface. There are also two other waves, at an angle of 45° on each side, which together form three parallel lines on the surface, down the length of the vein. The centre line is the centre of the interconnecting spirals and the width of the spirals is determined by the outside lines. The spirals may be healthy (white spirals) or unhealthy (black spirals), depending upon the subterranean rock and other factors. The distance from the centre line directly above the water to the outer parallel is the same as the depth of the vein (*see Figure 61*). This is used by water diviners to gauge the depth of subterranean water sources.

When some types of ley comprising individual vertical waves (overgrounds) encounter the outside of such a spiral, they automatically tune into its centre, giving a powerful 'hot spot'. A few decades ago, these overgrounds were mainly natural and the spirals were comparatively weak, but in this modern age we have 'artificial leys' from other sources: nuclear submarines and missile stores, radar stations, microwave towers, television repeater stations, electric sub stations and power station generators, for example. In addition, we have an increasing amount of disturbed Earth energies from quarrying, deep mining and in particular open-cast coalmining (oil drilling may also be bad, judging from a conversation with an oil-rig employee). These activities create micro-seisms and draw unhealthy sub-surface Earth currents to the surface and on their journey across country to eventually earth themselves, perhaps in a quarry, they focus on the centre of black spirals. Basically, the more electricity we use and the more we disturb the planet, the more powerful these telluric spirals, both black and white, become.

Figure 60: A microwave tower.

Figure 61: A subterranean vein of water or pipe emits energy vertically to the surface and also one wave to each side at an angle of 45°. The centre wave is the centre of a series of overlapping spirals whose width is determined by the two outside waves. Incoming leys (arrows from right of illustration) of vertical waves of energy are automatically drawn into the centre of the spirals (also known as vortices). In this illustration the spirals are clockwise from the centre, showing that they are malevolent, not conducive to health. Spirals such as these can occur anywhere in a house, as a house itself has little effect on the energies from subterranean sources. The vertical waves of energy from the ley, however, will not pass through glass windows or mirrors, ceramic tiles in kitchens and bathrooms (although they will pass between the tiles). Natural Earth energies such as these seem to be part of poltergeist phenomena, demonic attack and various illnesses.

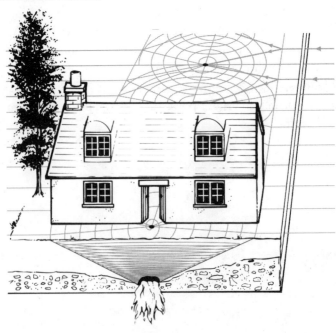

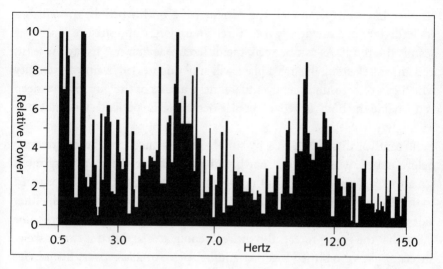

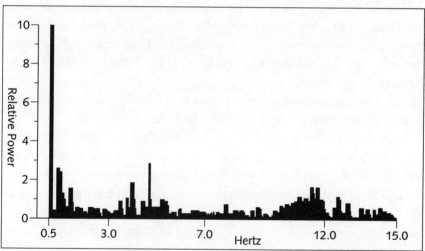

Figure 62: Two brain scans taken of an individual at different locations. The top one was taken in a 'healthy' place, tellurically speaking, and the bottom in the patient's bed, above an underground stream.

Living, and especially sleeping, above a subterranean fissure emitting such vortices can have a profound effect on our brainwave patterns, as you can readily observe in Figure 62. The top scan was taken in the clinic of a complementary practitioner and shows the normal electroencephalograph readout of a patient. Knowing about geopathic stress, the practitioner took another EEG, this time with the patient lying on his bed, below which a water diviner had previously discovered an underground stream. The lower scan is the result. As can be seen, the difference is marked, to say the least, and anyone sleeping in such a place will suffer depressed brainwave activity which can only result in an eventual illness, as one of the purposes of sleep is to enable the body to repair cellular damage. The patient's wife, not surprisingly, had ME.

Recently, I discovered that by simply placing sheets of glass or mirrors below a bed where strong Earth radiations from faults, underground streams, etc. were causing health problems, the lines could be safely warped to one side. A long mirror from an old bedroom sideboard is ideal, either side up, since it is the glass which deflects the radiation, but care has to be taken that the glass protects the entire sleeping area and that if two or more sheets of glass are butted together another piece of glass covers the join, as the vertical line of radiation will automatically adjust itself to pass between the sheets. If you are able to dowse for Earth energies, you will find that any black line or lines from a subterranean fault, cavity or stream will be neatly warped to one side and any black spiral in the bed will be pushed away from the sleeping position.

This has not yet been tried out with people suffering from ill-health, including cancer but is worth experimenting with.

According to Chinese *feng shui*, flat mirrors deflect the noxious *sha ch'i*, or Earth radiation, and concave mirrors absorb it, whilst convex ones reflect and disperse it, which I agree with. There is much scope here for others to research, but protecting a bed with glass is so simple that it is well worthwhile – be careful to use a type which is not easily broken – old car windscreens are useful – and I am so convinced that it works I take care that my own bed is protected in this way. We must remember, of course, that smoking, bad diet and chemical insults to the body also play a large part in ill-health.

THE GHOST CARS OF LOCH TAYSIDE

As well as affecting health, these powerful vortices, the incoming over-grounds and the veins of water beneath them, may be partly responsible for phenomena of various types, which I have been investigating for some years. The first is the hologram type of incident.

In Perthshire, a Loch Tayside farmer and a neighbour, driving out of a field, saw a friend's car travelling along the long straight road at the foot of Ben Lawers on the north side of Loch Tay. They stopped and waited for it to pass, but no car appeared – it had vanished and there was nowhere it could have gone. A number of cars have been seen to skid to a halt on this stretch of road for no apparent reason and it may be that the drivers have also seen something odd.

At the same spot a lady was looking for her pet terrier about midnight when she saw part of the fence 'about the size of a dinner table' lit up but not casting a shadow. There were no vehicles in the area at the time. It may also be relevant to point out that there is some seepage of water from the field onto the road at this point, possibly forming one of T. C. Lethbridge's 'Naiad fields' which we will investigate later *(see p.230)*.

This length of road coincides with a large telluric circle, which is composed of interconnecting spirals around its perimeter. Several old homesteads are situated on it. The energy may have been emitted from a beautifully carved engraving, deeply etched in a garnetiferous mica schist boulder. This stone has telluric links with the outside perimeter of spirals, although it is not in the centre of the circuit, as I would have wished, but at the periphery. The energy is a standing wave, amplitude 13 inches (33 cm), wavelength 95 inches (241 cm).

Figure 63: This petroglyph on a stone near Loch Tay may be part of a puzzling phenomenon.

'LIGHTS, LIKE THOSE ON AN OLD-FASHIONED CAR'

A local couple asked me to check their house for unhealthy energies as their little boy was 'dying before their eyes'. There were two burial-grounds nearby and unhealthy leys were passing through their house from both of these into their own home.

The family also had another problem. Originally their house had been a school, which had a playground at the rear. This was now used as a car park, with access from a narrow track passing close to the kitchen. On a number of occasions the wife had noticed headlights passing up the lane and into the car park and gone out to investigate, but nothing could be seen at all. One night, the husband also saw the car park lit up with powerful lights and went out, expecting to welcome visitors. He saw two headlights 'like those on old-fashioned cars' streaming light across the courtyard. As he watched, they switched off and slowly faded away. There was nothing there at all – no car, nothing. There are other stories of lights following cars along straight roads in this area.[1]

Since this took place at the crossing of two leys it would be reasonable to think of the car lights as a form of hologram. Possibly, a car had driven into the car park, perhaps many years ago, and the energy in these two leys had split it, like a hologram, and memorized the picture, to replay it from time to time.

THE GHOST TRAIN OF BALQUHIDDER

In a similar vein is the interesting story which Brian Maddison and his wife related.[2] They were driving south on the A84 Lochearnhead to Balquhidder road late one starry night in 1997 when they heard the whistle and chuff of a steam train near the old station at Balquhidder junction. To the north they could see a line of moving lights which they took to be carriages. When they told Mrs Maddison's father about the event, they were astounded to find that the line had been closed over 30 years ago after a landslide. (See also Chapter 17: Lethbridge's Legacy.)

The ley which may be responsible for this phenomenon comes from Killin stone circle (see Figure 63a). To recap, from the top (north) the cup-mark ley enters the circle and is then warped up and over the hill to Loch Larig-Eala, down the now disused railway track towards Balquhidder

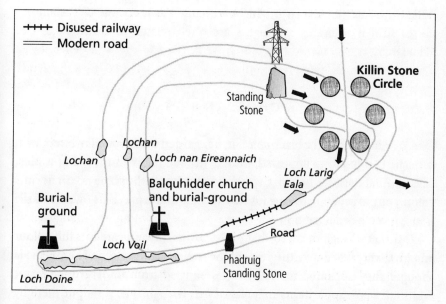

Figure 63a: This is a stylized map of the ley circuits from Killin stone circle. Note the outlying standing stone which acts as one of the original crossing-points. The three small lochs to the left are situated at the top of hills to attract the cup-mark ley up and over the top.

church and burial-ground, up over the hills to Loch nan Eireannaich and back to the stone circle for another circuit outside the original one.

This second circuit also travels up over the hills to pass close to Loch Larig-Eala, then runs down the modern road to Balquhidder station before being warped around Balquhidder church and over the hills to another small lochan, then down to the stone circle for the final circuit, which crosses the first two via a modern hydro-electric suspension tower and an outlying standing stone.

The disused railway line has the first circuit of the powerful energy ley running down it, while the road (A84) runs roughly parallel and quite close to it on the next circuit. This is where the working edge of the ley of the second circuit and its companion waves are tightly packed together at the south side of the road, just where Mr Madison and his wife's car was.

The phenomenon could at least partly be explained by information picked up by the first circuit (one of the many trains following the path of the ley in the past) and the occupants of the car somehow tuning in on the nearby second circuit, at a much later date, long after the rail track had been pulled up. Alternatively, it might be explained as a seismic disturbance – noises similar to trains and lights are often related to earthquakes *(see Chapter 17)*.

A GHOST IN SEPIA

One lady in Perth had a black spiral in her garden where an old woman with her hair tied in a bun appeared, head bent, walking with the aid of a stick. The unusual twist to this story was that the lady saw the scene not in normal colour, but in sepia. Later she found that one of the previous owners of the house fitted her description.

T. C. Lethbridge believed that ghosts originally appeared in full colour and gradually faded over the years to the traditional grey, white or green. He thought they appeared in the energies emitted from underground water and that many apparitions may have been thought imprints put there by someone in the past.[3]

DOUBLE MURDER

A house I investigated had an unhappy history. The occupant had shot his wife and her friend dead in a macabre incident. The next couple to rent the house were alarmed when one of their children reported seeing two apparitions – one sitting at the end of his bed, apparently in conversation with another at the foot of the other twin bed. The beds had been left in the same position since the shooting, and it was suspected that the apparitions were of the husband and wife having a heated argument in the past.

I found numerous small black spirals in the house and the area around it. The apparitions were, presumably, of the repeating hologram type.

The ley came from the nearby stone circle of Dalchirla, which is now ruined *(see Map 9)*. Two of the stones are missing and the two which are left are in line with the house, focusing their energies into it and on to Moncreiffe stone circle, south of Perth. Prior to the murders, this stone circle had been removed to Moncreiffe House, which must have altered the local energies dramatically.

CAUGHT IN A BLACK HOLE

I have already mentioned the powerful energy ley which runs from Comrie's Braefordie standing stone down Crieff High Street to two standing stones in tandem, one at Aberuthven and the other at Dunning. This also passes through Crieff's old parish burial-ground *(see Figure 54)*. A local lady, walking past this disused burial-ground with her husband, suddenly found herself enveloped in almost pitch darkness, even although it was a bright November afternoon. Terrified, she could just see in front of her a young girl, aged about eight, whom she instinctively knew was herself (she had had a frightening experience at this age). Eventually, after about five minutes, she managed to free herself and walked through into the light again, to find her husband walking a few yards in front of her as if nothing had occurred. When she asked him what had happened he was quite puzzled – he had noticed nothing at all. Time, apparently, had stood still for her in these few minutes.

When I checked the site of this occurrence I found that not only had she been on the Braefordie/Dunning energy ley, but also that she had been standing above one of the many underground streams which run under this hill town.

Another surprise was in store for me when I checked her house – there was a black spiral in her bed, at her head. Sleeping under the influence of this black spiral for some eight years, she could well have become hypersensitive to such unhealthy energies, and walking into an even more powerful spiral from the underground stream next to the old parish burial-ground could have triggered the hallucination, which to her was very real.

Another fact which may be relevant is that the burial-ground had recently been landscaped using heavy machinery and the gravestones removed to the side, which might conceivably have disturbed something – who knows what?

Four months later, the lady was still in a state of shock and spent much of her time in her house lying on a settee, crying. Shortly after I had shown her what had happened and referred her to others who had shared a similar experience, she recovered.

It is an intriguing possibility that people who believe they have been abducted by aliens or suffer other phenomena of a bizarre nature might also be under the influence of nature's energies, the event itself taking place not necessarily in bed, where they may have been sensitized to these malevolent energies, but at another power point elsewhere which they happen to walk into at the wrong time.

A BLACK WHIRLWIND

Telluric energy may also account for other unusual phenomena. One particular ley from the mausoleum at Ochtertyre has its burial-ground in constant use and one local lady told me an unusual story. She had been attending her sister's grave when the blue sky turned unusually dark and a fierce wind arose. She suddenly noticed that the bushes around the area were laid flat with the wind, but only in that small area. Terrified, she put her son in his pushchair and tried to get out of the narrow gate, only to find that the wind seemed to be trying to separate her from the child. She struggled desperately to get free and ran several miles to her home. She has not been back to visit the site for 30 years.

I had already investigated this ley and had followed it to the north-east, to a large slate quarry. Mile after mile, walking along, I found other small slate quarries, with the varves, the leaves of slate, in line with the ley. Some 15 miles (24 kilometres) from Ochtertyre Mausoleum, the waves became highly distorted, but nevertheless I followed them to the twin stone circle at Tullybelton. The reason for the distortion was that the circles have been completely flattened and were not working properly. As I approached the ruined circles I was amused to note that more outcrops of slate showed just above the ground on the nearby worn track.

Another factor to be taken into consideration is another ley, this time from Cairnpapple henge, well to the south, which crosses through the mausoleum.

A HAUNTED HOUSE

Two girls gave me descriptions of several ghosts in their isolated cottage in Perthshire. A figure of a monk entered one wall to exit by the opposite wall and early one morning a figure of a very small Roman centurion appeared. Alarmed at the intrusion, one girl attempted to strike the apparition, but her hand went through him. Despite this, the girls felt the centurion was benevolent.

An apparition which was unpleasant, however, was that of an old man, partly decayed, with flesh hanging from his body in shreds and some bones visible. One girl saw the phantom and the other was made aware of its presence by the smell of decay.

Other unusual events occurred. The girls heard a noise like a rat climbing up one wall and down the other, but not on the roof. This grew in intensity as time passed to become quite loud. Mysteriously, the telephone bill was astronomic, although the instrument was rarely used, and the same applied to the electricity bill. The girls also suffered some illnesses soon after moving into the cottage and one developed a violent allergic reaction.

On investigation, I found the little cottage had been built over a wide tunnel, partially filled with water, with black spirals travelling vertically upwards into the house, and had a buried 3-foot (1-metre) diameter hydro-electric water pipe running very close to it. To further exacerbate the problem, an electrical sub-station was located just 100 feet (30 metres) away, also above the tunnel. Another interesting point is that the tunnel acted as a waveguide, the wavelength being decreased and the amplitude heightened, rather like the overgrounds down the Electric Brae.

Some 10 years later, the present occupier has also noted apparitions. When he walked past the kitchen one day he was surprised to see, out of the corner of his eye, a figure in blue dungarees at the sink. When he went back to look, of course, there was no one there. When I rechecked the house, I found the centre of a black spiral near the sink, just where the figure had been seen. The owner asked me to look up at the ceiling, at a large green patch of damp mould, painted over. This was where the moisture from the tunnel had been sucked up into the house by the spiral. 'Often wondered why I couldn't get rid of that,' he said.

SPONTANEOUS WATER

ANNE SILK

There are many other reports of water appearing as if by magic at certain spots, often over several centuries. These places, often given religious significance, are known to produce water with special properties.

Condensation is not necessarily the answer, although it can be one obvious option. The reason may lie in a combination of air pressure, outgassing and base rock, whether of granite, sandstone or limestone.

Spontaneous water warrants further examination, as if the special conditions which appear to apply could be replicated, it may be of real value in arid regions.

A World-Wide Phenomenon

The following sites have seen the spontaneous appearance of water, but there are many others:

Aberfeldy, Perthshire, Scotland

A cup-marked stone near here is always more or less full, even in the driest of weather, and presents a glistening appearance from a distance. The locals travel to this stone on the first day of May every year and wash their faces in it.[4]

Arles-sur-Tech, at the eastern end of the Pyrenees, near Narbonne, France

In the fourth-century abbey here there is a stone chest or sarcophagus which is free standing and holds some 40 gallons (182 litres) of water. This is clear and fresh at all times and for centuries has been considered to be holy water. Small bottles are constantly filled with this water, yet the sarcophagus is always full.

In 1794 members of the Republican Army, the Pyrenées Orientale, on their way to Spain, emptied the stone sarcophagus and filled it with refuse. After cleaning it, several women observed that their dusters became moist when in contact with the walls and bottom of the tomb. The immense lid was replaced and within a month it was found that there were 10 inches (25 cm) of clear water in it again. In the presence of clergy, lawyers and council men, the limestone tomb was examined at great length, but no pipes or holes were detected, neither was there a false bottom. Throughout this testing, which lasted several days, the water continued to accumulate.

Most curiously, analysis has shown that this spontaneous water is not of the same composition as the normal town water. It should also be noted that the tomb is located in the driest district of France. Aix-les-Thermes is several miles away and here 60 warm springs have a high sulphur and fluorine content.

Ayers Rock, Australia

The annual rainfall here is about 5 inches (12 cm) and often fails altogether. Nevertheless, there are three places at which there are permanent pools of water.

Fladda Island, Western Isles of Scotland

There is a stone on this island in the chapel dedicated to St Columba which is always wet, whatever the weather.

Fontainebleu Forest, Paris, France

Deep in this forest there is a stone shaped like a dish and, whatever the weather, it is always full of water.

Jastrzebie, Poland

Here in 1985, on 21 June, in a third floor flat on a bright sunny day, 'suddenly, jets of water of great intensity spouted out of all impossible places',[5] i.e. ceilings and walls. Emergency water services were called in and turned off the mains water. This had no effect at all. For many days the water jet phenomena continued and it was realized that the 12-year-old son of the family, Arthur, was the centre of them. He was seen by several doctors, four priests, the police, the building manager, etc., but no one could effect a cure. It was found that he appeared to be in a light trance during these watery episodes.

Pozzuoli (Latin Puteoli, Greek Dicaearchia), to the west of Naples, Italy

Around AD 90 in the Grotto of the Nymphs there was a jar of white stone containing water which neither flowed over the edge, nor was depleted if it was drawn from. Damis and Demetrius discuss this mystery at length in *The Life of Apollonius*. It should be noted that present day Pozzuoli is seismically very active and has been since Roman times, the whole bay area of the Phlegrean Fields, having risen and fallen many feet over the centuries.

Noirfontaine (Black Fountain), France

If the word *noir* (black) in a placename refers to water, as in the black fountain above, it may be a link with some unusual geological feature. At Noirfontaine a stream of water fell from a stationary point in the sky for 48 hours in April 1982.

Rochdale, England

Peter Hough, an experienced investigator known to Anne Silk, was asked to visit the Gardener family at their home in the town in August 1995. The house is on a hilltop and the family had found water dripping from the ceilings during a summer so hot and dry that there was a hosepipe ban in force. The water appeared to start on the ceilings, yet when local Water Board and council officials investigated, there were no leaks and the floor and the joists of the rooms above were perfectly dry. This had been going on for some 10 months when the investigator visited. Then the water began to take form, flashing horizontally across the ceiling. The edges were 'jagged, like broken glass' and the water ingress 'finished in a point'. Then the kitchen door appeared to become wet on its lower section and suddenly, whilst under observation, 'thousands of tiny droplets instantaneously covered the entire door'.[6]

Interestingly, two people, at different times, heard their names called when no one else was in the house. This is a known medical effect and indicative of an electrical surge in the brain.

If readers know of other places where a constant clear supply of water appears with no apparent explanation, the authors would be pleased to hear of them.

HEALING WELLS AND HOLY WATER

In the UK, as with all countries world-wide, there are thousands of wells and springs which have had the name 'holy' bestowed on them and which have been considered sacred since time immemorial. To take just one county, in Cornwall alone there are over 300 holy wells, many with the names of saints. Over centuries these have attained reputations for particular therapies, in particular for helping skin problems, scurvy, wound healing, eye infections and, more rarely, psychosomatic problems. Some have very special properties. To take one example, in New Zealand, a land with many ancient volcanoes and major faulting, some 84 miles north of the city of Canterbury lies Hanmer Springs, discovered by a settler in the 1850s. Since 1859 these hot mineral springs and pools have been used to treat wounded soldiers, alcoholics and mentally disturbed people. Also in New Zealand, the thermal waters of Rotorua are on the volcanic rift which runs from north to south across the country; again we find healing waters. Nearer home a Scottish colleague told me years ago that the Victorian hydro hotels, so fashionable in the nineteenth century, were always sited beside an ancient healing well or stream.

Some of the names of wells in the UK are indicative of their special or seasonal properties. There are many Wishing Wells, a Fairy Well, Blackwell, White(e)well, Summerwell (Glos.), Winterwell (Northleach), Milkwell, Rising and Falling Well, Dripping Well, Boiling Well, several wells called Hotwell, as at Bristol, and Lappingwell. A study of the local Ordnance Survey maps will produce many more.

Unusual phenomena are also known at well sites. The water level can rise and fall, which may relate to the water table itself or the syphoning action of the water entry. Bubbles can appear, probably due to gases such as methane leaching out far below. Strange smells can be noted at some wells, again possibly due to methane or other natural gases. More puzzling is the fact that well water can change colour, from clear to red (iron chalybeate suspension), white (chalk or limestone), yellow (sulphur deposits or clear particles), blue or black, both possibly due to deep disturbances.

Wells have also been seen to emit beams of light and have been heard to hiss or moan. If an electrical discharge (like quartz fracture and piezoelectric energy release) takes place below a water surface, a blast wave is formed by the expansion of the arc channel, called the electrohydrodynamic effect. Such a blast wave propagates concentrically to the discharge channel, generating photons as it goes, which, with the boundary condition of the walls of the well, allows a vertical beam of light to emerge. In the same way, wells act as waveguides for acoustic energy from seismic activity.

When we add together the many factors in well water, for example the mineral and trace elements, the gases in suspension, the fact that they are often sited at faulted areas or at a junction of differing strata, then we are seeing a synergy which can validate the ancient claims of healing wells.

Attributes of the Water

There are countless stories and reports of the efficacy of water from healing wells and spas. Whilst it would require an academic treatise to examine all the sources, it is interesting to look at the chemical and mineral analyses of these wells, where available. The vogue in the 1990s for drinking bottled mineral water has far more ancient reasons than clever marketing by super-markets and bottlers.

So what are those virtues attributed to water from wells? The obvious ones are clarity and taste and the less obvious ones are gases in suspension in the water, chemicals, minerals and trace elements, and lastly radioactivity from natural sources in the water. There may also be bacteria and plants, algae, etc., from growth at the edge of a well.

Before considering these, a personal experience is relevant to the gener-ally unconsidered properties of water. For a few years we took our holidays in Morocco and one of the pleasures was to drink the special bottled water from the Lalla Haya (Lady Haya) spring in the Rif Mountains to the east of Tangier. But year after year I became ill at the end of the week. After the third year my husband opined that it might be the water, as I drank it at every meal. He was never ill and drank tea, coffee or wine, like me, but never the water, as he dislikes sparkling water. The fourth year I gave the water a miss – feeling very deprived – and had no tummy troubles at all. The fifth year likewise. What I had not realized was that the water was radioactive to a small degree from a volcanic area of the Rif Mountains.

There can be a great deal, apart from natural radioactivity, in water. The multiplicity of chemicals below – all natural – comes from an analysis of UK, French and Italian bottled mineral water labels in 1998 and 1999, together with one or two from nineteenth-century Malvern water: magne-sium bromide, magnesium chloride, magnesium bicarbonate and sulphate of magnesium, carbonate of iron, muriated nitron, sodium chloride, sodium sulphate, bicarbonate of lime, potassium sulphate, potassium chlo-ride, ammonium chloride, calcium fluoride, ferrous bicarbonate, ferrous sulphate, ferrous chloride, calcium bicarbonate, silica, oxygen, nitrogen, carbonic acid, lithium fluoride, fluoride, zinc, copper, lead, barium sul-phate, gypsum and strontium. There is one analysis which lists 'traces of rubidium'.

So we see in natural waters fluoride, now known to preserve healthy teeth, lithium, now used to treat certain types of depression, lead, now known in quantity to be neurotoxic, and so on. Magnesium is known to be essential to brain function and potassium for cell metabolism, etc., etc.

Healing Waters in Greece and Italy

Near Helice in the Mediterranean is the River Crati and the Spring of Sybaris. This water has curious properties. Ovid mentions the vast numbers of fish to be found in the river which, he writes, has miraculous properties, Aristotle also wrote that those who drank of the waters of the River Crati 'became timorous',[7] whilst Pliny, writing two centuries later, noted that 'the water turned horses white'.[8] Whether this was a bleaching of the coat of the horses or a talc-like deposit in their hair after they had been in the water is not clear. Either way, there are indications that the water has special properties.

Some 25 miles north-west of Rome lies Trevignano. There a spring runs out of a hill. The Etruscans believed this water cured sterile women. It is known as *l'aqua delle donne* (ladies' water).

In *The Fountains of Rome* (Michael Joseph, 1966), H. V. Morton has gathered together many local and centuries-old reports of the special properties of fountains and springs. He lists the Spring of Forgetfulness and Memory at Lebadia, the rain-making springs at Mt Lycaeus, the saltwater springs at the Acropolis in Athens and also at the Temple of Poseidon at Mantinea. At Epidaurus, he describes how the patients at the great healing temple fell into the 'temple sleep' after drinking the water. Vitruvius wrote that certain fountains in Greece bore notices warning travellers to avoid them.

At Delphi, another great healing centre, the Castalian Spring had one fountain which was sacred to the Oracle at the foot of Mt Parnassus by the Via Sacra (Sacred Way). On the island of Chios, the waters were reputed to 'fossilize the brain', a phrase which presumably refers to memory loss, slowness of thought. But the water from the fountain at Clitor in Arcadia would ruin the palate for wine; indeed, it was called the 'vine-hating' fountain.

On the road to Tivoli, there is a pungent smell, as of sulphuretted hydrogen (as at Harrogate in the UK). In Roman times, this was the only place where ivory did not discolour over time. But it was also a very good place for the skin, Morton reports.

There was an ancient belief that the River Alphaeus on the island of Ortygia, off Syracuse, was connected to the fountain of Arethusa on Sicily by a 400-mile (645-kilometre) long fissure or tunnel beneath the sea. It was said that a cup cast into the River Alphaeus would be recovered later from Arethusa. As Mt Etna is an active volcano, the possibility of a lava tunnel must be considered.

Pliny the Younger, writing to Clausius Gallo in AD 100, comments that Lake Vadiman (now known as Lago di Bassano) in Umbria is a holy lake, so no boats sail on it. It is, he says, a complete circle and its sacred waters will heal fractures.

Some waters are thermal, as at Bath and Harrogate, and are mostly the result of volcanic rocks far below the surface heating water in the deep aquifers where giant natural reservoirs dwarf any man-made reservoirs above. Such thermal springs are generally either acidic or rich in hydrogen sulphide, which makes them sulphurous, as at Yellowstone in the US, Solfara in Italy and Pozzuoli in the Bay of Naples.

There is a large literature on wells and water and these notes are intended only to indicate some reasons why the subject is worthy of deeper study in relation to Earth energies.

PHENOMENAL ELECTRICITY BILLS

Let us return to the case of the two girls who experienced ghostly phenomena and poltergeist activity in their house above the waterlogged tunnel, the same house which had the black spiral in the kitchen. One of their problems was the electricity meter, which ran out of control, giving them astronomical bills.

There is a logical explanation to this phenomenon when we look at free natural sources of energy and their effects on metals and other materials.

When the Danish physicist Hans Oersted proved that a current flowing through a wire produces a magnetic field surrounding that wire, the English physicist Michael Faraday, in further experiments, proved that a magnetic field moving by a coil produces an electric field. Faraday constructed a simple dynamo, consisting of a metal disc which rotated over a coil of wire. The coil was electrically connected to the disc and the shaft brushes. As the disc rotated, a current was passed through the coil, which in turn induced a magnetic field aligned with the axis of the coil. This is precisely the same alignment as used in gauges connected to electric meters. Spin imparted to such a disc by external forces produces the same rotary motion and thus turns the disc, controlling the record of the total electricity or gas used. As Faraday found, as long as the disc kept rotating, the magnetic field could be maintained indefinitely. Thus, by the same process, as long as the magnetic field is applied, the disc will continue to spin. That is to say, in cases of abnormal electricity bills, it will incorrectly record the electricity being consumed.

The meters in the UK are made to a standard pattern. One manufacturer is Sangamo of Felixstowe, Suffolk. Called Floton, this meter is designed to run at 240 volts, 20–80 amps at 50 hertz and revolve at 166.66 revs on magnetic bearings. The thin aluminium disc, sitting on its bearings, is parallel to the Earth and rotates slowly on its spindle, turning the meter, which records power consumption with the trip counter.

The question is, in the cases of houses with exceptionally high meter readings, from where does the external magnetic field to spin the discs originate? No one in their right mind is going to apply a ceramic magnet to increase the meter reading and thus vastly increase their electricity bill. But many cases have been reported in the UK of phenomenally high meter readings (and thus bills).

SEISMIC DISTURBANCE

There is one source of magnetic fields, however, which is common to all these cases, and that is seismic disturbances, deep movements of the Earth far below our feet.

If two plane waves – seismic waves are of this type – are travelling in opposite directions, and if they both have the same amplitude, phase and polarization, the electromagnetic fields will add and the magnetic fields will cancel. This leads to uniform electric field excitation. Alternatively, when both waves have the same amplitude and polarity, the magnetic fields will interfere positively and the electric field will be nullified.

Metals are not unique in reacting to an external magnetic field. Certain ceramic materials known as ferrites, used in portable radios, television and other types of electrical equipment, will react with electromagnetic waves at microwave (GHz) frequencies and also exhibit interesting non-reciprocal properties when they are also under the influence of an external DC field. This latter is precisely what we are considering in relation to Earth energies. The gyromagnetic effect in ferrites and in para- and ferro-magnetics means that energy will be imparted to any freely suspended artefact, such as the revolving disc in an electric or gas meter.

Natural electric currents are always present in the Earth. Whilst 500 microVolts is more usual, currents up to 1.8v have been observed. Small potentials not exceeding 100 microVolts, and often less, can accompany ground water flow, but this depends on the type of rock and ions in the porewater and is generally stronger in the region towards which the groundwater is flowing, rather than the source area. Put simply, this means that near springs and streams the Earth is more electropositive. In the more conductive parts of the ground, eddy currents induce secondary magnetic fields which, in a near vertical sheet-like conductor, flow in rotational or spiral paths and themselves produce secondary magnetic fields (black and white spirals).

If a house with an electric meter is situated over such an area, we have an ideal situation for far greater spin to be imparted to the aluminium disc in the meter and hence far higher bills, as in the case of the two girls mentioned earlier.

ELECTRICITY METERS KEEP WORKING IN VILLAGE WITH POWER OFF

In the village of Flaminze, in the Moldavia district of Romania, in October 1990, all the fuses blew at the same time. The local electricity authorities investigated and found, to their amazement, that all the domestic meters showed power was being consumed (discs spinning), although all the power in the village was off.

It is no coincidence that at Cluj, in this highly seismically faulted area, there had been a large earthquake on 20 and 21 October, and there had been seven earthquakes in the Pyrenees between 22 and 26 October. These generate long amplitude waves. Very low frequency (VLF) seismic waves will induce eddy currents in the more conductive parts of the ground and will generate secondary magnetic fields with the same frequency as the primary VLF, but with a different phase.

In 1991 a house in Somerton, Somerset, showed phenomenally high readings, which the local electricity board investigated, reading 2,160V in a field measurement at the house. In another case at Ryde, Isle of Wight, in 1975, when the bills were impossibly high, especially indicative of an external power source, the SEB fitted a new meter with a special sealed unit to prevent tampering and to the astonishment of the fitter, the 'highly efficient mechanism disfunctioned even as they watched', even though the meter was apparently 'impossible to interfere with'.

REFERENCES

1   Personal correspondence
2   *Phenomenal News*, Autumn 1997
3   Guy Underwood, *Patterns of the Past*, Abacus, 1970
4   *Proceedings of the Society of Antiquaries of Scotland*, Neill and Company Ltd, 1888
5   R. Bugas, 'Two water poltergeist cases', *Journal of the Society for Psychical Research*, October 1996, 235–42
6   P. Hough, 'Wet, wet, wet', *Fortean Times*, 89 (1997), 23–6
7   Aristotle, *De Mirabilibus Ausculationibus*, 169
8   Pliny, *Natural History*, XXXI 9:13

16

POLTERGEİSTS

Some Insights into Various Phenomena

There are no unnatural or supernatural phenomena, there
are only very large gaps in our knowledge of what is natural,
particularly relating to rare occurrences.

US ASTRONAUT EDGAR MITCHELL,
MIND AT LARGE (PRAEGER, 1979)

Poltergeists seem to be of two basic types, either of natural origin, from seismic disturbances, which can be explained rationally, or semi-intelligent malevolent forces capable of using these same energies for their own purpose.

Their activity, like that in the haunted house above the tunnel in the previous chapter, usually begins with faint scratching, building up to rappings and eventually very loud noises which cannot be traced. The energy appears to follow its own course of evolution and may become powerful enough to cause objects to disappear and reappear in a different place. Stones appear in mid air and drop to the ground, and puddles of water or other liquids can be found in a house. Spontaneous fires may break out, although they usually do little damage, and objects can be flung forcibly at the occupants of the house and at researchers, usually without causing harm. Ghostly figures may be seen.

The childlike quality of poltergeists is usually apparent and one of the 'rules' appears to be that no harm comes to the occupants of a dwelling, although there are exceptions. When the entity evolves further, it can communicate with a simple one rap for yes, two for no, or by writing, and may even speak in a synthetic manner. The communications are mostly typical of the childish malevolent quality of the low entity, or lower self, usually being blasphemous and incapable of telling the truth.

TWO EVIL AND TWO GOOD SPIRITS IN ONE HOUSE

One case I have been involved with for over five years is that of a family and their friends in a fairly old one-storey house. To preserve the identity of this family, I will call the mother Anne, her son John and his friend Robert. Robert and John have some psychic powers and were later to help control the entity and communicate with another friendly spirit who was there to help. Robert's mother I shall call Joan.

The house had two spirals, one healthy, the other unhealthy. The unhealthy one was in the centre of the living room and spiralled vertically upwards into the centre of the bed where Anne slept. She complained of headaches and permanent ill-health. Footsteps were heard on the ceiling at this spot (I contacted the previous owner who had heard them too) and loud bangs on the ceiling made the light shake. Downstairs, near the black spiral, a picture was once thrown from the wall into the spiral's centre. At the same time Anne and her family felt a 'presence' whirl around them and exit via the door.

Most of the paranormal occurrences took place at the centre of another spiral in the young lad's bed. Very unusually, the overgrounds, both healthy and unhealthy, were warped away from it.

Directly below the bed was an electric cooker, also in the spiral. The thermostat had burned itself out some time previously, because of the poltergeists' activities, and John had taped black insulation beneath the switch so that it could not be switched on. Despite these precautions, occasionally the tape had been physically removed and the switch left in the 'on' position, with the rings glowing red hot. That was when Anne contacted me, frightened in case of fire.

The bed itself figured in the activities. The mattress was rolled back at one time, and on another occasion, hearing a noise, Joan looked in, knowing that the room was empty, to see the bedclothes moving. It was here, on an earlier occasion, that she saw an amorphous blob, shaped like a 6-inch (15-cm) long snail jump off the bed. Afterwards it could not be found.

There were many other events: a female voice could be heard singing soprano in the wall cavity; ice cubes were thrown to the floor in their holder and talcum powder was thrown over the son's head. The entity used talcum powder, taken from the bathroom, rather a lot. Robert had his chest covered with powder as he lay sleeping and talc would occasionally be scattered in the hall. Slippers, beer cans and the pet dog's bouncy balls were thrown at John in the hall and on separate occasions the dog and Anne were locked in rooms, the doors of which had to be forced open.

Early one morning, John was woken by loud thuds on his bedroom door and when he went to investigate he found two large kitchen knives embedded in the wood. Looking out of the window to find a means of escape, he decided it was too high and spent yet another frightening night in his bedroom. Apports – objects disappearing and reappearing some time later – were quite commonplace, mainly relating to Joan, the lady of the house's friend. For example, a dish disappeared and three months later reappeared on the draining board.

One other noteworthy incident occurred. When the young son was in town he had been told that a friend had been attacked and injured. At the same time, back in his kitchen, drawers were mysteriously thrown onto the floor in the centre of the spiral.

The Good Spirit Appears

As it grew more powerful the original entity revealed itself as a tiny indistinct figure with burning red eyes. Its size was about that of a small dog, quite surprisingly small. Worse was to come when another similar figure appeared! To compensate, however, two other entities, this time benevolent, entered the house and Robert was eventually able to communicate with one simply by leaving sheets of A4 paper and crayons for what he came to call the 'good side' or spirit to write upon. The evil side, naturally (or supernaturally!), stole the crayons to write occult symbols and messages in the bedroom and also wrote the message 'Come and join me' next to the kitchen knives, which had been formed into a hexagonal shape with a shovelful of earth nearby.

Over the years the messages from the good spirit built up to a pile almost a foot high. It is interesting to watch the evolution of the communication over a period of time. It began one evening when Robert heard footsteps in the bathroom and the door slam with unaccustomed violence. Knowing the good spirit was active, he went into the bathroom to find no one there, but there was a message scrawled on the bathroom mirror: 'Please help me.' The spirit had used Robert's mother's brown foundation cream, so he replied using the same tube of cream on a sheet of paper. Eventually, after running out of cosmetic creams, he tried leaving coloured crayons, which the good spirit accepted.

Figure 64: Notes from a poltergeist written in crayon on A4 paper. The spelling has been left as per notes. Note how the strength of the writing is decreasing towards the end. Names have been deleted.

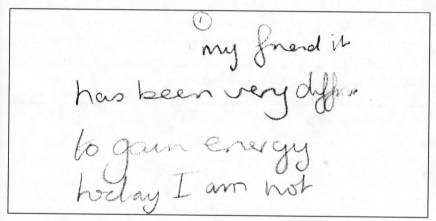

my friend it has been very difficult to gain energy today I am not

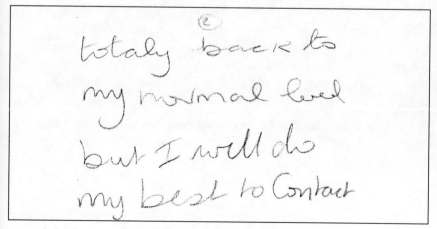

...totaly back to normal level but I will do my best to contact...

③

*you for just now
anyway No Richard
nothing comes easy
and it is going*

...you for just now anyway No Richard nothing comes easy amd it is going...

④

*to be very difficult
because there are
two of them drawing
our energy now*

...to be very difficult because there are two of them drawing our energy now...

...I will help you all I can but right now I am weakening but I can feel a lot of...

...turbulance going on right now my friend but I will try and contact you later. Bye my friend.

The sheets, as you can see, are numbered, apparently to keep them in order because the poltergeists occasionally found them and furiously threw them around the house. The good spirit always began the letters with 'Robert my friend' and ended with 'Bye for now'; the style of writing was modern and flamboyant, and Anne's name was never spelled out fully, being given simply as a capital 'A' with a circle around it. This is explained by Robert once running out of space in a letter and shortening Anne's name to 'A'. The spirit wrote back, 'Why are you so angry with the letter "A"?' After that, the good spirit always referred to Anne as 'A', with a (protective?) circle around the letter. When evil was mentioned, it was with a capital 'E', the word usually being heavily underlined.

Sometimes the writing, which was very large, petered out after a few pages, due to loss of energy by the entity. Only on occasion did it use a pen and the spelling was occasionally incorrect, usually confusing 'ei' and 'ie', which is a very common mistake anyway. It is interesting that the entity, despite having a reasonable command of spelling, occasionally used the phonetic spelling of difficult words, such as 'Spiritualists' ('Spira chulists'), and spelled 'totally' with one 'l', just as the two lads did, which, with other similarities, leads me to think that the entities were at least partial exteriorizations of the two young men, although their writing is incompatible (see Figure 65). This is emphasized by one event, when John, late one evening, began to drink a few cans of beer. As he got progressively more inebriated and excited, so did the poltergeists.

Poltergeists are 'God's Cast-Offs'

In the correspondence the good spirit said it had been sent to help. The evil spirits were 'God's cast-offs', which could lie dormant in a house for a long time waiting for the right victim. All of them had been around for many centuries. Good spirits could flit from one house to another – most houses had them, but they tended to keep very quiet – and the evil ones gained their power from those who took drugs or used ouija boards, and from the waxing and waning of the moon. This was when the good spirit felt the 'turbulance' (sic) getting high.

When I placed a cup-marked stone outside the building to warp the unhealthy energies around it, the good spirit commented that 'the man with the divining rods' had 'a lot to learn' and it wasn't sure just how much Earth

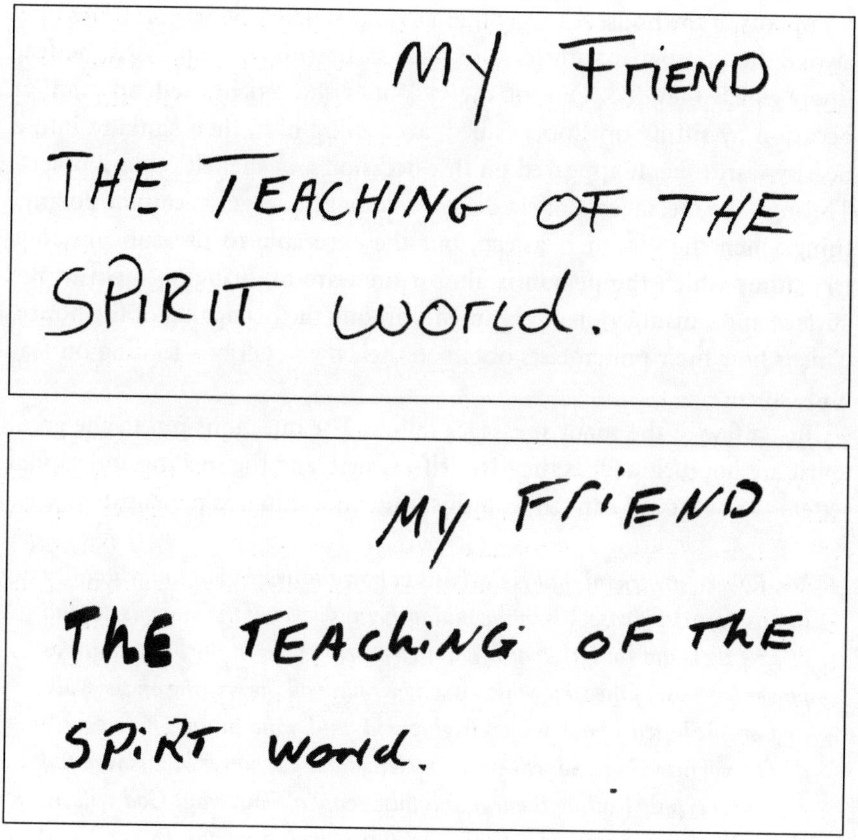

MY FRIEND

THE TEACHING OF THE

SPIRIT world.

MY FRIEND

THE TEACHING OF THE

SPIRT world.

Figure 65: Samples of writing from Robert and John.

energies played a part in poltergeist effects! Well, I knew I had a lot to learn, anyway, but it is interesting that the entity was unaware of the effects of Earth energies – perhaps it simply used the power without being aware of its source.

Another message, in reply to a query on standing stones, said that they had little to do with spirits, but that some of the energies were unhealthy and caused problems. There had been a man in the house who knew about them, but had a lot to learn. (This refers to the unfortunate author again!) It also pointed out that poltergeists were so devious they could easily alter Earth energies to confuse me.

Apparently, the disturbances were worst around the full moon and the evil presences projected their shadows on the wall to make themselves look huge and menacing. Another trick they used was to upset and irritate the occupants of the house, causing them to argue violently. Several times they awoke the occupants with loud crashes so that they could instil the fear upon which they fed. One of the evil ones showed himself on another occasion by sitting on Robert's bed, awakening him, then slinking into a nearby wardrobe. It appeared on this occasion as a shapeless black object. Through the messages, Robert discovered that poltergeists cannot do anything when the victim is asleep, but they are able to use subconscious irritations which the person is almost unaware of, bringing them to the surface and causing violent arguments among the occupants of the house. This is how their poltergeists obtained their own energy – feeding on fear and violence.

Just a few of the many messages follow. The questions put to the good spirit are not included, as they are self-evident, and the spelling and capital letters are, as far as I can tell with this difficult writing, as per copy:

Yes, Robert, my friend that is the basis of how this works but unfortunatley in this particular case A is in the middle because even if the moon is not full or new there are [ouija] boards and drugs being used in the block so it has power for most of the time which is why we have all the writing on the walls and stuff Shifted about which frightens A and your mum These people don't recognize God and will go to any lengths to get power but as you and I know it is only leading them into a false sense of Power but God will see these People are punished for these activities they carry out. But as I said Robert, my friend every Case is different that is why I Can't really help you until I know the Situation if you get your first case whenever then I will help you all I can with it but it would all depend on the people whether they were believers or non believers, where the house is situated and what took place there before. these are all important factors when dealing with this sort of thing. Good Luck my friend

Bye for now

My friend these people who practice the Cult rituals are thinking they have Power, but all this does is give them a buzz they get no power from it All they are doing is going against Gods word, And you and I both know how dangerous this can be As it brings out much Evil But really my friend this does not have much to do with what we do or have power to do

Bye my friend

Robert my friend
Spirits can walk through walls and doors without opening them that is why
you would never see a ghost either because although they take form like me
and other Spirits we [here 'we' is overwritten with a capital 'I'] can move
through walls. The red eyes you seen that night were definatley not evil my
friend it was me. you don't have to contact me all time my friend I will
always be here for you

My friend people can't bring Poltergiest into a house, they can some-
times contact Spirits in which some are Evil Poltergiest are thoroughly bad
you get no good Poltergiest as you do Spirits.

There are several interesting anomalies in these notes. When the power is high the writing is clear, bold and flamboyant, and when very low it can be much more crude and rather smaller (six lines to the page instead of three/four). The words 'occult rituals' and 'poltergeist' have been mis-spelled, and the phrase 'the red eyes you seen' is grammatically incorrect – an import from America some 15 years ago which has since been included in many younger people's vocabulary. The spirit makes the point that it has been around for centuries and one must question where it gets its com-mand of English – apparently from listening to the conversations of the occupants of haunted houses.

In one message, the spirit said it had to go back to 'God's Resting Place', but was furious at the action of desecrators. After more questioning, the resting place turned out to be the local graveyard, which had recently been vandalized.

Spirals as Primitive Radios

When I investigated the energies in the bedroom, I leaned back against the wall, deep in thought, and my divining rod bumped against it. I was rather taken aback when there was an equally gentle, but audible bump in reply! It seemed to me at the time almost as if the spiral in the room was acting like a primitive radio receiving and transmitting sounds. Robert told me that he had tried to communicate with the good spirit at an early stage in the pol-tergeists' career by jangling his car keys, and there was an immediate reply – obviously the entity repeated the noise as it did not have time to search for another set of keys!

This is similar to the story told to me by a lady who complained of a Christmas party – or rather the sounds of a Christmas party – in her house. The noise seemed to be coming from a particular room, but when she opened the door, all was quiet. Perhaps a line of spirals had been passing noises of a real Christmas party from a nearby house into hers.

I have noticed that the line of energy directly above an underground stream or fissure *(see Figure 61)* is involved in some cases of 'paranormal' occurrences. For instance, a girl who heard the sound of footsteps and drawers opening in her kitchen had this type of energy passing through her armchair from the kitchen.

In another case, that of a house in Paisley where a previous owner, Robin, had committed murder and then suicide, a line from a girl's bed passed through the telephone and television, which often malfunctioned. When she was in bed she sometimes told 'Robin' to behave, whereupon they would function normally again. This type of line, measured by Alf Riggs, a fellow researcher, has been measured as a 12-volt DC field, wanders around at random, just like a subterranean fissure, and may be a link between the person involved and some forms of phenomena. Certainly, and more importantly, I find in cases of severe illness, like ME, this line often runs the length of the victim's body, and if it also happens to be the focal point of a spiral, the problem is exacerbated. Many cases are not ME at all, but are more correctly called 'post viral fatigue syndrome'. ME is an inflammation of the brain and spine, perhaps caused by the 12-volt field running down the head and spine.

POLTERGEISTS THROWING OBJECTS

Reverting to the poltergeist which threw pictures, these effects could be explained more rationally by poltergeists using Earth energies, or simply Earth energies on their own, without a discarnate spirit. Take John and Robert's case. The picture in their sitting-room, I noticed, had been thrown into the centre of the black spiral, and the kitchen drawers had been thrown into the spiral in the kitchen.

As already noted, overgrounds do not normally pass through glass, but are diverted to one side. Glass and its derivatives, like tiles, mirrors, etc., act like insulators to some types of telluric energy. Incoming unhealthy waves, striking this barrier, are normally diverted to one side, but under exceptional circumstances may have sufficient pressure to cause the glass and picture to be hurled into the centre of the spiral. Perhaps the exceptional conditions are the energies from discarnate entities amplifying them, although there may be more scientific explanations which we will address shortly.

Much of the poltergeist's arsenal of weapons is composed of glass, or china, although other items can be involved – bottle tops unscrewing themselves, for instance, which may be caused by the anti-clockwise spiral. This may also cause kitchen and bathroom taps to turn on.

Another feature of the objects which attract poltergeist phenomena is that many of them are resonant cavities: jugs and ornaments, for example. As we have already discovered, cup-mark leys tune into resonant cavities and there must be other energies which I have not yet studied which do likewise, as I have noticed that reports of ball lightning often show it seeking out chimneys, stoves, aircraft fuselages and ships.

THE CASE OF THE LEVITATING LAVATORY PAN LID!

There was a series of amusing poltergeist incidents in an office in the city of Perth. Customers' files mysteriously disappeared from their cabinets and, after frantic searching by the secretaries, reappeared several days later in the most obvious places. The room in the basement was exceptionally cold and had been the embalming room of the previous occupant, an undertaker.

The one feature which occupied everyone's attention was the ladies' lavatory pan, whose lid mysteriously and repeatedly lifted itself wide open when no one was around! The secretaries could hear every little movement in the basement, yet no one ever heard the phantom loo vandal at work. The ladies left the lid firmly down, but when they came back a short time later, it was equally firmly wide open. Whatever agency caused this effect was extremely quiet, since the lid had to be lifted very carefully. Too far and it would fall against the cistern, not far enough and it would crash back onto the toilet.

There was a black spiral centred on the lavatory, perhaps attracted to the bowl itself, and it may have been this spiral, possibly triggered by one of the girls in the office from an adjacent spiral, which lifted the lid. The incidents were most severe at times of stress, when a new manager was taking over, for instance, or when the offices were being renovated.

HOW TO REDUCE POLTERGEIST ENERGY

The best way to avoid a poltergeist's power escalating, according to Robert, is to go out for a walk and calm down. When he does this, on his return the infestation has subsided, due to lack of energy. Other tips from Robert are: never go into these situations tired, as you are vulnerable, never underestimate them, and stand your ground. Exorcisms are usually of little use, and don't allow anyone to take photographs and investigate with electronic equipment – it leaves things worse for those who are left.

When Robert asked the good spirit for advice, the reply was in three parts (spelling is as per copy again):

1 Close thier minds to all evil.
2 When Evil is active ignore it.
3 Be happy.

Apparently evil spirits do not like happy people!

Apart from the above case, most cases of poltergeist activity I have been involved with are of rather mild character and at least some can be understood simply in terms of the behaviour of natural Earth energies, as we shall see. The more evolved, speaking type of poltergeist, one capable of communicating, lifting heavy objects and producing a variety of objects out of thin air, hints at the power of departed spirits and of youngsters around puberty, perhaps in association with natural and artificial electric and electromagnetic fields.

Other phenomena similar to poltergeist hauntings have occurred. The recent publicity about the house at Moel Fanog, a farmhouse on the Brecon Beacons, is only the latest in a long line of similar incidents. Utility bills there have been as high as £750 per quarter, even when the family had been on holiday; telephones ring when no incoming calls are being made, electric doorbells ring when no one is there, light switches frequently move to the 'on' position and have to be taped down to prevent being switched on spontaneously, TVs and radios come on even when the power is unplugged, hair rollers heat with no power applied, and other poltergeist phenomena and apparitions have been reported.

TYPES OF MAGNETISM AND THEIR EFFECTS

There is a logical explanation to at least some of the poltergeist-type phenomena when we look at free natural sources of energy and their effects on metals and other materials which may be involved in poltergeist infestations, but first of all we must examine the various forms of magnetism.

Oxygen, sodium, salts, iron, nickel and oxides of nitrogen are paramagnetic where the magnetic field of a magnet induces magnetization of the substance or metal in the same direction as the original magnet.

Glass, water, mercury and most gases are diamagnetic, that is, they act to repel any magnetic field in which they are placed. Thus a force is experienced by any artefact such as glass, etc., when it is exposed to a magnetic field gradient. This force seeks to move the glass from where the magnetic field is relatively strong to where it is weaker. In glass, magnetization is negative; in other materials, positive.

Iron, nickel, copper, cobalt, with all of their alloys, rare earth metals, oxide of iron and lodestone are all examples of ferromagnetism and are always attracted to the strongest part of the magnetic field.

When a ferromagnetic substance is magnetized, it changes length slightly, either expanding or contracting. Iron, for example, contracts in a weak field and expands in a strong field. This is called magnetostriction.

Non-magnetic objects can be repulsed by the induction of eddy currents in the metal conductor by the original magnetic field. This sets up a contrary magnetic field which pushes against the original source.[1] Could these properties relate directly to equipment which refuses to function in haunted places and authentic crop circles, etc.? Cameras and video recorders, for instance, are very sensitive instruments machined to close tolerances, which could easily be affected by magnetostriction. Also, in 'haunted' places, often in public houses, glasses will, apparently of their own volition, move along the counters, perhaps because of the diamagnetic effect. This may, as we have already observed, be another explanation as to why pictures are flung from walls in some poltergeist infestations.

In one case in Crieff, a girl sitting on her bed drying her hair with an electric drier was horrified to see the duvet beside her being depressed, almost as if an invisible body was sitting on it. There are many cases of this type, which include the mattress being found rolled up in John and Robert's house, and other reported incidents where a person lying in bed has the sensation that the bed is bouncing up and down, often with the feeling that the bedclothes are being pulled off.

Here again the physics of resonance and forced oscillations has a direct bearing on this phenomenon, once we take into account the possibility of ambient piezo electric and magnetic fields.

RESONANCE

First, however, a note on resonance. Any mechanical system which can vibrate has a natural frequency at which it will vibrate if displaced and then released. Such a system may be forced to vibrate, however, at a different frequency called the forcing frequency. If this forcing frequency becomes equal to the natural frequency, then very large vibrations will occur and there is said to be resonance. The amplitude of response at resonance depends upon the amount of energy dissipated during each vibration.

Everything under the sun has its own resonant frequency, from every cell in your body to the glasses in your drinks cabinet. Even vast man-made structures will, given the correct frequency and amplitude (strength), resonate and shake to destruction. A familiar example is the wine glass which shatters spontaneously when the singer hits a very pure, coherent note which is exactly the same as the resonant frequency of the glass itself.

The Tacoma Narrows Bridge in the USA may be less familiar. On this long metal structure, in 1940, the combination of a steady wind and traffic set up an oscillation which from a swinging movement soon accelerated to a gigantic oscillation which destroyed the bridge, throwing cars into the river below.

Another extreme example of resonance was reported in *The Times* in 1997. New radar domes fitted to Concorde were disintegrating at high speeds. Happily, new materials and bonding techniques were developed by a British company to safely eliminate the problem.

Bouncing Beds

A most interesting bouncing bed was reported, also in *The Times*, on 4 April 1997. A couple in Ottery St Mary, Devon, had bought special beds which were supposed to lull them gently to sleep. Presumably they had low-frequency motors incorporated into them. Within a few days of buying the beds, the couple had an ordeal which a judge in the court case which followed described as 'like being haunted by an electronic poltergeist'. The beds would start moving spontaneously in the middle of the night, as if there was an earthquake. 'Sometimes it would get faster and faster as if you were trying to get to sleep on a jet which was revving up to take off,' the lady said. 'You never knew when they were going to come on.' As there were two separate beds, each with its own separate control device, this is a very strong pointer to a local hotspot of energy which, perhaps due to interference effects, caused energy input to the bed systems and thus the extraordinary activity of the beds themselves.

Vertical springs in a mattress can be forced to vibrate, not only by the sleeper, but by an external force which we shall call F. If F has a frequency different from the natural frequency of the springs (which may number in the hundreds and are all of very similar dimensions), the amplitude will be small. Under certain circumstances, however, the addition of a small input of noise to the larger input signal can greatly increase the output signal.[2] This phenomenon is called stochastic resonance.

PHANTOM FOOTSTEPS AND OTHER
AUDITORY PHENOMENA

There are thousands of reports in phenomenological literature detailing sounds heard which are impossible in the given environment, with footsteps being one of the most common. John and Robert's case started with footsteps on the ceiling and other reports tell of 'steps as if on stone floors' when the house is fully carpeted, the sound of distant engines and cars when there is no road for a car to drive on, the sound of music and singing, even choirs, when there is no one present, just like the sound of the woman singing soprano in the wall cavity.

In checking through the many reports of ghostly steps, it will be evident that they are usually described as slow, measured, dragging, etc., rarely as running or rushing. It is also strange that if two people are in a room, perhaps a bedroom, often only one will hear the phantom steps.

The study of acoustics is fascinating and crosses the barriers of several scientific disciplines. Strange sounds can be caused by distant earthquakes, distant waterfalls and wind blowing across open wells, chimneys and pipes, quite apart from the common water knock in house plumbing.

Wells, chimneys, corridors and tunnels act as wave guides and allow sounds to be heard out of place, as it were. If you take a milk bottle and blow gently across the top, a low sound will be produced. If you listen with your head in your fireplace (with no fire in the grate, we might add!) you can hear conversations, birds singing, distant trains and so on, which are so faint as to be imperceptible when standing in the same room.

If you hold a seashell to your ear the sound of the sea is well known. In reality, you are hearing the pulse of blood pumping round your blood vessels. The swooshing sound is very like the swoosh of pebbles on the beach as the waves wash back to the sea. Likewise, if you wake in the night with an ear pressed against the pillow, your own pulse can be heard. Indeed, due to the shape of the ear itself, a very strong amplification of such sounds can occur. The heartbeat and the circulation of the blood continue from before birth to death, with, fortunately, very few hiccups. Sometimes one feels a racing pulse, sometimes a missed beat, but rarely major problems. So the occasional audible sound of a heartbeat, whilst unexpected, is normal, although rare.

The Electric Light Connection

In the dozens of reports of 'steps' heard by people in bed, two stand out for accuracy and implication. The first is taken from Ian Wilson's book *Worlds Beyond* (Weidenfeld & Nicolson, 1986), a serious analysis of cases from the Society for Psychical Research. It is the case of the strange occurrences at the Lodge of Ardachie House near Spean, Inverness.

Husband and wife Bill and Frances Matthews had answered an advertisement for a caretaker/housekeeper in the *Evening Standard* in 1953. After a long journey they arrived at the Lodge, talked with their new employers and retired early to bed.

Wilson writes:

As explained by Frances Matthews, husband Bill had just gone to sleep when she heard footsteps coming up the stairs just outside their bedroom door. The steps appeared to go into the unoccupied room opposite their own. A few minutes later the same sequence was repeated and Frances awoke husband Bill, only to find that he seemed to think that the footsteps were coming from the wall next to their beds.[3]

Later on, after reporting the 'footsteps' to their new employers, and having eliminated the Lodge's electric generator and the pet dog and cat as the source, the Matthews returned to bed. However, having gone back to bed and turned off the light, rapping had begun from behind the same wall which Bill Matthews had thought he heard footsteps. Although this continued when he got out of bed to get to the light switch, it ceased the moment the light went on. Bill again went to the McEwans, the owners of the house, and now very frightened, they enlisted the help of Peter McEwan, who happened to be a member of the SPR, who suggested that the two men should return to the bedroom, switch off the light and await developments.

The two men sat in the darkness for a full ten minutes but they heard absolutely nothing (note that the men were seated upright in chairs, as against lying flat in bed, as was the case when the sounds were heard by the Matthews). Well past midnight it was decided that the Matthews should sleep in a room at the front of the Lodge, two staircases and corridors removed from their first room. Again, after retiring to bed for the second time that night, both Frances and Bill heard 'a faint but distinct rapping above Frances' head'.

Wilson writes:

As, bleary eyed, the two couples once again gathered in the passageway ... suddenly Frances stiffened with horror. She could now see a figure crawling on her hands and knees with what looked like a candle stock in one hand. Peter, however, could see nothing.[4]

The story continues with other visitors to the house who had also heard taps and footsteps, in situations where no evident cause could be found.

In his book *In Search of Ghosts* (Weidenfeld & Nicolson, 1986) Ian Wilson gives further valuable and personal pointers to the brain and eyes to auditory phenomena. In June 1988 a long-standing friend of Wilson's, Dr Michael Clift, sent a report to the Society for Psychical Research regarding happenings he experienced while staying at Bearwood College, Sindlesham, near Wokingham, in 1983:

On Wednesday, 27th July of that year I was visiting an old friend, Lieutenant Commander Michael Hayes, who was history master there and lived in the Tower flat. The house, a splendid example of Victorian Gothic, was built around 1873 for the (then) owner of The Times ... but has been a school since the 1920s. On several previous occasions I had stayed there overnight, always in the same dormitory on the top floor ... I had never felt any unease, and had always slept well. On this completely windless summer's night it was different. As I was dozing off, I was roused by a lot of noise like that of furniture being moved nearby. I thought at first it was caused by cleaners on the floor below, then by my friend moving about in his flat, then by a lorry discharging planks on the gravel below the dormitory window. None of these survived investigation. I got up three or four times and it was only on the last occasion that I realized the noise came on when the light was out and faded away when I switched it on. There was a clear relationship between the two, and then I felt so fearful that I went downstairs and slept until dawn in my car.[5]

We have here a direct association between the endogenous (natural) alpha waves of the brain and perception. What is the relationship between vision and hearing? A close analysis of the many reports of auditory hallucinations, if such a thing were possible, could throw new light on cross-perceptions (synaesthesia) when the body produces such odd effects as the feeling of nausea in the leg or seeing words in colour in the brain.

A further example of auditory phenomena occurred in December 1531, at Guadalupe, Mexico. Juan Diego, an Indian, was walking from Quahutitcan, near the present-day Mexico City, to Tlatiloco, passing a hill called Tepeyacac. As reported in *La Estrella del Norte de Mexico* (Florencia, 1669), he was walking by the hill when he heard 'exquisite, entrancing bird-like music coming from the top of the hill. Then the music stopped and he heard his own name being called. Then on the top of the hill he saw a radiant apparition of a woman, dark in colour, like a native, which spoke to him in the native dialect called Nahuatl, and said she was the Blessed Virgin Mary, and that she wished a church should be built on the hill called Tepeyacac.' When Juan Diego returned to the hill later, he found flowers growing there out of season instead of the usual cacti and weeds. Some flowers were picked and taken to the local bishop, which produced a great flurry of activity amongst the Catholic clerics of the area.

Another interesting sound has been heard at Dunter, a castle on the

Scottish border.[6] This is a constant rhythmic noise 'like the grinding of seed in a hollow stone mill'. Local reports consider it to be an evil omen.

A lady known to Anne Silk recorded a strange experience in a Jewish Hassidim class. During the discussion for the group the teacher began to hum. At the same time the lady was aware of a strong emotional change and a weird feeling in her brain. She described it as 'a peculiar effect'.[7]

Another woman told of her feelings when a Tibetan bowl was struck when she was visiting a teacher. Again she was instantly aware of strange feelings in her brain, but instead of the weird, unpleasant sensation of the first person, she felt a great surge of energy and love.

In both these cases we are looking at the systemic effects of eddy currents and resonance in the brain. Sound and music were both known to the ancients as having the ability to engender specific feelings. There are several factors which possibly combine here: the notes played and their harmonics, the volume (amplitude) and the beat (rhythm) of the sound. This subject is beyond the scope of this book and is a vast and largely uncharted sea for the interested researcher.

One of the most interesting reports of poltergeist phenomena, containing virtually the totality of perceived effects, is that of the Hislop family at Oldmeldrum in Aberdeenshire. They had moved into an old house and experienced nine months of weird happenings. If these are considered in the context of ambient energy effects on the brain, there may be rational explanations:

Effect	Probable Cause
Strange violin music.	Auditory hallucination.
Faces at the window.	Visual hallucination.
Room becomes very cold.	Vortex – air pressure.
Pervading smell of roses.	Stimulation of limbic region.
Voice calling 'Marjory' three times.	Sub-clinical effect.
Feeling of strangulation.	Stimulation of brain stem.
Red marks around neck.	Histamine.

There are other strange instances where a person hears their own name, even pet name, called out loud. If this happens when there is no one else in the house, with the victim wide-awake, then indeed it can be a frightening experience, but it is simply one of the many tricks the brain can play on us.

OTHER STRANGE HAPPENINGS

Car Problems

Modern car speedometers sometimes show dozens of miles travelled that are quite impossible in the real time frame, but one answer probably lies not in the paranormal, but in the laws of electromagnetics.

Speedometers usually work through a square-shaped cable which runs from the gearbox to the back of the instrument in the dashboard. The faster the car goes, the faster the geared cable spins. At the dashboard end, the cable has a small bar magnet attached, which sits inside a rotating aluminium speed cup, which in turn sits within a stationary magnetic ring. The cup is a magnetized piece of aluminium connected to the rear end of the speedo spindle, to which the speedometer needle is fixed. As the magnet spins, it sets up an electromagnetic field which induces eddy currents in the non-magnetic but highly conductive material of the speed cup, which tries to spin with the magnet, taking the speedo spindle and needle with it. So an externally applied magnetic field will, under certain circumstances, override the system and impart spin to the spindle, showing vast, apparently impossible mileages on the mileometer, according to Professor H. Burke from MIT and Stanford Universities in the USA.

Abductions

There are reports of people who believe they have been abducted and suffer from perceived missing time, like the case of the lady who was walking past the old cemetery. This is a known effect in neurology when the time sense seems to slow right down under the influence of magnetic fields.

The brain can be influenced in other ways. A couple were motoring along the Loch Tummel road in Perthshire when the lady saw an enormous gold-coloured crystal dome shining in the glen. Inside were little houses, also made of crystal. The vision lasted only a few seconds and her husband, who was driving at the time, saw nothing. She wondered whether she had seen something from the past. The glen had been formed by a glacier only a few thousand years ago, so it could hardly have been part of an ancient golden age and it is unlikely that it is part of the future. There are, however, three powerful hydro-electric dams and power stations in the area, within a radius of 6 miles (10 kilometres) of the site of that incident and it may be that she had found herself in a very localized hot spot, which caused her to have a waking dream – a powerful hallucination, in other words.

Demons

A lady in Edinburgh telephoned me for help. Her story was a horrifying one. Almost every night she was being savagely raped by an invisible entity. She described it as a bestial, determined and impersonal attack, which took place even when her husband was with her. She had also been attacked when she lived at previous locations and kept shifting her bed in an effort to thwart the creature, but it always caught up with her.

There was a black spiral in the living-room, in front of the television set, and the real culprit, another black spiral, in the centre of the couple's bed, at the level of the solar plexus. Both husband and wife told me that, occasionally, they felt as if many sharp nails were being driven into their solar plexuses. The husband told me that he had also been attacked by the entity on one occasion. This may be a result of stimulation of the septal region of the brain.

I put one of my cup-marked stones down, which eliminated much of the black energy, but unfortunately, to my horror, made things worse! Then I put the wife in touch with an Arabian gentleman who eliminated it with a form of ceremonial 'magic'. He told me, 'The people in the UK do not know very much about these things!'

Sisters Attacked

Later, I had a request from two sisters in the same area. They were being attacked in a very similar manner. In this case, the black spiral was in the bed of the younger sister, while the older sister, who slept downstairs, had the spiral about a yard away from the foot of her bed.

They also told me of another unusual occurrence, when a very bright disc-shaped light flew across Edinburgh with incredible speed. Watching it through their window, they were horrified when it sped towards them, then seemed to settle into the house, the furniture and room glowing orange, which slowly dissipated.

The younger of the sisters described the experience which followed as an invisible and personal assault, while the elder, with the centre of the spiral beyond the foot of her bed, found the attacking force could only shake her bed. Both had decided not to tell the other about the problem, which lasted for some months, until finally, at the end of her tether, one told her sister the story.

Presumably, the phenomenon was a form of Earth energy which had to earth itself into the most attractive spot in the vicinity. The electromagnetic fields and static may have caused the ladies to have powerful hallucinatory dreams – or was there some form of entity which actually attacked them?

REFERENCES

1   M. Burke, *Handbook of Magnetic Phenomena*, Van Nostrand, USA, 1987

2   M. Nelkon, *Advanced Physics*, Pan, 1987

3   Ian Wilson, *Worlds Beyond*, Weidenfeld & Nicolson, 1986

4   Ibid.

5   Ian Wilson, *In Search of Ghosts*, Weidenfeld & Nicolson, 1986

6   P. Allardice, *Myths of God and Fantasy*, Prism Press, UK, 1991

7   Personal communication to Anne Silk.

17

LETHBRİDGE'S LEGACY

...Like Peris' Wands, when pointing out the road
(Thomas Moore)

ANNE SILK

The origin of the laws of physics comes down to
information: the information we try to prise from
Nature by making observations and the information
Nature has, but is reluctant to part with.

ROY FRIEDEN, *PHYSICS FROM FISHER*
INFORMATION (CAMBRIDGE UNIVERSITY PRESS, 1998)

Dr Tom Lethbridge was a great man, in every sense of the word. Professionally, he was an archaeologist and Keeper of Anglo-Saxon Antiquities at Cambridge, but he was also an historian, a practical visionary and a dowser. Above all, he had curiosity. By the time he died in 1971, he had written several books on a variety of phenomena from a strictly observational and analytical point of view, in addition to many research papers. He listed, in the clearest possible language, all the effects, both good and bad, of Earth energies that have ever been published. With the immense progress in geophysics and seismology in the years since his death, it is now time to look again at his work and set it into the framework which, ahead of his time, he did not live to see realized.

Let us look again at the places where Dr Lethbridge and his wife Mina experienced strange occurrences and at the analyses he gave of perceived phenomena. With hindsight, we can consider the effects on the brain and emotions from high-energy seismic sites. These can be, as both Lethbridges found, very localized.

Ladram Bay

27/1/63

This is a highly faulted area on the coast of the English Channel, 2 miles south-west of Sidmouth. The geology is red sandstone. Lethbridge wrote: 'I passed into a kind of blanket of fog, depression and fear.' His wife said, 'Something frightful is here. I can't stand this place any longer.'

3/2/63

At the same place, Lethbridge again felt the same depression, just over the point where a streamlet ran over the pebbles into the sea. At the other end of the beach he wrote that the feeling was at its worst. 'It was so strong as to make me feel almost giddy. It felt not unlike one feels with a high temperature when full of prescribed drugs. It had definite limits which you could step over in a single stride. There is an air of unreality about it.'

Hole House

21/12/63

This house, Lethbridge's home, is on the north–south uplift on the coast in this area. Both Tom and Mina noted that they experienced blurred vision here.

Skellig Michael

On this tiny island 6 miles (10 kilometres) off the Kerry coast in Ireland, Dr Lethbridge was standing on top of the cliff, looking out to sea. Suddenly he experienced a total collapse and 'fell flat on [his] face in the grass'.

If the motor cortex in the brain is subjected to a transcranial magnetic field of specific strengths, both the muscle behind the tibia in the leg and the soleus, the muscle in the calf of the leg, will contract sharply, leading to collapse and fall, if the person is standing.

As Dr Lethbridge was climbing down the cliff he had another experience, and felt 'as if someone wanted to push me off'.

He is not the only person interested in archaeology to have felt this effect. John Sharkey, writer and lecturer, was sitting alone inside Barpa

Langas, a chambered cairn close to the 20-stone circle of Pobuill Phinn (People of Finn, yet again), on the island of North Uist, listening to the tick of a Geiger counter, when he was flung violently across the little chamber by a vicious 'kick' in the kidneys. He wrote:

> I was lucky to escape with minor injuries from the large, protruding stones, but the sudden nervous shock and a sore back for a few days afterwards were more than sufficient to repay me for my morbid curiosity. The radiation reading was no higher than outside, but in fact nearly a third lower than in the evening, so I can only guess that at dusk there was a kind of shift in the accumulation of energy in the stone funnel...[2]

If the ulnar nerve connected to the spine gets a zap of energy, however sourced, the individual will feel as if they have been pushed from behind, exactly as both Lethbridge and Sharkey described.

The effects Lethbridge reported in these places are as follows:

'Ghouls' (his term for oppressive feelings).
Self-harming/suicidal thoughts.
Drop (physical collapse) attacks.
Visual hallucinations.
Auditory hallucinations.
An immense feeling of sadness.
Sudden extreme depression.
A sense of presence.

He came to the view that the medium involved in these effects is some form of the natural electric field, closely associated with water or a damp atmosphere.

MOOD CHANGES IN NATURAL ELECTRIC FIELDS

The brain is a never-sleeping electrochemical factory, producing neurotransmitters, enzymes, essential chemicals such as melatonin (a cancer-preventing agent) and serotonin (involved in sleep and emotions). These chemicals and the functions control all human emotions: happiness, ecstasy, panic, depression, violence, and so on. If the production of serotonin (an amine neurotransmitter) is suddenly either accelerated or depressed, certain effects on mood, sleep, attention and memory can be triggered.

Both serotonin and noradrenaline are used in two very particular but enormously widespread pathways in the brain. The cell bodies of both systems lie in small clusters deep in the brainstem, at the base of the brain, so a sudden change of current can affect emotions and mood. Putting it simply, as Professor Colin Blakemore writes, 'Depression is due to under-production of serotonin and noradrenaline, and extreme behaviour is due to their over-production by the brain.'[3] So we may visualize the Lethbridges walking along the beach and by the streams, being subjected to a momentarily high electric field from the ionized water flow and equally momentarily undergoing extreme depression, gloom, even an urge to commit suicide – in their words, encountering ghouls – yet finding that these feelings of dread pass rapidly on leaving the bad zone. It gave me (Anne) great pleasure to realize that the very clear, but at that time anomalous, descriptions of such emotions by Tom Lethbridge, fitted exactly with what the Romans called the *genius loci*, the spirit of place.

Interestingly, blurred vision is another effect of abnormal serotonin levels, as is the weird effect of looking at a scene or street where all appears dead. One's limbs may appear distorted and a veil-like lacy curtain can appear over objects. These are all transitory effects and are apt to be misinterpreted as paranormal.

DOWSING

Professor Trazska of the Environmental Protection Agency in Poland made many highly relevant observations on dowsing at a scientific conference on Biomedical Effects of EM Fields in October 1995. He stated that in a series of tests, dowsers were found to display sensitivity to hydrogen resonance (1,420 MHz) at a sensitivity far below 0.01 microV/m. He found that it was the magnetization of water which the dowsers were able to detect. Further, the relaxation time was proportional to the applied magnetic field intensity. In other words, he found a sensitivity to magnetic fields far below those generally considered to be applicable to man. We may call this 'hypersensitivity'.

Were Lethbridge still alive he would have been highly interested in these findings and also in the solid scientific text *The Biological Effects of Environmental Electromagnetism*, written by Professor König (Munich University), Dr Krüger (School of Public Health, University of California), the late Dr S. Lang and Dr Walter Sonning (of Munich). In the 280 pages of this extremely well researched text, Lethbridge would have delighted in such chapters as those on ionized columns of energy from faults and flowing water, biological reactions measured at these sites, natural electrophysical forces and biological activity of static fields. It is explained that not only is the walking speed of the biolocator (dowser) vital to perception, but magnetic saturation (very high field levels) can negate the effect.

The human body acts as an antenna, and will pick up and absorb both Earth and man-made energies, depending upon the polarization (direction) of the energy and the height and position of the body itself. The prone or sleeping body will maximally absorb horizontally polarized energies and the standing body will maximally absorb the vertically polarized energies. Then there are elliptical circular polarizations with varying effects and absorption rates. However, this is not the place to go into eddy currents in the brain and effects of energy on deep structures such as the amygdala (emotions such as fear, terror, etc.), the hypothalamus (the temperature control of the body), the pineal (which produces melatonin, an oncostatic agent) and the pituitary (which produces many hormones, neurotransmitters including those affecting food demand).

THE SENSITIVITY OF MAN

Imagine how strange it would be if you could only see those people whose names began with 'M'. You would never see Queen Elizabeth, Elton John would be invisible and the humour of Rowan Atkinson would be wasted on you. Madonna, Maradona, Mozart and Marilyn Monroe, however, would all be there. So it is with the visible part of the electromagnetic spectrum. We see one another through a tiny window of visible light, yet there are infinitely wider frequencies: the non-ionizing, from static, RF, microwave, infra red and the ionization from UV through X-rays to gamma rays. Until fairly recently, conventional science maintained that the lower regions of the spectrum were virtually imperceptible to man. That is now no longer so. Static electricity from Earth energies and magnetism has been felt by man since he stood upright and walked on the Earth. Animals which walk on all fours are hypersensitive to such energies. For those whose knowledge of electricity stops at pushing the TV switch, it may come as a surprise to realize just how responsive the human body is to ambient electrical and magnetic fields.

Evidence continues to accumulate in scientific papers, such as that by Professor Baker, which states: 'Magnetite has been found in man in the sinus region above and behind the nose and in many other places. In this area deposits of ferric iron have been measured up to 13 times the amounts of other parts of the body.'[4]

Interestingly, in some people the levels were very low. Is it possible that those who are unable to dowse or who dowse poorly may be anaemic?

Prior to his death in 1990, I had the privilege of working on seismic energy with the late Dr Bill Sutherland, the medical physicist. He was a brilliant scientist working in oncology and also a dowser with extreme sensitivity. We were working on 'hot spots' or 'clusters', where the incidence of a specific condition is statistically very much higher than average. With his specialized knowledge and equipment, Bill was able to bring frequency analysis to his findings, a very significant factor in health effects, both adverse and beneficial.

Are dowsers also working along these lines? Energies may be positively charged, negatively charged, even nulled, and magnetic fields will vary depending on the type of rock, buried ore bodies and type of fault. These magnetic gradients are of the greatest significance to body charge and the production of eddy currents in the brain as the body moves across a gradient.

POSITIVE AND NEGATIVE POLARITY IN HUMANS

Branscombe Mouth, under 1 mile (1.6 kilometres) from Hole House, where Lethbridge's dowsing and psychic knowledge became so keen, is on an especially important axis of uplift running north–south, with a 20° dip fault where chalk is on a junction (discontinuity) with Upper Greensand, according to the British Geological Survey. Further, the little River Bran runs down the valley to exit on the beach.[5]

As the seismologist Bryce Walker has stated:

With its layered panoply of materials, the earth responds to the impact of an earthquake by vibrating in a maelstrom of wave forms of all frequencies. If the frequencies were audible it would be as though a full-sized symphony orchestra was blaring out all the notes of all its instruments at once, every instrument playing fortissimo in every possible key, producing utter cacophony. When depicted visually on a seismogram, the earthquake's tumult of conflicting and overlapping seismic waves presents an apparently bewildering hodgepodge of zigzag lines.[6]

FAULTS AND PHENOMENA

Far below us, sections of the Earth are slowly grinding along each fracture. You will have heard of the San Andreas fault in America, and we have already discussed the Great Glen fault in Scotland, which stretches down from Inverness to Islay. You may not know of the hidden bands which run across Greenwich under the Thames. Another runs under Tower Hill from Deptford and on into Essex. Hundreds of these seismic faults have been found in the UK and it is the energy released when they move which concerns us *(see Map 21)*.

I must stress that we are not looking here at the great works of nature and eruptions of energy from major volcanoes and earthquakes, but at the subtle energies. In the UK the energy is way down in the extremely low frequency, very low frequency and radio frequency bands. Rarely can it reach up into the microwave bands. Acoustic energy is transmitted and thus is heard by some (depending upon the frequency) as a groaning or crying, or as musical tones, murmurs, the sound of breaking glass, a railway engine or a squadron of Lancaster bombers. Much depends on the type of rock or earth below the ground *(see Natural Earth Wave chart, pages 259–60)*.

Map 21: *Major faulting in England, Wales and Scotland.*

Earthquake Noises

It was Pliny the Elder who wrote in the first century AD:

> [Earthquakes] are ... preceded or accompanied by a terrible sound that sometimes resembles a rumble, sometimes the lowing of cattle or the shouts of human beings or the clash of weapons struck together, according to the nature of the material which receives the shock and the shape of caverns or burrows through which it passes, proceeding with smaller volume in a narrow channel but with a harsh noise in channels that bend, echoing in hard channels, bubbling in damp ones, forming waves in stagnant ones, raging against solid ones. Accordingly, even without any movement occurring a sound is sometimes emitted.[7]

This description of earthquake noises is one of the best, most exhaustive and scientifically profound descriptions that has ever been composed. Not only does it give a vivid image of the intensity and the character of the sounds, but at the same time it explains in an understandable way how much the quality of sound varies with the structural form and the material composition of the environment. This remarkable description did not overlook the fact that earthquake noise frequently begins several seconds before tremors become perceptible and that ground noises occasionally appear without Earth movements.

It is interesting to compare the modern perceptions of this intensive acoustical experience. Charles Davidson, who from 1889 to 1916 evaluated about 20,000 reports of earthquake noise, came to the conclusion that it was usually a dull-sounding rolling noise resembling distant thunder or the noise made by a heavy vehicle rolling past. His seven-point scale also includes sound impressions that resemble the sounds made by a load of coal being tipped out and by a giant flock of partridges.

Several people who told Prof. Tributsch of their earthquake experiences compared the sensation to that of suddenly finding themselves in a mighty train that was hurtling over such bumpy rails that they were thrown about helplessly. The earthquake noise which accompanied the Ligurian earthquakes towards the end of the nineteenth century was compared by alert, technically trained observers to that of a train rushing past an observer in a tunnel.

An anecdote which a railway engineer told the seismologist Mercalli shows how accurate this comparison is. It seems that a signalman happened to be in the 8,300-foot (2,530-metre) railroad tunnel between Joppoli and Ricadi, Italy which runs through a rock formation, when the earthquake happened. The sound effects of an onrushing train were so genuine that the signalman gave the prescribed signals. He was terrified to hear the noise passing without seeing a train!

Despite the many earthquakes which happen every year, science has only very sparse hard evidence of the accompanying noise. The pride of earthquake researchers is a catalogue of 13 accidentally recorded tapes which produce, through the screaming of people and the falling of dishes, some 'genuine' earthquake noises. Still, the representation of earthquake noise has been remarkably well developed, thanks to careful laboratory experiments, accurate theoretical examinations and a tape recording which caught several miniquakes.

Since earthquake noises are generated when vibrations of the Earth's surface transfer pressure waves to the air, the key to these sound phenomena lies in the knowledge of the vibrations which can be produced in the Earth before and during a 'quake. We know today that there are many mechanisms which can evoke them.

Earthquake waves themselves vibrate at frequencies between 0.1 and 10 hertz (Hz). This frequency range is followed (up to several hundred hertz) by the more rapid vibrations of the microquake. A human, whose hearing threshold lies around 16 Hz, can, theoretically, hear the waves of smaller earthquakes. On top of the frequency range of these microquakes are the frequencies (up to 3,000 Hz) of still other kinds of vibrations. These are produced by breaking rock.

Since sound is produced in all major earthquakes, the source of the vibrations must not be neglected. Laboratory experiments show that before rocks break, fine hairline cracks appear in them. In the process, ultrasound signals are emitted at frequencies which can reach 100,000 Hz (100 KHz). The sound frequency varies with the size of the tears which are being produced and thus with the kind of rock in which the cracks appear. It follows, then, that almost any sound frequency may be emitted in an earthquake, from infra sound to the extreme ultrasound. But a concert of this kind would hardly have been compared to the growling of thunder or the passing of a train in a tunnel – rather, one might think of the rattling of tin cans, breaking glass or screeching brakes.

The reason for the great difference between generated sound and perceived sound in an earthquake is that rock swallows much of the generated sound energy. This muffling effect is not equally strong at all frequencies, but is proportionally stronger in the higher frequencies. Whereas sound of 10,000 Hz travels 656 feet (200 metres) in typical bedrock, sound of 100 Hz covers 12 miles (20 kilometres). As sound travels through the bedrock, ultrasound frequencies are filtered out drastically, so that only the deeper earthquake tones remain. In order for ultrasound signals coming from the developing hairline fractures in rock to be detected, the events must be taking place 32.8–328 feet (10–100 metres) away. Since the origins of earthquakes generally lie many miles beneath the Earth's surface, and since very shallow earthquakes are rare, ultrasound signals as earthquake signs are barely worth considering. This is confirmed by the fortuitous tape recordings of three small earthquakes in 1975 in the Imperial Valley of California; the measured acoustical frequencies are indeed limited to the very low frequency range between 50 and 70 Hz.

However, earthquake noise is not always limited to this narrow frequency range. If a small 'quake happens in a bottom layer of granite or lava rock, people living above it may perceive very high-pitched noises. This is because small earthquakes produce high frequency tones and because these travel well through this kind of crystalline rock. A similar earthquake under a layer of ocean sediments, which swallows higher frequencies more easily, would sound muffled and deep.

The acoustical measurements of the Imperial Valley noises yielded a surprise bonus of a very special kind. Since antiquity, witnesses have always maintained that earthquake noises have appeared several seconds before the tremors. Even the Italian researcher Luigi Bossi experienced and described the phenomenon – according to his observations, aftershocks of the earthquake wave of 1808 in the Piedmont came with and without noises; when noises did appear, they preceded the earthquake by about 2 seconds. If the dramatic descriptions of earthquake noise deserve to be taken with a grain of salt, then the claims that sound preceded the 'quakes deserved even more scepticism. But the measurements from the Imperial Valley confirmed these old reports. The earthquake noise began about 2 seconds before the onset of perceptible Earth movements and was already waning as the latter were gaining strength.

The explanation turned out to be the simplest one imaginable. The earthquake waves proper (the S waves), which are felt by humans and which oscillate at right angles to their direction of travel, are preceded by the compression waves, whose vibrations, much as those of sound waves, run parallel to their direction of travel. These P waves are about 70 per cent faster than the S waves, and when they arrive at the surface from below, they set the surface vibrating so that it radiates sounds vertically into the air. On the other hand, the S waves, from the other direction, cannot impel pressure waves into the air. However, if the earthquake waves arrive at the surface at an angle, then only that part of the forces which move the ground at right angles to the surface will have an effect. Thus, people hear the earthquake wave which they cannot feel and feel the wave they cannot hear. Only if an earthquake is stronger than magnitude 3 do the P waves become somewhat perceptible.

After scientists had poked around the secret of the sound-producing P waves for the first time, in 1975, the stories of how country folk recognized the phenomenon centuries ago and had used it prudently to save lives in the last seconds before a quake made sense.

An observation by Alexander von Humboldt in 1799 in Cumana, Venezuela, supports this view:

It is widely believed in Cumana that the most destructive earthquakes are announced by very weak oscillations of the ground and through a howling, and something like that does not escape people who are used to such incidents. In such moments you can hear the cry everywhere: 'Misericordia! Trembla! Trembla! Trembla!' ('Mercy, it is quaking, it is quaking!') and it is rare that a false alarm is set off by a native.[8]

If it is possible to hear an earthquake, it is possible to 'hear' not only its distance, its intensity and the direction of its source, but also the ground through which the sound travels and the Earth's surface which transmits it into the air. Water conducts sound much better than rock and also radiates it differently. Its presence gives a different voice to an earthquake.[9]

PHYSICAL EFFECTS ABOVE GEOLOGICAL ANOMALIES

Curiously, one of my own patients who had been aware of unusual visual effects told me of her feelings at a small village at the end of a valley north of Buckfast. She said she and her family became aggressive when they visited the village and frequently heard a buzzing in their ears. While staying in the house of a relative, they were awakened by knocks on doors when there was no one there. My patient and others found certain places extremely cold and in general, although the village was pretty and unspoiled, they felt gloomy and depressed. My patient's wristwatch also misbehaved when she stayed there.

By sheer chance at a City dinner some years after this, two colleagues were discussing the *genius loci*. One said that as a boy he used to stay with a relation in this same village during his holidays. He told me that he always felt cold, angry and 'different' when he stayed there. Now, this could be attributed to missing his family, who were abroad, and natural resentment, except that he made it very clear that when he stayed with another relation in the north he had none of these problems.

This village is situated on a sandstone bed 100 feet (30 metres) deep, in rock which contains many large quartz pebbles. In addition, there are areas of strontium, a radioactive ore named after the village of Strontian in Scotland, where it was first discovered. The synergistic effect of radon gas and ELF waves might well have produced the symptoms described.

GLENCOE, THE GLEN OF WEEPING

Many visitors have written of the heavy feeling of gloom and depression when driving through or walking across Glencoe in Argyllshire. Even if the sun is shining, the feeling of depression is present. It certainly was for me when I drove through it *en route* to Mull some years ago.

Glencoe is an interesting place, geologically speaking, part of a cauldron fault, or caldera. Below ground, a cylinder of ancient lava rests on schist rock, the whole bounded by a ring fault. In *Tertiary Volcanic Districts of Scotland*, it is stated that the area 'has subsided thousands of feet between the schist walls'.[10] Simultaneously, magma rose up the circular fissure around the cylinder to spread across the surface (imagine dropping a can of fizzy drink into a pot of viscous paint).

David recalls how, on several occasions, he walked the ring of peaks comprising this fault – the path narrows to about 4–5 inches (10–12 cm) wide at one point, on the Aonach Eagach 'toothed ridge' on the north side, with the Glencoe road far beneath one's feet. The only sensible way over is to sit astride the path and bounce across, which makes this traverse interesting, albeit a little airy. On the north side are the impressive peaks of Bidean nam Bian, the Buachaille Etive Mor and an interesting glaciated hanging valley, the Lost Valley.

Figure 66: Bidean nam Bian in Glencoe, Argyllshire, the rim of an ancient volcanic caldera.

THE LITTLE PEOPLE

Lethbridge was convinced that there are several types of Earth field connected with different elementals: water fields (he called them Naiads); Oreads, associated with open spaces and mountains; and Dryads, associated with woodlands. He writes:

> Little people are seen now and then by many races of Man. They are seen in Africa, where they are just tiny Africans. I do not doubt for a moment that they are seen, but I do doubt the interpretation placed on the seeing. Ordinary men and women all over the world have seen these little people, but I do not believe they really exist as such ... they have seen something which appeared to their minds as a little man.[11]

This may be attributed to micropsia, the medical term for the apparent perception of tiny figures and minute images. The opposite, macropsia, describes the hallucinatory appearance of giant images, perhaps the 8-, 9- and 10-foot (2–3-metre) monsters of folklore still encountered even to this day.

Lethbridge proposed that the force fields of the Earth are concentrated in certain natural features such as waterfalls, springs and streams. He thought that the human body could interact with the natural force-field at these sites. Flowing water carries energy and creates negative ions (the 'good' ions), as against positive ions ('bad' ions). The magnetic field in the UK is at an average of 50,000 nT (50 mG), but both highs and lows are found, especially over basalt, haematite and magnetite. A massive sulphate deposit containing pyrrhotite would be dense, and both magnetic and electrically conductive. At these places compasses may swing, watches, cameras and video recorders may malfunction, and the sensitive human body will give several signs of magnetic gradient.

As Lethbridge wrote, 'Both archaeologists and anthropologists have become so specialized that few men or women remain who are capable of letting their minds range widely about the world.' Nearly 30 years after his death there are many other specialities where his comment applies more than ever. Nevertheless, at the end of the twentieth century some are 'letting their minds range widely'. Tom Lethbridge left clear signposts for paths of future research 'like Peris' Wands, when pointing out the road'. How far along this path have others travelled?

REFERENCES

1   Many reports refer to 'radiation readings', using Geiger counters which measure ionizing radiations. However magnetometer readings and non-ionizing radiations (extremely low frequency, radio frequency and microwave frequencies) are hardly ever mentioned in UK reports.

2   John Sharkey, *The Road Through the Isles*, Keith Payne, 1985

3   C. Blakemore, *The Mind Machine*, Oxford University Press, 1990

4   R. R. Baker, 'Magnetic bones in human sinuses', *Nature*, 301:78 (1983)

5   *South-west England*, British Geological Survey/HMSO, 1975

6   Bryce Walker, quoted in *Earthquakes*, TimeLife, 1982

7   Pliny the Elder, quoted in H. Tributsch, *When the Snakes Awake*, MIT Press, USA, 1983

8   Alexander von Humboldt, quoted in Bruce Bolt, *Earthshock*, Sphere, 1980

9   H. Tributsch, op. cit.

10 J. E. Ritchie *et al.*, *The Tertiary Volcanic District of Scotland*, British Geological Survey, 1987

11 T. C. Lethbridge, Ghost and Ghoul, Routledge & Kegan Paul, 1980

18

BALL LIGHTNING
AND EARTH LIGHTS

Unidentified Aerial Phenomena

> It is useful to be assured that the heavings of the
> Earth are not the work of angry deities. These
> phenomena have causes of their own.
>
> SENECA, THE ROMAN ORATOR AND WRITER

Natural ball lightning, or Balls of Light (BoLs), are some of the most mysterious manifestations of nature. They can be as small as a pea or larger than a house, can glide silently and disinterestedly past an observer or brush affectionately past their ankles. They may circuit rooms and factories and hover around aircraft, entering the fuselage or vanishing silently or in a puff of smoke. They can waft through doors and windows without causing any harm or break trees into thousands of splinters. They seem to favour the month of July and areas of natural Earth disturbances. Sometimes animals are terrorized by them and at other times are quite nonchalant. Sometimes they strike and kill humans, but mainly no effects are felt. They may be brilliantly coloured, opaque or translucent, like bubbles. Their movements in the dark resemble ghostly incense censers being swung.

Some of the properties of BoLs are as follows:

Time:	Of 100 reports taken at random, 26 were in July and 25 in August, with very few in the other 10 months.
Place:	BoLs may be seen outdoors, indoors or transiting the two.
Colours:	Pale yellow, yellow, red, orange, pink, white, grey, silver, ruby red, bright green, blue, pale blue-green.
Appearance:	Dazzling, brilliant, transparent, opaque, translucent, blinding.
Size:	3–12 inches (7–30 cm); 2–3 feet (0.6–0.9 metres); 8 inches (20 cm); 10 feet (3 metres); the size of a tennis ball, an egg, a billiard ball, a football, a large orange, a fist, a bus.
Shape/features:	Ball has 'white, well-defined bands'; 'stick crystals', 'a blue halo'; 'writhing strings of light'; 'aerial bubbles, transparent, like immense soap bubbles'.
Smell:	'Ozone', 'stench of sulphur', 'odour of electrical discharge'.
Sound:	'Silent', 'like a rifle shot', 'hissing', 'swishing', 'pop', 'terrible noise', 'like heavy rain pounding'.

(The fact that not all reports mention all of the above features may be a reflection of the report or a lack of noting by the observer.)

It is notoriously difficult to judge size and distance when out of doors, especially in flat, open fields with no clear frame of reference – is the BoL near you? A hundred yards away? A mile away? The bouncing behaviour, however, runs through very many reports, as does the apparent and, some think, human-like affinity for people. BoLs can curl round people's legs, circle their cars, go round and round a group of people, then pass through walls and windows without leaving a trace...

There are two factors which can give clues to this strange phenomenon. One is the fact that in almost all of the following reports a thunderstorm has just happened or is still happening. Secondly, and especially in the Australian reports of the phenomenon, the aurora is mentioned. This is a display of glowing light in the night sky, mainly in regions near the Earth's magnetic north and south poles. The aurora borealis (the northern lights) is most spectacular in Canada, Alaska and northern Scandinavia, while the aurora australis (southern lights) is at its best in Antarctica. The moving, shimmering glow may resemble clouds, arches or draperies of red, yellow or green.

Auroras are probably produced when streams of charged particles (mainly electrons and photons) from the sun collide with molecules of nitrogen and oxygen in the atmosphere, around 60 or more miles (100 kilometres) above the Earth. The charged particles are trapped by the Earth's magnetic field and guided towards its strongest area, the north and south magnetic poles.

The orange glow of a neon sign is produced in much the same way, by the collision of molecules of neon gas with electrons supplied by an electric current.

The categories of BoL are as follows:

- Ordinary: cases are typical in size, colour structure, duration.
- Repeating.
- Forced entry: where BoLs penetrate screens, windows, aircraft fuselages, etc.
- Giant: luminous spheres larger than 3 yards (1 metre).
- Rayed: luminous spheres with spikes, knobs, ray-like protuberances.
- Ball: with internal structure.
- Aerial bubbles: floating dimly-luminous spheres which appear transparent.
- Bizarre shapes: e.g. ribbons, columns.

The Min Min lights in Australia certainly come into the category of Earth lights. In her excellent book *The Mystery of the Min Min Lights* (M. Kozicka, 1994), Maureen Kozicka has assembled and carefully documented many hundreds of reports, both ancient and modern, and analysed and mapped them. Several points are worthy of special note: in Australia the Min Min lights have never been known to harm any person or animal, although on occasions animals have shown great fear, but this is by no means general. A curious fact is that, when first seen in the distance, on many occasions the light has been taken for a shining lantern swinging as if held by a walking man.

Sightings of dome-shaped lights in the air close to earthquake epicentres have been reported for centuries. These rise from both the ground itself and from the sea. Associated with these lights, peculiar electrical effects may also occur, such as radio and television anomalies, compass disturbances, etc. The latter probably relates to the magnetic fields associated with all electrical energy. Erickson, an American geophysicist, states that such lights are due to friction at the fault face heating up a thin strip of surrounding rock, which vaporizes the water, forming an insulating barrier around the slipped section of the fault itself. The rock shear and water vaporization then generate an electrical field which discharges vertically into the atmosphere as sheet lightning.[1]

Many explanations have been proposed, including plasma spheres, anti-matter meteorites, cosmic radiation, etc. It is relevant that Prof. Sir Basil Schonland, of the Institute for Geophysical Research at Witwatersrand University, South Africa, in his book *Flight of the Thunderbolts*, devotes six pages to verified reports of BoLs.[2] He quotes diameters from half an inch to 6 feet (25 mm to 1.8 metres) and duration of visibility from a few seconds to several minutes. Rate of travel varies from a walking pace to a running pace.

In *The Lightning Book* the physicist Prof. Veimeister states there must be a non-nuclear non-chemical process that feeds energy to a BoL if its long life is to be explained. He points out that as they float and are not in contact with a conductor, the energy must come from the absorption of intense radio waves or electromagnetic radiation. Hallways and chimneys would act as wave guides (perhaps also aircraft fuselages).

STRUCK DEAD AT THE DINNER TABLE

There have been many reports of BoLs over the centuries. In Sir Robert Atkyns' *History of Gloucestershire* there is a report of one at Little Sodbury Manor which 'rolled in at the parlour door at dinnertime as a fiery sulphurous globe. It struck one dead at the table and caused the death of the rest.'

In London in 1773 a case is reported by Rev. Wainhouse of Steeple Ashton in Wiltshire of 'a ball of fire between them at face level, the size of a sixpenny loaf, surrounded with dark smoke'. When it burst, it filled the room with a disagreeable smell, resembling sulphur, vitriol and other minerals. The Rev. Pitcairn, the other man in the room, said he saw 'a great quantity of fire of different colours vibrating swiftly, both backwards and forwards'.

According to Camille Flammarion, a French astronomer, in 1897 at Linguy a couple were sleeping in their beds when ball lightning entered their bedroom from the chimney and passed over their beds before squeezing through a partition and entering the adjoining dairy. It carried a whole row of milk

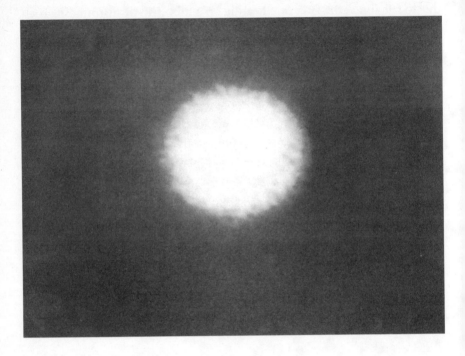

Figure 67: A 'spook light' in Long Valley, New Jersey, USA. According to local legend, this is a lantern swung by a dead railroad conductor, 'the Hookerman'. In 1976 Vestiga research group showed that the light was an organized form of plasma produced by seismic pressure.

cans from one side of the dairy to the other, breaking the lids, but without spilling a single drop. It also broke four plates out of a pile of 12, knocked off the tap of a wine barrel, tore bricks out of one wall and embedded them in the opposite wall, and shattered all the windows to fragments except for a mirror, which was flung from the wall and left on edge on the floor.[3]

A retired Glasgow policeman relates a previously unpublished story of ball lightning when he was living at Torchuillin, a cottage overlooking Loch Duich. In 1963, he and his family were sitting in the cottage watching the wildfire as a storm brewed up. Suddenly, in the darkness and gathering storm the policeman noticed a ball of light wandering aimlessly across the loch. He watched with interest for some time, thinking initially that it was 'those daft Mac...s fishing for salmon(!)' until it approached the house, still wandering in a haphazard fashion, and then, some distance away, steadied itself and came directly up the shore, straight to the house.

He got the impression that it had somehow sensed something in the house, which it entered via a small window. In typical Highland fashion, as soon as the storm started, the family had opened all of the windows of the house to give free access (and more importantly, departure!) to this phenomenon. The BoL entered the house, spluttering furiously and smelling 'like a car battery being charged' (ozone). It went across the room to the policeman's invalid mother, who was sitting in her wheelchair wearing a steel calliper on her leg, bounced against the lower part of the calliper, then 'evaporated' as it hit the stone-flagged floor.[4]

RAF LAUNCH DAMAGED

Not many people have witnessed ball lightning, but Robert Brydon of Edinburgh has done so no less than three times! The first was when he was serving in the RAF at the Skipsey air/sea bombing range at the time of the Korean War. He was on a high speed launch, monitoring the strikes from Meteors and Vampires against ground targets. It was during February, around 13.00 hrs, with low-cast cloud, a light wind from shore and a slight swell. Between the launch and about 1.5 miles (2 kilometres) from shore there appeared an orange ball. It zigzagged towards them, at first 50–60 feet (15–18 metres) up, then came down to 5–6 feet (1.5 metres), half a mile (0.8 kilometre) from them, and on a collision course with the RAF launch. The officials on the shore had also seen the strange sight and were extremely agitated, while the crew of the launch discussed what on Earth it could be. About 20 yards (18 metres) away, travelling very slowly, now about 10 feet (3 metres) above the swell and 10 feet in diameter, it looked like a bright orange sun, hissing and still ominously heading towards the launch. Aware that it was about to collide, Bob looked around for the crew, only to find that they had disappeared down the hatch, and threw himself under the engine casing.

Everything happened very quickly after that. There was a loud scream from the radio cabin and the radio operator came rushing out, headphones on, with the plug disengaged. Then the radio mast and gear collapsed on to the deck, Bob felt an electrical shock and felt strange. Whether the ball had passed through the launch or had hopped over the top, he is still, to this day, unable to tell, but the object was now on the other side of the launch, gyrating as it landed on the water. Then there was an enormous ear-splitting explosion without any blast – he believes it is more correct to say an implosion – and the launch jumped in the water.

When the launch travelled the few yards to the site, all that was left was a strange oily slick on the water and vapour still hanging in the air.

TWO BOLIDES OVER EDINBURGH

Early in 1958 Bob was on the scene of yet another incident. He was sitting in a vehicle at Dreghorn Barracks in Edinburgh, on a day of low cloud, when the sky darkened. There was a bright flash and from the clouds two bolides, orange spheres with tiny dark centres, slowly floated down. Then came a loud bang, slates were lifted from the nearby roofs and the vehicle jumped in the air, as the launch had years before, as if the Earth itself had suddenly heaved. Soldiers, believing the ammunition store had exploded, were running around in all directions.

A few years later, in 1970, Bob was living in Corstorphine, outside Edinburgh, overlooking the Pentland Hills. Now interested in the BoL phenomenon and carefully watching thunderclouds for any further incidents, he was rewarded with another sighting. An orange ball floated down, hit a tree, which ignited, and then bounced. Bob had observed the bouncing effect before and he got the impression that these BoLs had little or no mass.[5]

THEORIES

Current theories for BoLs are many and varied – and none seems to cover all the known facts. Careful perusal, however, indicates that one possible contributory factor may be highly relevant and this is not covered in any theory as yet. This is the contribution in a stochastic fashion of seismic waves, which are known to (a) bounce along the ground at varying distances (wavelengths), as noted in the previous reports from Bob Brydon of Edinburgh; (b) be polarized either horizontally, vertically, elliptically or in circular mode; (c) cover a wide waveband; (d) have nodes and anti-nodes (standing waves, which can show *all* electric or *all* magnetic areas).

Certainly, of all of the sites in the UK where BoLs have appeared, almost all are over known faults as detailed by the British Geological Survey. Further research would be needed to form an opinion on other sites world-wide.

Sagely, Maureen Kozicka, in her analysis of thousands of BoLs, has drawn attention to the nearby presence of dams, streams and boreholes as well as the rocks in the areas where lights are seen: granite, basalt, porphyry, etc. In the highly mineralized area of Queensland where the Min Min lights are common, and have been for centuries, there rises Mt Isa, with its very many old mines, and the whole area lies astride the Great Artesian Basin, a great water sump for the Australian economy.

The fact that so many BoLs 'switch off' at the side of a canal, river, or dam, may well link with natural S (secondary, shear) waves which cannot traverse fluids.

The main theories for BoLs are as follows:

1 Complex hydrodynamic forces in conjunction with electrical fields, with temperature gradients. BoLs act as if repelled by the Earth and well-earthed objects.

2 May be total electrical charge, excess charge being dissipated by aerosol droplets surrounding the ball.

3 Prof. Veimeister's theory (as a Russian physicist and Nobel prize winner, his views must be taken seriously): the ground and clouds act as partially reflecting surfaces for long wavelength radio waves produced by ordinary lightning discharge, thus standing waves can be created and the electromagnetic field trapped between clouds and the ground. At the positions of maximum amplitudes (anti-nodes) the field strength could be great enough to ionize the air and produce a glowing ball. Energy would be fed into the ball continually from the wave created and the electromagnetic field trapped between clouds and the ground.

4 Dr T. Ashby and Dr C. Whitehead, in *Nature*, described the possibility of micrometeors as antimatter, and gamma ray bursts from electron-positron annihilation events in the atmosphere.[6]

5 Prof. V. M. Batenin, in 'Superhighfrequency generators of plasma', describes mechanisms of discharges and plasma formations when superhighfrequencies and DC electric fields (as that of the Earth) are combined. This theory looks at molecular gases. The air pressures cited in his work range from 100Pa to normal atmospheric pressure.

6 Dr G. Egely and his team at the Hungarian Academy of Sciences have been investigating BoLs for several years. They have collected over 300 reports and have proposed a four-dimensional model to account for

the highly anomalous nature in energy, momentum and charge transport propagation. They feel that the BoLs have negative charge and very high internal energy density.

7 Dr D. J. Turner has put forward an approximate thermodynamic model, reconciling the best features of earlier models, whilst avoiding the conflicts with the basic laws of physics which have bedevilled other theories. Central to his model is a thermodynamic prediction that a hot air plasma (a gas of electrically charged particles) can be held down against buoyancy in wet air. Electrostatic repulsion can explain why BoLs fall from cloud bases and are therefore heavier than air.

BoLs can form at the end of a 'stepped leader' (the series of jumps and steps taken by lightning as it approaches the ground). Turner believes that electrostatic forces are repulsive as long as the ball is floating 3 feet (1 metre) or so above the Earth, but some effects may involve ion motion, with temperature and humidity gradients. It is possible that BoLs are stable only over a limited range of water vapour pressures or partial pressure gradients. In fact, a 'window' effect is postulated as in other electromagnetic researches.

Professor Ohtsuki of Waseda University, Tokyo, and his colleague, Professor Ofureton of the Tokyo College of Aeronautical Engineering, were reported to have produced many types of plasma discharge using a magnetron (a microwave oscillator) and an air-filled waveguide.[7] The microwaves were reflected up and down the cavity, setting up standing waves with six anti-nodes, points at which the field intensity was strongest. Amongst the phenomena produced were fireballs and moving flames. The plasma fire colour varied from red to orange, was observed to pass through a solid ceramic board and exhibited the ability to travel along the wave guide against a strong wind blown into the cavity.

Essential to a plasma is what is known as the boundary condition, that is to say, a wall, or magnetic 'bottle' or containment within which the plasma can form and circulate. We are familiar with plasmas in fluorescent lights and neon tubes, where the ionized gas produces brilliant light. Plasmas can also form naturally, given the right circumstances, and it is possible that BoLs are generated when natural currents, air pressure, humidity and the geomagnetic field all come together at one point in space. In the case of higher, apparently compressed, saucer-like plasmas, radar ducting (waves flowing along a defined channel) may be of direct relevance to the observed phenomena.

PHENOMENA OVER AIRFIELDS

This is not the place to go into this possibility, but of the hundreds of reports of visual phenomena in the UK surely it has been noted that great numbers are above or near airports, both civil and military. The ducts of pulsed radio frequency energy in the atmosphere, invisible to humans, but not to a radar beam, which can extend for many miles and may be line-of-sight, as an aircraft approach beacon, or oscillating fan-wise as with other systems, will energize the molecules in the air they traverse to some extent. If, in their near horizontal travel, they meet and interact with a natural ionized column from a fault, thrust or underground stream, what complex anomalies may be produced? Also, what of the vertical ascent from the ground of a lightning streamer?

Lightning is essentially a discharge of electrical energy. A violent stroke of lightning produces a powerful electro-hydrodynamic flow of charged particles. As ordinary lightning approaches the ground in a stepped leader, positively charged streamers arise from the ground, trees or tall buildings to meet it. When such a streamer contacts the ionized leader, the electrons along the leader channel flow downwards, thus the path of the electron flow goes ever upwards and the discharge between the two is called the return stroke. This powerful surge generates photons, hence the bright flash we see in lightning storms. A typical discharge can be between 10 and 100 million volts, and up to 300,000 Amps of current (consider that in most ordinary household appliances the power is only 220–250 volts).

It is now thought that BoLs may all be electrically charged, with the excess charge being spread about the aerosol particles which surround the ball – many reports describe this 'halo' of luminance and also an associated spinning motion. This spin would then create a magnetic field which would draw the charges together at the equator of the spin.

A Selection from Thousands of Reported Cases of Balls of Light to Show the Variation

Month	Year	Outdoors/Indoors	Colour	Size	Thunder
–	1556	O/I	'Fiery sulphur ball'	–	Yes
July	1665	O	Grey	–	Yes
July	1763	–	–	–	Yes
–	1843	I	Bright and shining	9" (23 cm)	Yes
July	1868	O	–	3" (8 cm)	–
August	1868	O	Bright red	2–3" (5–8 cm)	–
–	1870	O	–	6" (15 cm)	–
March	1877	O	Red and yellow	–	Yes
September	1880	O	–	–	–
September	1883	O	Yellow	–	–
July	1892	O	–	–	–
July	1893	I	–	–	–
April	1894	O	Ribbon of dazzling light	Yes	–
July	1897	O/I	White, brilliant	Egg-size	–
Summer	1911	I/O	Bright green	–	–
July	1921	I	Various colours	like aerial bubbles	–
August	1925	O	Brilliant red	12" (30 cm)	–
June	1929	O/I	Orange	–	–
–	1938	I	–	–	–
Autumn	1940	O	Smoky grey	6" (15 cm)	Yes
World War II		O	–	Grew in size to 10 feet (3 metres)	–
March	1963	–	–	8" (20 cm)	Yes

ople and Objects, their Sizes and Colours

Comments	Location
The BoL rolled in through a door: eight people killed.	Chipping Sodbury, UK
Killed one person, burned others.	Norfolk, UK
Hit a church and exploded.	–
Came down a chimney, played around the feet of a man, rolled around and went back up the chimney.	France
Excavated a 10-foot (3-metre) long trench in the ground.	Guildford, UK
Bounced down a mountain, buried itself in the bank of a stream; 20-foot (6-metre) peat ring turned up on the bank.	Glendown Mountains, Ireland
Floated with an undulating motion, getting smaller each bounce.	
Travelled several miles! (Royal Meteorological Society report)	Pyrenees
Like immense soap bubbles.	Vence, France
Fell into a pond, killing over 100 fish.	Hendon, UK
The size of a cricket ball.	Banbury, UK
Fell into a lake; 60-ft (18-metre) column of water visible.	Liverpool, UK
A dark space fringed with crimson appeared in a kitchen, then burst.	Epping, UK
Great damage to a barn.	Dunstable, UK
Danced in the air 'like rooks at play', entered a barn, floated upstairs, exploded in a bedroom; sulphurous smell; paint flew off a wall.	Suffolk, UK
Floated indoors then out again. Exploded.	Newport, IoW, UK
A large number of very bright BoLs entered from the air inlet of a large stove with a small wood fire burning.	Grindelwald, Switzerland
Travelled 100 yards along a road. Hissed and exploded.	Yarmouth, IoW, UK
The doors of a slaughterhouse 'flew open', the BoL entered the and left by another door.	Morecambe, Lancs., UK
BOAC plane flying in rain at 8,000 ft (2,440 metres). One BoL entered the cabin and burst with a 'resounding bang'. A few minutes later a second one passed through the cockpit, burned the pilot's eyebrows and some hair, and exploded in the rear cabin.	In BOAC plane
Bounced 'like a rubber ball' and climbed a hill with a 3-foot (1-metre) high bounce every 10–20 ft (3–6 metres).	Berwyn Mountains, Wales, UK
Zig-zagged across the water to a motorboat, growing larger as it approached. Hit the boat and exploded; the launch jumped in the water. All the crew's hair stood on end.	At sea
In flight, NY–Washington. The BoL left the pilot's cabin and passed down the aisle of the plane.	In US plane in flight

Month	Year	Outdoors/Indoors	Colour	Size	Thunder
–	1973–81	–	–	–	–
August	1977	O	Brilliant yellow-green and transparent	'A bus'	–
Summer	1977	I	Red	–	–
June	1977/8	–	–	–	–
July	1978/9	–	–	–	–
September	1981	–	Dazzling white	A large orange	Yes
May	1985	I	Orange	A table tennis ball	Yes
August	1992	O	White with blue halo	A football	No
–	1993	O	–	–	Yes
July	1994	I	Opaque reddish-gold	A car tyre	Yes
October	1994	O	–	Like beach balls	–
February	1995	O	Transparent but white, well defined bands	12" (30 cm)	Yes
January	1995	I	Bluish-white	–	Yes
June	1996	O/I	Blue-white	–	Yes

Comments	Location
Prof. Harley Rutledge observed many BoLs and felt that they exhibited synchronicity between themselves and the observer, that 'they seemed aware'. From a physicist such comments are factual.	USA
Seen by a coastguard. Floated down a hillside; severe static on BoL bounced off objects and the ground. Cattle and seabirds very disturbed.	Fishguard, Dyfed, UK
Whilst speaking on the phone, a woman heard a crack 'like a rifle' hissing and 'the phone came alive in my hand'.	Haymaked, Virginia, USA
The same woman was hit by a BoL in the same house on the same date one year apart. The BoL hit her chest and fell to the floor.	
The same house in the South of France was hit by BoLs on the same date one year apart. The BoLs rolled along into the living-room.	Midi, France
Gave the appearance of dozens of stick crystals 0.2" (5 mm) in length.	Berkhamsted, Herts., UK
All the plugs were blown out of a wall; a hole 3 x 4 x 1.5" (8 x 10 x 4 cm) deep appeared in the wall by the plugs. The BoL hit a girl; a red five-pointed star burn appeared on her shoulder.	Garton on the Wolds, UK
Struck an oak tree, split the bark, showered wood over 50 yards (46 metres), rolled down the tree and dispersed in flashes.	Conwy, Wales, UK
The BoL danced across an aluminium roof and excised a piece of round glass, which was found unbroken on the carpeted corridor.	A school in NSW, Australia
A shaft of light entered through an open window and formed itself into a white ball which bounced up and exploded with a 'terrible noise'.	South Leigh, Witney, Oxon., UK
Many BoLs flew up out of the river into the sky and out of sight. An annual spectacle for years, always at the same time, full moon, duration 30 minutes!	Mekong River, Thailand
BoL rolled off the road 20 ft (6 metres) to below a car. Rear of car jumped 2 ft (0.6 metres). No damage at all.	M23 nr Crawley, UK
A brilliant light in the bedroom awoke the wife, she woke her husband, both saw the source of the light within the bedroom lamp near the ceiling. Faded slowly, lasted 10 seconds.	Barkham, south-east of Reading, Berks., UK
Forks of lightning hit a USAF jet at the tail end. Immediately after this, a BoL bounded along the roof of a factory into the building, through an up-and-over door, and flew along the girders, lighting them with 'unbelievable sparks'. Seen by 40 people.	Tewkesbury, Glos., UK

'ISLANDS' FLOATING IN NEAR-EARTH SPACE –
A NEWLY DISCOVERED NATURAL PHENOMENON

In the 1980s and 1990s, observations from Russian satellites have found large-scale non-linear phenomena in the topside ionosphere, which lies 185 to 60 miles (300 to 100 kilometres) above the Earth and, circulating as it does around and over the Earth, may be considered as relevant to Earth energy.

The lifetime of these 'new' geophysical objects is about one hour and they are able to influence radio signals in different frequency bands. As Prof. Kalinin states, 'It should be remembered that the motion of these ionization islands can increase the instability of transionospheric UHF signals by several orders of magnitude.'[8]

These vast bodies have similarity of shape function at differing heights. Vertical size is one of the criteria for identifying them, as they are some 185 miles (300 kilometres) in height. As is known, there is always a threshold sensitivity for any method of detection of localized objects. Using complex mathematical analysis, these rotating objects are said to be 'statistically infrequent, but not exceptional events'.

The theory that Russian scientists put forward is that the surrounding medium (the topside ionosphere) produces a substance from which the isolated large-scale non-uniformities are created. Interestingly, they have found no link between emergence of these islands and the geophysical indices for solar and magnetic activity.

If we consider gas clouds in the ionosphere, a number of chemical reactions at high altitudes are known to take place. If we further consider the ionization of gas as chromatic (having colour) changes will occur.

Interestingly, the Russian work indicates that these 'plasma islands in space' above the Earth travel at approximately the speed of sound. Also that the axis of the line of travel is directed along the lines of force of the Earth's magnetic field. The shape described is remarkably like that of the typical UFO. Is it possible that a similar but stochastic effect will occur far closer to the surface of the Earth when random events combine to produce an ionized gas plasma? Coloured lights, a domed top, radio interference and extremely rapid travel are reported in these events. Again, the fact that so many are reported near military bases and power stations world-wide may not be just coincidence.

EARTH LIGHTS – NATURAL SOURCES

Earth lights have been seen since time immemorial in all countries of the world. They can take many forms and colours, from floating figures which appear to have no heads to great glowing spinning tops like that photographed at Banbury *(see plate section)*. They may be green or white or scintillating with many colours and they may take the shape of vertical aerial columns which descend to the ground.

We have become used to considering light as the visible spectrum, that which can be seen and measured with photometers, but in the last 100 years the ionizing radiations beyond the visible spectrum have been studied by scientists with the discovery of X-rays, gamma rays, beta rays, etc. In ionizing radiations the wavelengths are billions to the metre, whereas at the lower end of the non-ionizing radiations, radio frequencies beat at thousands or tens of thousands a second (Kilohertz or Megahertz), and extremely low frequency waves run from 1 Hz per second and below to 300 Hz. (1 Hz means one beat per second; 100 Hz, 100 per second.) It is relevant that our brain waves also cover the ELF end of the spectrum.

It is important to note that lights apparently in the sky may in fact be endogenous effects from stimulation of the brain, e.g. the visual cortex, temporal lobes, retina, etc. If the perceiver projects these into the surrounding space they will be reported as external phenomena which may explain why sometimes in a group of people only one or two people will 'see' something. Magnetophosphenes (tiny brilliant flashing lights) are another example of this.

Nature has many tricks up her sleeve in relation to Earth lights and luminous phenomena. The following list describes the major sources, which range from crystallography and geology to electricity, biology, chemistry and acoustics.

When studying Earth lights it is wise, again, to first start by looking at the ground and type of rock found in the area, and then address the geological fault system in the area. The British Geological Survey at Keyworth in Nottinghamshire and Edinburgh have very detailed analyses of every area in the UK, covering geophysics, geology, seismology, mineral deposits, water, etc.

Major sources:

- Triboelectricity
- Piezoelectricity
- Sono-acoustic electricity
- Chemical: e.g. sulphur, phosphorous
- Outgassing – ignition
- Outgassing – ionization
- Electrical – St Elmo's fire
- Lightning
- Balls of light
- Biological – Lycopodium, fireflies, glow worms
- Bacteria, fungal skin infections
- Fractoluminescence

Some of the most important are:

Fractoluminescence

Recent work by Professor Kawaguchi of Hiroshima, Japan, has added a new explanation for some Earth lights. They can be due to the fact that when silica (quartz is a form of silica) fractures in stressed rocks, light is emitted a millionth of a second after the silica starts to fracture, starting as a red glow (650 nm) and 10 milliseconds later turning blue. This is a brilliant but very short event and is quite different from rock fracture due to thermal causes, where charged particles also emit light. Indeed, Kawaguchi is to experiment with granite, which has a high quartz content, to ascertain whether this might be relevant to warnings of imminent earthquakes. Work at the Chugoki National Research Institute at Hiroshima continues.

Triboelectricity

The concept of triboelectricity is vital to the understanding of Earth lights. This is the electric charge generated by friction between higher and lower valence materials.

Triboluminescence

This is the glow given off by some crystalline materials when they are crushed. It occurs in a wide range of materials. A very simple example is the tiny flashes of light which you can see if someone near you in a darkened room crunches mint sweets between their teeth.

Flashes will only occur in crystals if they contain certain impurities and when the crystals do not have rotational symmetry, that is to say, the flash occurs when the positive and negative charges in the crystal recombine. Crystals without rotational symmetry are piezoelectric and when they are stressed, for instance by grinding or under extreme pressure, a voltage is generated across them. If the crystal fractures, the parting surfaces carry opposite charges, positive and negative, and these charges can then recombine. The resulting electrical discharge then excites molecules of gas such as nitrogen, which then emits energy as fluorescence.

Rarely, some crystals, despite having no rotational symmetry, do not exhibit triboluminescence. This may be due to very high conductivity, which allows the separated charges to leak away rather than to recombine and emit light.

There is an interesting experiment which can be carried out at home, or in lecture halls, providing the room is completely dark. Take two large crystals, one amethyst and one quartz, for example, and, holding one in each hand, rub them briskly together. After a few seconds a cold glow will illuminate the crystals and your hands. This is not the hot glow of friction, but triboelectricity in action.

This experiment is a miniscule example of what occurs when rocks are under strain. The area of strain may run for hundreds of miles and may be from either deep Earth movements or man-made, as in new hydro-electric reservoirs, where millions of gallons of water are dammed and exert enormous pressure.

Triboluminescence may be responsible for such anomalous lights as those seen at Stokesay Castle in Shropshire on several occasions during 1997 and 1998.

Forewarning of Earthquakes

Earthquake precursors also involve electrical effects in the Earth. There are three main precursors to deep Earth movements:

1 Radon gas increases.
2 Soil conductivity increases.
3 The water table rises.

As ground currents of electricity are mainly carried by ions moving in porous waters, the rising water table must then affect natural electrical currents.[9]

Piezoelectricity

In rocks with a piezoelectric coefficient like quartz, 500–5,000 v/cm has been measured. At half the seismic wavelength the generated voltage is 5 x 10v, which is equivalent to the voltage responsible for lightning in storms, which can reach from 10,000 v/m to 100,000 v/m. There will be electrical precursors to earthquakes due to changes in rock stresses near the foci. There are many reports of sudden lightning and storms when archaeologists move standing stones and excavate Stone Age barrows, etc., and it is possible that such local stress shifts trigger this mechanism.

There are also reports of enhanced luminosity of rocks, especially chalk, during earthquakes and electrical storms, and this effect is reported to be strongest over buried ore bodies, e.g. ironstone bands and magnetite. It was first recorded in Germany in 1747 and more recently in North America. At Shide on the Isle of Wight, UK, after dull damp days, a very large chalk pit was known to exhibit a flaring luminosity. In 1911 Dr John Milne, a famous geophysicist, provided photographic proof of this effect. He used a slowly rotating cylinder lined with photographic paper in a dark chamber at the end of a tunnel deep in the chalk pit. On developing the paper there were three faint dark bands and it was suggested at the time that the effect was electrical.[10] The explanation is probably electrochemical.

The interaction of mechanical and electrical stress-strain varies in a medium. Compression of a quartz crystal or Rochelle salt generates an electrostatic voltage across it and conversely application of an electric field to the crystal may cause it to expand or contract in certain directions.

Piezoelectricity is only possible in crystals which do *not* possess a centre of symmetry. Quartz has a natural resonant frequency (as does everything else under the sun) and if the ambient field is made to alternate with the same frequency, the crystal will respond with a vigorous resonant vibration. This may explain why some people, especially if they have sensitized their bodies by learning to dowse, or have had a severe electric shock or lightning strike at some point in their lives, experience such a marked reaction when touching certain outcrops of rock, standing stones and many other structures of the megalithic age.

Luminescence

A property of certain minerals, luminescence is caused by the change into light rays of various kinds of energy (e.g. thermal, luminous, electrical, chemical and mechanical). In mineralogy the most important is photoluminescence, originating after some minerals have been exposed to ultraviolet light of a wavelength of 253.7 or 336 nanometres. It occurs only when the mineral contains a trace amount of an activator, usually manganese, copper, lead, silver, uranium, elements of rare earths, water molecules, etc. Since only some specimens of the same mineral may produce coloured luminescence, it cannot be used as a reliable clue in mineral identification.

QUARTZ SANDWICH, ANYONE?

Quartz under pressure or strain, then, exhibits many effects, some at least of which must have been known by our predecessors, but were lost until they were rediscovered in scientific laboratories during the sixteenth to twentieth centuries. The alchemy of the earlier centuries was itself transmuted into science at this time and as the cracks of knowledge widened, so researchers such as Paul Lavoisier, Michael Faraday, Hans Oersted and many others opened up and utilized the vast powers locked in nature.

In 1917, Paul Langevin, who for many years assisted the Curies in their laboratory work on radium, explored a particular feature of piezoelectric crystals – the fact that under pressure they emit an electrical charge. He produced what came to be known as the Langevin Sandwich, a layer of quartz trapped between two layers of steel. Zapping the quartz with an electric charge made it change shape regularly, thus causing it to resonate. When placed in the hull of a ship, for instance, the outer steel layer transmitted a powerful undulating signal into the water (in early water tank experiments, many fish were killed). When the signal hit any solid object, a submarine, shoal of fish or reef, for instance, the echo bounced back, creating vibrations in the steel plate. This caused the quartz signal in the sandwich to resonate, setting up an electrical charge which produced a 'ping'. Thus was born sonar, which is used to locate underwater objects.

Again we see this sandwich effect in domes and tumuli was understood, at least in practical terms, by our ancestors. The ancient Chinese used quartz in a more artistic sense – it was crushed and added to pigment for painting, and the crystals, like little diamonds, gave a wonderful illumination to pictures.

PHENOMENA ABOVE A FAULT LINE

The first author recalls more phenomena. Closer to home, again near the haunted house above the underground tunnel outside my home town of Crieff, I parked my car to go sea-trout fishing at midnight one summer's night. As I began to put my waders on and assembled my fly-fishing tackle, I noticed a very bright orange light, partially masked by mist, about 50 feet (15 metres) above the small hill on the other side of the river. Thinking it was simply a flare, I paid little attention to it, until several minutes later I realized that it had not moved, and was possibly an anomalous Earth light, as this part of the river runs down an old fault line at the foot of the haunted house. Frantically, I ran up the riverbank to a shallow crossing and hurried through thick undergrowth to get closer, but the light died out, and although I fished around that same spot until daybreak, nothing untoward happened.

It is possible that a fault movement was causing the glow in the sky, since this area is also part of the Highland Boundary fault. Oddly, at the time of the event I heard two children speaking, the sounds gradually fading away. The words were very indistinct, there was no torchlight in the heavily overgrown and wooded area, and the riverbank where the voices were heard was rather dangerous. Although it is not impossible that there were two children there, it is unlikely, as the place is very isolated – perhaps it was a result of the Earth energies causing an hallucination.

At that same spot, the local gamekeeper once saw a ghostly figure, which slowly faded away, beckoning to him, and a few miles upstream another fisherman saw a circular shape spinning amongst the trees. This was later verified by the local police, who found trees there with their branches singed.

PILLARS OF LIGHT

An electronics engineer and his wife gave a very clear written description of a light phenomenon which was associated with a visible and long duration oscillation on an overhead telephone cable. In Kinross county, on a summer's evening, about 10 p.m., they saw 'five strange vertical pillars' alternating in and out of their vision. They were smoky grey, about 18 feet (5.5 metres) in height and 12 inches (30 cm) in diameter. They appeared to be 'emerging and receding' in a full cycle of 30 seconds from being very faint to developing full capacity. Whilst this was going on, the multicore telephone cable which was strung on nearby telephone poles was seen to be vibrating markedly, although there was no wind. Specially curious was the fact that the only section of the long line of cable to act in this manner was close to the vertical lights, the others being quite still.

There are many reports of a different form of 'pillars of light', vertical shafts of light known as 'sun pillars', in atmospheric science. Just as sunlight or moonlight can refract or bend through ice crystals as through a prism, so light will also reflect off crystals. As the tiny plate-like ice crystals fall to the ground when the sun is setting or when the moon is low in the sky, light will be reflected from each crystal. These columns of light will mirror the colour of the sunrise or sunset, appearing to be red, orange or yellow. They can sometimes be seen even when the sun is below the horizon. On cold winter nights when the air is full of ice crystals, even lights from distant street lamps can give rise to light pillars.[11]

All around us people are seeing strange things – lights, flashes and columns which have been traditionally looked upon as being supernatural. When viewed in relation to geophysics, deep Earth movements and the marvellous works of nature, rather than in relation to specific belief systems, whilst our terror at the unexpected may decrease, our profound awe at the marvels of nature can only increase.

REFERENCES

1   J. Erickson, *Volcanoes and Earthquakes*, McGraw Hill, USA, 1988

2   Prof. Sir Basil Schonland, *Taming of the Thunderbolts*, Oxford University Press, 1964

3   Camille Flammarion, *Thunder and Lightning*, Chatto and Windus

4   Personal correspondence from James Wotherspoon, Glenrothes.

5   Personal correspondence from Robert Brydon, Edinburgh.

6   T. Ashby and C. Whitehead, *Nature*, 230:180, 1971

7   *Nature*, 350:139

8   Yuri Kalinin and A. A. Romanchuk, 'Large scale isolated islands of ionization in near Earth space', *Cosmic Research* 33:4 (1995), Institute of Applied Geophysics, Moscow

9   J. Milsom, *Field Geophysics*, Oxford University Press, 1989

10 J. Milne, 'Earthquakes and Luminous Phenomenon', *Nature*, 87:16, 1911

11 R. D. Sampson, *Earth*, October 1996

BIBLIOGRAPHY

Specialist authors and research bodies have studied and analysed BoLs and the interested reader is recommended the following:

Dr J. D. Barry, *Ball Lightning and Bead Lightning*, Plenum Press, New York, 1980

W. Corliss, *Lightning, Auroras, Nocturnal Lights*, Sourcebook Project, USA, 1982

P. Davies, *Fireball*, Heinemann, 1987

D. Elson, *TORRO*, Geography Unit, Oxford Brookes University, Ox. 30 Bp

Dr T. Meaden, *Journal of Meteorology*, UK

Sir Basil Schonland, *Flight of the Thunderbolts*, Clarendon Press, Oxford, 1964

Prof. Singer, *The Nature of Ball Lightning*, Plenum Press, New York, 1971

P. Veimeister, *The Lightning Book*, MIT Press, 1961

19

EARTH GASES AND
VOLCANIC TUBES

Spontaneous Combustion and Strange Mud Springs

Once the question can be properly framed,
the answer is never very far away.
PROFESSOR JEAN AUBOUIN, *GEOLOGY:*
PRINCIPLES AND METHODS (METHUEN, 1990)

North Sea gas comes to us, domestically, at the touch of a switch in the home. It is, so to speak, always there. We shall, however, give a little thought to its origin, as it is, indeed, a most ancient form of Earth energy.

The Earth's natural gases are to be found in pockets deep within the planet. These can be released by earthquakes, volcanoes and can even themselves be the source of disturbances. Dr Thomas Gold of the Astronomy Department at Cornell University calls these zones 'Pore Space Domains'. They become unstable at a certain depth, whereupon the upper pockets will collapse and release gas (outgas) along the crustal faults and fissures.

Gas can be associated with petroleum, although some oil fields have very little gas and some gas fields yield no commercial quantities of oil. Chemically, natural gas is a mixture of the lighter chemicals found in petroleum: methane, butane, propane with carbon dioxide, hydrogen sulphide and helium. Most gases are odourless, but some smell of sulphur, garlic or rotten eggs.

Gas can escape from rotting vegetation – some council tips in the landscape have an eerie plume of flame at night burning off the methane and other gases produced from the decay of rubbish. Gases in artesian basins are mixtures of several other gases and are probably a contributory factor to the strange Min Min lights in Queensland, Australia. A particular combination of humidity (or lack of it), air pressure and gas and rock types combine on occasions to throw one form of balls of light into the near-Earth atmosphere.

Janet Bord relates the story of a smoking tree near Cowes on the Isle of Wight. Firemen were called over a period of three days, but could find no cause. Bord hypothesizes that it could have been gas, not smoke, coming from the tree and also cites trees in the Ozark mountains in the USA which were found to be emitting gas from areas near the roots which burned with a yellow flame if ignited.[1]

At the time of writing, sulphur dioxide is outgassing from Paracutin volcano, Mexico City, at the prodigious rate of some 25,000 tonnes per day.[2] The link between the vast pancake of pollution which hangs over Mexico City and visual phenomena increasingly being reported as 'lights in the sky' may well relate to a stochastic combination of deep Earth movements from the nearby volcano and ionized gases from the same source, added to the exhaust fumes from thousands of vehicles.

SPONTANEOUS COMBUSTION

A rare example of outgassing is by spontaneous combustion. In 1560, for example, a coalbed ignited spontaneously in the north-west area of Xinjiang, China. This was reported by Reuters to have been finally extinguished on November 1997, 437 years later.

Another example was that of a large iron ore open-cast mine at Mt Newman, Australia, in 1986, where workers were amazed to witness the quarry face they had just exposed glowing red, starting to smoke, then spontaneously catching fire. Since the rock, which had a high sulphur content, was of no commercial value, it had to be loaded into trucks and dumped elsewhere.[3]

More locally, at Ringstead Bay in Dorset, in 1826, the shale spontaneously ignited and burned for four years. The area came to be known as 'the Burning Cliffs'.[4]

Figure 68: This giant excavator uses its 30-ton capacity grab to load burning sulphurous rock into trucks for disposal.

GASES FROM WELLS AND FAULTS

Outgassing from wells can explain some phenomena. For example, at Bath, gas is periodically vented naturally from the wells deep below the city. Of these gases, some 10 ccs per litre are noble gases and of these 1.6 cc per litre is helium. This gas, just like spring waters, will take the easiest route to the surface, running along discontinuities between strata.

In the Szechuan province of China, in an area called the Black Bamboo Ravine (Heizugou), for centuries both animals and people have vanished. In 1995 two interesting features were reported in this valley. First, the rotting plants in the ravine were emitting toxic gases 'suffocating people, where-upon they fell into the abyss'. In addition the magnetic field there is very strong, although measurements were not given, and is considered 'likely to disable compasses and cause plane crashes'. There is a similar valley in Java known as 'the Poisoned Valley'.[5]

There are very many reports of places where nothing ever grows. This may apply where lightning has struck the Earth, but it would be interesting to check ambient gases at such sites. A good sniff first might be a good pointer. Both yeasts and fungi feed on escaping hydrocarbons – this, too, might be a clue.

Another example of outgassing is at Lastingham church crypt in North Yorkshire. The crypt is very simple, being built right into the hillside. Author Philip Heselton described how his friend, when visiting the church, felt 'such powerful energies in the Crypt that she was unable to speak'.[6] Heselton also experienced this sensation, but in a less pronounced form:

> It was as if the energies within my brain and body were reacting to the energies within the crypt and a flowing, pulsing feeling of warmth came over me. I was unwilling to move for many minutes as I experienced the power present in that place. After perhaps 10–15 minutes the feeling faded, although I did not wish to speak and made my way outside.[7]

We have here a very clear description of the phrase 'struck dumb'. Next Heselton took Paul Screeton to the crypt. 'He got a buzzing feeling and thought the place quite extraordinary.'[8]

Lastingham is located on a deep ironstone band which runs from Rosewell Abbey, miles to the north. Lastingham is also known to affect compasses strongly, indicative of a high magnetic field.

The Delphic Oracle is the genius loci par excellence. Joseph Fontenrose, who spent many years working at Delphi, quotes the phrases used by classical authors to describe the effects produced on people at the Temple of Delphi: pneuma enthousiastika (to be inspired), spirutus (a breathing) and atmos entheos (possessed by a God). Several authors dismissed the possibility of outgassing here, as no fault has been visible over the years, however, very recent work by Dr Jelle de Boer, a geologist from Wesleyan University in Connecticut, has uncovered evidence that corroborates the reports of such writers as Plutarch, who wrote that the exhalations of the Earth came from a chasm below the temple where the Pythia sat to prophesy. De Boer found an active fault to the east and west of the temple, only recently exposed by roadworks. He also found another fault running north to south which intersects this one, below the temple. He reported to a recent meeting of the Geological Society in London that the two faults produce fissures in the rock which can open and close with earthquake movements.

Of special interest is the fact that far below the surface lies limestone rock which is rich in hydrocarbons. Such rock strata can release trapped gases, including ethylene, methane and hydrogen sulphide, which travel to the surface through the fissures. If we then add in the extremely low frequency waves in active fault zones, which are in the same frequency bands as natural brainwaves, we have a potent mixture with the ability to bring on hallucinations and affect emotions, and just as effective today as it was then.

PHENOMENA AND FAULTS

The following chart shows the scientifically recorded wavelengths due to distant Earth movements. It is not necessary for the movements to be under the area where phenomena manifest, as several factors will affect perceptions, including whether or not the area is on sand or rock and at the end of or in the middle of a fault, as well as the depth and strike (angle) of the disturbances and, last but not least, the mindset of the individual.

Natural Earth Waves, Known as Body Waves: Types and Wavelengths

Type of Wave	Description	Hertz
P (Primary or push)	Longitudinal compressional sound waves – acoustic.	1–20
S (Secondary/shake/shear)*	Polarized at 90° to the direction of propagation.	1–100
SH (Horizontal)	The horizontal component of S waves; particles will oscillate on the horizontal plane.	1–100
SV (Vertical)	The vertical component of S waves; particles will oscillate on the vertical plane.	1–100
L or Q (Love or Querwellen) (Cross waves)	Particles will vibrate transverse to the direction of travel, but there is no vertical component. Propagated in a medium with a reflecting surface and equivalent to SH waves reflected up and down within layers of the Earth's crust, e.g., rock/air. The British geophysicist Augustus Love calculated in the nineteenth century that as earthquakes send up-and-down ripples shuddering through the mantle, a secondary set of	0.3–1

* S waves will not traverse fluids.

	side-to-side vibrations should propagate through the relatively thin crust.	
R (Rayleigh)	These are elliptical waves and are described in the vertical plane to the direction of propagation. Their movement may be described as 'push-pull-up-and-down' in a retrograde ellipse.	0.7–2.5
H (Hydrodynamic)	A type of wave first seen after the A-bomb test in New Mexico on 16 July, 1945.	
C (Coupled)	An interference effect linked to controlled explosions.	
Stoneley	Guided waves of special condition.	100–500
Guided	Found when constraining channels (mines, wells, etc.) act as waveguides. Also coal seams, boreholes, interfaces of dissimilar strata. Typically propagate over 328 ft (100 metres).	
Standing	Interference pattern where plane waves of the same frequency, amplitude, wavelength and speed, but travelling in opposite directions, meet at one point in space. A standing wave will form with nodes and anti-nodes.	
Seismic	Waves from an earthquake or explosion. High-magnitude events generate waves which travel through and around the Earth.	
SR (Schumann Resonance)	Low-frequency standing waves in a global circuit, bounded by the Earth and the ionosphere.	7–50
SES (Seismic Electrical Signals)	These occur as precursors to earthquakes, where telluric currents are disturbed and ground resistivity is altered.	
Body waves from the Earth	These are elastic waves (the term 'elastic' here means that both wavelength and amplitude will be time-varying), thus can vary over quite short periods.	
Lightning flashes (100 per second, globally)	Constantly excite SR – like a hammer hitting a bell – so amplitude of SR is dependent on incidence of lightning.	

Read now the comments made in 1716 by the Rev. Samuel Wesley and his family after disturbances at Epworth in Lincolnshire and then check his remarks with those in the chart.

The Rev. Wesley wrote: 'The door in the yard, the latch whereof was often lifted and the door pushed violently [with] sounds as if several people were walking over our heads.' The sounds were 'as if somebody had emptied a bag of money at my feet' and 'as if all the bottles under the stairs had been dashed into a thousand pieces'. Perhaps most telling of all is 'a noise like the winding up of a jack'.[9]

In Colline, Kirkcudbright, in 1695, at a house owned by a certain Andrew Mackie which had long been considered by the local people to be haunted, a variety of effects were seen and reported not only by one cleric, the Rev. Alexander Telfair, minister of the parish, but also by the ministers of Kells, Borg, Carmichael, Parton and Ketta parishes, the Laird of Colline and the Laird of Millhouse. Amongst the phenomena, which began in February and ended in May, metal objects were hurled about, sparks were seen (static discharges?), cattle panicked and escaped their sheds, men were 'pulled off their feet' and metal pothooks and hangers swung of their own volition. It is noted that one outbuilding in particular was affected. It would be interesting to know whether any metal ore body or magnetite was below the ground on this site, now marked as a ruin on the OS map.

Remembering that some of the farm workers at Colline were 'pulled off their feet' in 1695, it is interesting to read of the very similar disturbances in 1971 in a military village in northern Brazil. Here brooms leaning against walls spun, flew and fell, bottles with soft drink in them shook and vibrated against the walls of houses, an armchair turned itself over and a bucket of water 'rolled downstairs'. Many people in the village said they felt 'a strong punch' in their backs.[10] As noted earlier, the sensation of a punch on the back or shoulder will result if the ulnar nerve is stimulated by an external magnetic source, which can occur as a surge when Earth energy is high.

'Figures Dancing, Holding Torches'

The following report shows both the visual and behavioural effects very clearly. It comes from a GP and his wife on the Isle of Wight in 1969. We should first remember that Mersley is situated over an active fault and Newport is on the transverse fault which runs across the island.

Dr G. (a pseudonym) and his wife were driving from St Helens to Niton via Ashey Down late one summer's evening. On reaching the hilltop at Mersley Down they saw ahead of them hundreds of orange lights in the fields below, stretching towards Havenfield. They knew the route well and that this was a place of pasture and open fields. Trying to explain the lights, the doctor became, as he says, very irritated, as he could find no rational explanation, the more so, when, as if by a switch, all the lights went out at the same time, leaving the fields in darkness.

Puzzled, the couple drove on towards Mersley. At the right-hand turn to Mersley, off the main road where they knew fields stretched across to Newport, they again saw hundreds of lights, but this time they also saw 'figures dancing, holding torches'. So far, so good, except that one figure danced through the car bonnet and vanished! At the same time (and this is highly significant), the doctor's wife became aware of a strong sense of evil and extreme depression. There were about 100 figures of men, all holding flaming torches, dancing back and forth across the road. At the Hare and Hounds pub all the lights and figures suddenly vanished, leaving only the car lights illuminating the dark country road.

However, all the foregoing becomes explicable when we realize that Mersley is on a band which is on a most unusual horizontal fault running across the Isle of Wight. This fault band is quite narrow, but the GP and his wife were, in fact, driving along it, thus we may have a completely rational explanation for the microwave-generated lights and the spinning gaseous forms and helixes. Of course, the electrical discharge at the highest point of the gaseous form is the electrical current discharging into the air, St Elmo's fire.

Figure 69a: 'About 100 figures of men, all holding flaming torches, dancing back and forth across the road.'
b: Himalayan foothills – small figure holding lantern above his head.
c: In 1620 a 'radiant figure' holding a golden sword was seen above the tomb of Mohammed.
d: In 1886 ghostly rowers were seen in the mist on Lake Tarawera in New Zealand. Later the same day great seismic disturbances occurred and the level of the lake rose by many feet.

(a)

(b)

(c)

(d)

Madonna Lilies

To illustrate the linkage between phenomena and mysterious perceptions, here are further examples from the Isle of Wight in the twentieth century, and from Epworth Rectory in 1716 and from Eggardon Hill in 1675.

The following is related by Alasdair Alpin MacGregor, drawing on personal reports from Lady Marjory Leslie, who lived at the much haunted Billingham Manor for a while:

> ...the following night Lady Leslie was awakened by a commotion in the next bedroom and hall. It sounded as though furniture was being hurled around. She slammed home the bolt on her door, and as she did so there was a blow on the outside of it, followed by a sound like a sword being drawn from its scabbard. The next morning not a stick of furniture was out of place and all the doors and windows were secure. Later that week the children's nanny had the latch of her door lifted, saw chairs she had put against the door pushed aside, and heard what seemed to be the thud of a falling body, at which point the air was filled with the heavy scent of 'Madonna lilies'...[11]

This perfume has often been smelled in the house at Billingham by visitors over the years. In 1949 again the sound of furniture or other heavy articles being moved in the middle of the night was heard by a housekeeper.

Both the springs in wind up clocks and the quartz crystals in automatic clocks will react to strong magnetic fields. Indeed, an horologist told me once that it was a not uncommon procedure to use a magnet to de-gauss faulty timepieces (that is, neutralize the magnetism in them by encircling them with a current-carrying conductor).[12]

Magnetism

At Newport on the Isle of Wight, in the early spring of 1976, work was proceeding on converting a Texas DIY store, known to be an eerie place at night, into a larger unit. Workmen reported doors opening and closing when no one was to be seen and footsteps walking when no one was there. When the new floor was laid, a vast sheet of polythene 'moved oddly in a manner which could not be explained by draughts ... more as if an unseen entity were walking across it'.[13]

At 4 a.m., in the presence of two workmen and a policeman, an unused hosepipe lying on the floor 'suddenly rose from the ground and leaped around', as the manager Raymond Pearson said at the time. Modern hosepipes are by definition flexible and around the polymer inner tube there is sufficient metallic mesh to give firmness to the pipe itself. We do not know what type of metal the mesh was, but if it was a metal which reacted to a strong magnetic field, as most do (apart from Mumetal), this could account for the phenomenon, just as the scaffolding leapt about at the St Anne's brewery site at Exeter *(see p.30)*. There are probably many other examples of this anomalous behaviour, but the 'hard hats' are not likely to chat about them too much.

Eggardon Barrow

In 1675, Dr William Sydenham, an early 'barrow digger', wrote to his uncle in London to tell him that as he had been excavating a barrow on Eggardon Hill with his team of workmen, he came across a hole, deep in the earth, 'perfectly like an oven, curiously shaped around', yet extremely hot to the touch.

If we exclude the possibility that he had stumbled across a seventeenth-century cremation, we are left with the possibility that the barrow was acting like a battery and generating a current, or alternatively, a capacitor, capable of storing energy. Barrows date from about 5,000 years ago, so it is unlikely that any fire lit in the year 2500 BC would still be hot! If the barrow had been built over a seismic source which emitted infra-red or geothermal energy, however, then the 'trap' of that barrow, comprised perhaps of earth, flint, organic and inorganic matter would emit thermal energy.

SEA LIGHTS

Of recent years many reports from mariners and aircraft pilots have been made of lights apparently emitted from the sea. This 'sealight' phenomenon has been closely monitored by William Corliss, a scientist in Maryland, who has collected, collated and analysed hundreds of journal reports.

In water, sound waves (acoustic energy as from deep Earth movements over faults, undersea volcanoes, etc.) can create gas bubbles which both heat up and emit light as they collapse, a phenomenon called sonoluminescence. The more pressure in the bubbles, the hotter they become. However, depending on the type of gas in the bubble, this heat is variable (for example bubbles of oxygen or nitrogen do not get hot). This is now thought to be due to the fact that oxygen and nitrogen turn into free radicals and react with the water.

MUD SPRING SWALLOWS ANIMALS

At Wootton Bassett in Wiltshire, there is a curious mud spring. This has, over decades, swallowed animals and lorryloads of rubbish, all vanishing forever. Surprisingly, many shells and fossil ammonites are welling up from the spring. Neville Hollingworth of the UK Natural Environment Research Council is quoted in *The Times* of 2 May 1996 as saying: 'It is like a fossil conveyor belt bringing up fluids from the clay layers below, and then washing them out in the nearby stream.' In 1974, when this was first observed, Wessex Water workmen were clearing a channel in a small stream called Hancock Water, which was obstructed by a grey heavy clay. When they dug this away, grey liquid mud spouted out a foot into the air, at a rate of 14 pints a second. The mud gushed in pulses, bringing up with it sticks, stones, fossils, cow bones and some artificially sharpened stakes, in an area 100 by 50 feet (30 by 15 metres).

Outgassing has been called the murderous vapour, due to its ability to first render unconscious and then kill small animals. One report by the Abbé de St Non related his stay in Italy between 1759 and 1761. At the Cave of the Dog, near Naples, at Lake Agnano, he was shown how at 10 inches (25 cm) above the floor of the cave, spiders and dogs first became comatose and then died within minutes unless removed from the site within two minutes. No dog, however, could withstand more than a few demonstrations by the Lazzarone before it died.

'TREACLE MINES'

'Treacle mines' is the collective name for a rare phenomenon, where tar and pitch seep from the Earth and can form their own wells. Historically, this was brewed into medicine and pastes for skin conditions.

One place where this happens is at Pendle Hill in Lancashire, at Sobden. Another is 3 miles (5 kilometres) west of Winder on the farm of Phil Chandler, in Georgia, America, a mysterious site of ancient terror known as the Nodoroc. The former director of the Barrow County Historical Society, Fred Ingram, said, 'It's real dangerous, if you step off in some parts of that soupy mess, you're gone.' It was a sinister place, with a reputation amongst the Native Americans in the area as a burning lake of fire. Few signs remain today, but the area was once a bubbling cauldron, a mud volcano from which a steady stream of foul gases ignited into a plume of black smoke which was visible for miles, according to the many accounts from settlers and Creek Indians inhabiting the area in the late 1700s. Over the intervening years the Nodoroc slowly declined in intensity and one day in the 1800s it blew up in an awesome explosion of mud and heat.

There are also treacle mines or Pitch Lakes in Trinidad and Venezuela, whilst in California there are asphalt pits. A gloomy pool in Trinidad covers 109 acres (45 hectares) and its slimy contents plummet to 271 feet (82 metres) in depth. The surface of the lake is solid enough to walk upon, although it occasionally bubbles and plops as sulphurated gas forces its way out. The lake has been quarried for its contents for over 100 years, but the asphalt soon oozes back into any trench that has been dug and fills it in again. Interestingly, like the UK site at Wootton Bassett, sea fossils and shells come to the surface. The use of this pitch for caulking ships was described by Sir Walter Ralegh in 1595. He wrote:

> At this point called Terra de Brea or Piche, there is that abundance of stone pitch that all the shippes of the worlde may be therewith laden from thence, and we made triall of it in trimming our shippes to be most excellent good and melteth not in the sunne as Pitche of Norway.[14]

GASES AND OTHER FORMS OF LIGHT

Gases, when ionized by whatever means, have the most interesting property of changing colour. So, a puff of gas from a cemetery (caused by the decay of bodies), a well or a fault, can, under certain circumstances, appear as a swaying column of green or white. This could explain why at least some ghostly figures seldom have heads and why they tend to vanish at the same place over a period of time. If the fissure in the Earth which allows the gas to escape vertically ends at, say, a rock face or stream, then the travel of the gas column is spatially limited. More gases are as follows:

> *Nitrogen*, when subjected to electrical discharges (Earth currents), is elevated to a metastable state and will produce a soft white glow which can be visible for some time after the discharge of gas has been terminated. This is called activated nitrogen and will readily combine with other atoms, whereas ordinary nitrogen does not. When it combines with hydrogen it forms ammonia, and when it combines with oxygen, nitric oxide (NO). Below 15° centigrade it will unite with other gases to form nitrobenzine, an oily substance with a strong odour of bitter almonds.
>
> *Artesian Gas* can be trapped in artesian basins. It is a mixture of several gases in varying percentages, with methane being the most common.

Compounds of carbon (C) and hydrogen (H), called hydrocarbons (e.g. methane, CH_4, and ethane, C_2H_6), burn. Other gases do not. These are mainly nitrogen, carbon dioxide and hydrogen sulphide.

Any gas rising to the surface would tend to rise vertically, unless deflected by an impenetrable geological layer. The gas from springs and boreholes that can be smelled as rotten eggs is hydrogen sulphide (H_2S) but this does not burn, although hydrogen phosphide (phosphine) is found in some artesian gas. The smell is of garlic. Phosphate deposits below ground can emit phosphene.[15]

Bombarding water with ultrasound creates air bubbles (cavitation); as already mentioned this is called sonoluminescence. Under certain conditions these bubbles will collapse and emit photons of light as flashes. Visible (photon) energy can be generated from frequency change of acoustic energy. Neodymium isotopes are found in certain rocks and when subjected to a certain frequency will generate laser-like beams of light.[16]

Lycopodium

This is a fine powder formed by the ripe spores of this species, a genus of the perennial plant club moss. In the last century its luminous properties made it useful for stage lightning and, surprisingly, as an absorbent of blood and fluids in surgery.

Lightning Bugs

On very rare occasions, fireflies have been known to flash in unison, causing a strange sheet of transient illumination over a large area. In 1904 A. H. Allard observed this near Oxford, Massachusetts, after a heavy thunderstorm. As he wrote, 'From time to time, as if moved by a common impulse, great numbers would flash closely in unison over the entire field, so that an extensive sheet of tiny points of light would gleam upon the vision for a moment, then vanish.'

A colleague saw such a firefly display in Boxmoor, Herts., when a young boy and so vivid was this that he has never forgotten it.

Luminous Bacteria

Luminous bacteria, live on fish and marine animals – when fish and whales are swarming there can be a bright glow from these mobile luminous areas. They are not only interesting from the point of underwater luminescence, however. Now they have a new and useful property: in the US Naval Research Laboratory in Washington, DC, recent work has found that when pollutants are present in water, whether chemical, pesticide residue or heavy metals such as zinc, copper, cobalts, etc., the bacteria glow is much fainter. Thus they have a new role for the environment as biosensors.[17]

VOLCANIC TUNNELS WITH GLASSY WALLS

In cultures world-wide there are stories of tunnels far below the ground which lead to the dwellings of monsters of various types. In Greece there are the Echidna, in Europe the ogres and dragons, in Scandinavia the trolls and in Japan more dragons.

By repute, these dwell in the centre of the Earth and often send vast rumbling sounds and ghastly smells ahead of their visitations to the upper world, together with smoke and fire (in folklore smoke and fire pour from the mouth and nostrils of the dragon).

In Hawaii, some parts of the United States, Italy, South America and Japan, we read of 'tunnels with walls of glass'. The well known Swiss author Erich von Daniken once wrote that these tunnels, which in fact can extend for many miles below ground, were so perfectly made that they 'could not have been made by human hands'.[18]

Indeed not, but these tunnels are both completely natural and of very great antiquity, in the order of four billion years – and nature is still working on them. In Iceland and Hawaii, to mention just two areas, where the volcanoes are still very active, new tunnels/lava outlets are still being developed. In geology these are known as Thurston Lava Tubes, and in the United States, rather affectionately as 'Firehose Entries', due to their regular shape. If you saw Harrison Ford as Indiana Jones in the film *Raiders of the Lost Ark* running frantically down a tunnel to escape the vast stone ball hurtling after him, you have some idea of a lava tube.

The walls, indeed, are glassy, due to the vitrification of the basalt by the extreme heat from upwelling magma. This emanates from the liquid magma bubbling away miles below ground in areas of volcanic activity.

Figure 70: The Herdsman, the strange basalt columns on the island of Staffa.

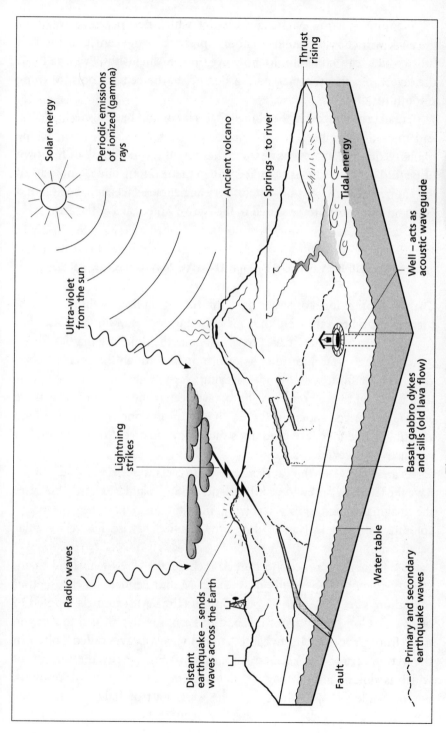

Figure 70a: Natural Earth energies.

The outer portion of the lava cascade which has forced its way over the rock will cool and solidify more rapidly than the centre of the lava tube, which can continue to flow ever more sluggishly. Eventually, as the lava cools and the magma ceases to rise, the centre cools, forming smooth tunnels.

The state of Oregon in the United States is covered by vast sheets of lava, and there are numbers of lava tubes and caves there. One open to the public, yet even now not fully explored, is found 11 miles south of the town of Bend. The main tube is 5,400 feet (1,640 metres) long and is only part of the enormous underground system. Very ancient artefacts have been found here and it is known to be sacred to the Native Americans of the area.

DEEP LAVA TUBES AND MAGMA CHAMBERS

There is another form of lava tunnel, this time from deep within the Earth. Magma chambers are well-known below Europe, Hawaii, the Cascades, Alaska and many other areas. Over millennia, the fluid magma has forced its way to the surface, forming its own tunnels through the ancient rocks. Over time, it shrinks and erodes, leaving glassy walled tunnels so regular that they might have been thought to have been made by man. Today there are 500 active volcanoes on the Earth and at any one time some 20 are erupting, while there are thousands more now quiescent or dormant, but very active in previous ages.

As an example of the capriciousness of volcanic activity, in the UK we have the Giant's Causeway and the islands of Staffa and Mull. In these cases the magma cooled slowly, evolving into the incredibly regular basalt columns we see now. Nan Madol in the Pacific, likewise, has very regular basalt columns.

Some other volcanoes and tunnels include: the Hawaiian island chain, which has round tubes with glassy sides; Mount Pendeli, on the Plain of Marathon, Greece; Mount Argathi, in the Himalayas; tunnels reputed to be 65 miles long running to the coast of Peru; tunnels alleged to run 900 miles from Cuzco, the Incan capital, to Bolivia; vast caves called 'Loltan' in the Mayan area of the Yucatan Peninsula; Mt Etna, Sicily, the summit of which is sinking after a magma chamber emptied in 1997; Mt Vesuvius, Bay of Naples, Italy; Vulcano, off the west coast of Italy, reputedly the home of the god Vulcan; the Lacher Sea, Mendig, north-west of Frankfurt,

Germany, where gases are still bubbling up; Yellowstone Park, USA; the Ape Cave, 12,810 feet long, south of Seattle, Oregon, USA; Mt Shasta, California, USA.

REFERENCES

1   J. Bord, *Mysterious Modern Mysteries of Britain*, Guild, 1967
2   Simon Lamb and David Sington, *Earth Story*, BBC Books, 1998
3   John Cowie, Crieff, former truck driver
4   R. V. Melville, 'The Hampshire Basin', *British Regional Geology*, HMSO, 1982
5   *World Press Review*, July 1995, p.27
6   Philip Heselton, *Earth Mysteries*, Element Books, 1995
7   Ibid.
8   Ibid.
9   Rev. Samuel Wesley, 1716
10 *Journal of the Society of Scientific Psychical Research*, 58–828
11 Alasdair Alpin MacGregor, *The Ghost Book*, Robert Hale, 1955
12 Ibid.
13 Gay Baldwin and Ray Anker, *Ghosts of the Isle of Wight*, 1977
14 Sir Walter Ralegh, 1595
15 A. R. Gray, Senior Geologist, Minerals and Energy Centre, Brisbane, quoted in *Mystery of the Min Min Lights*, M. Kozicka, 1994
16 Erich von Daniken, *Gold of the Gods*
17 J. Blitz, *Ultrasound*, Butterworths, 1963
18 S. Trento, *Field Guide to Mysterious Places of the Pacific Coast*, H. Holt, NY, 1997

20

CROP CIRCLES AND CHLADNI PATTERNS

Chaotic Systems and Natural Patterns

> No-one who has studied the faces of Nature can
> doubt that the world about us is a manifestation
> of something very clever indeed.
>
> PROFESSOR PAUL DAVIES,
>
> *THE FORCE OF NATURE*
>
> (CAMBRIDGE UNIVERSITY PRESS, 1979)

CIRCLES OF BIRDS AND ANIMALS

Some years ago, I saw what appeared, at a rapid count, to be some 80–90 large black birds sitting in a circle on the ground in a field near Thame, Oxfordshire. It was not possible to tell whether they were rooks or ravens, but it was certainly an astonishing sight to witness. Later, reading about this phenomenon, called 'the Parliament of the Birds' I realized that this behaviour was not so very unusual, but had been witnessed by many others. The reason for the circular sitting is not known, but in all reported cases the birds sit facing the centre of the circle, in the middle of which sits another bird.

I was told of another incident of the same type by a friend who had witnessed many cows walking slowly round and round in a field at Arbor Low in Derbyshire. Interestingly, my friend said that she had felt sick and panicky, and she knew she had to get away from the area quickly.[1]

Sheep circling slowly in a field have also been seen at Lockerbie on two occasions[2] and a further two cases were reported by Mr M. Belcher, who wrote to Dr Meaden.[3]

Out on an afternoon drive, Mr Belcher and his wife parked their car near the trigonometric survey point on Baildon Moor, near Leeds, Yorkshire, at approximately 14.30 GMT, facing north-east.

'Look at that circle of sheep in the field!' said Mrs Belcher. In the distance 100 or so sheep were in a circular formation, each animal more or less equidistant from the next. As Mr Belcher wrote:

> At the north end of the field some 20 or 30 cows were standing, grazing and chewing cud in the usual haphazard manner. The circular formation of these sheep was so unusual that I thought I was looking at bales of hay set out in the field by the farmer. Indeed, a Stone Age circle might have been more appropriate on this occasion. I looked around from north-west to north-east, and then espied a similar circle on a plateau opposite... In the sector between north and north-east, flocks of sheep were in other fields, but in no case exhibited the circular formation, being in their typically haphazard groups.[4]

In a second letter, Mr Belcher emphasized that the sheep in the two circles were variously standing, lying down or grazing, all quietly preoccupied but nevertheless forming this very regular circular formation.[5]

CROP CIRCLES

It is not only animals which form circles in fields, but the very crops themselves. 'Once the question can be formed, the answer is never very far away,' wrote the Canadian geophysicist Professor Jean Aubouin, rather simplistically in this case. So, we may well ask, 'What are crop circles?', or crop formations, as they are now known, due to their complexity and baffling shapes.

To date (1998), some 90,000 patterns have appeared around the world, most in England. However, thanks to the extremely silly hoaxers, analysis of the phenomenon is in chaos. Some people persist in believing that creating 'crop art' is a fun thing to do, despite the fact that it ruins not only crops but also the reputations of those scientists who do not understand that Mother

Nature does not hoax, only silly people do. One has only to surf the Internet to see the massive divergence of opinions, alleged Government/armed forces cover-ups, hoaxes, scientific evidence for and media coverage against the phenomenon to see what a morass the crop circle investigation is in.

So, rather than list the sites and patterns, and analyse whether they are authentic or not (something ably dealt with by other authors anyway), let us look at other patterns which Mother Nature can produce effortlessly on her own and then, assuming that at least some of the circles are genuine, try and explain them.

A well known circle researcher, an agriculturist, once said at a lecture on the subject, 'Nature does not produce straight lines.' He was wrong. There are natural straight lines running for hundreds of miles, visible to satellites but not on the ground. In the Central Desert in Australia, for instance, on the Nul Arbor Plain, there are lines 373 miles (600 kilometres) long and 10 miles (15 kilometres) wide – five running parallel to one another and visible only by infra-red imaging satellites. In the USA, meanwhile, a straight line of craters runs for hundreds of miles through the Midwest.

The vast scale of many of these lines is such that they have not been perceptible prior to satellite imaging, and in the case of geophysics, not until the masses of data collected could be analysed and collated. So, when in crop formations we see straight lines, we need not shout 'Hoax!', as the concept of straight lines being unnatural is an outdated idea which has been automatically accepted by many people without serious criticism.

'Lodging' is the term used by farmers to describe the flattened crops very often found when a sudden gust of wind has eddied around the corners of a field or sometimes in the centre. As I write, a cornfield half a mile from my home suddenly, overnight, produced two right-angled turns and two commas – not a crop formation, but very likely eddy currents of wind (which had been high), swirling down from the Chiltern Hills.

Who has not seen the dust devils and sudden dance and swirl of dry autumn leaves on the ground? It is quite eerie to watch a group of dry leaves in a corner suddenly become activated and do a merry dance on and just above the ground. They playfully chase one another round and round, up and down – and this is just ongoing wind energy. So, add in Earth and communications signals energies and we have a potent mixture all primed to react when matters reach a critical level.

RADIO FREQUENCY 'HOT SPOTS'

The chart below shows how man has added energies in free space since the turn of the century:

1890	Early experiments in radio transmissions
1901	The birth of radio communication
1920s	UK radio broadcasts commenced
1936	Early TV experiments; first UK TV broadcasts from Alexandra Palace
1940	Radio telegraph system, global coverage
1950	First UK television transmissions (black and white)
1960	First UK colour television transmissions
1960s	Military communications satellites in space
1970s	Communications satellites in space; ground based microwave transmitters
1990s	Mobile telephone communications base station transmitters

We should not, therefore, be surprised to see new phenomena appearing. The World Health Organization refers to 'radio frequency hot spots', small areas where several signals meet at one point in space at, or very close to, the same frequency and at peak envelope power.[6] In a high magnetic field, slow waves in the human brain increase the firing of nerve cells and increase their coherent activity. So, are UFOs ionized plasmas generated by local hot spots? Are the Greys and other aliens endogenous images generated by the brain when the temporal lobes are stimulated by external energies of radio frequency signals? The hundreds of reports of strange effects in crop formations certainly make interesting reading. (In the UK these reports are personally completed by those leaving formations on forms handed out by researcher Lucy Pringle and her team.)

It was Michael Green, the Centre for Crop Circle Study (CCCS) President, who was the first to notice, a decade ago, the close proximity of crop formations to ancient sites. Professionally an archaeologist working with English Heritage, Green is thoroughly familiar with ancient monuments in many countries, especially in the UK. The detailed maps he gave me started a train of thought – could it be that the known geomagnetic anomalies at these sites were interacting with the multitude of other signals to drive ambient fields, however sourced, into chaotic behaviour? We do not attribute the dazzling complexities of snowflake geometry to strange forces, nor the remarkable symmetrical lattices seen under the microscope when the commonplace bacteria *E. coli* and salmonella are subjected to agents that cause them stress.

To my knowledge, two factors have not been considered in crop formations: first, the very high natural geomagnetic fields which are found at the time of the equinoxes; second, the fact that signals, whether man-made or natural, rising into the ionosphere and oscillating in sympathy with other electromagnetic waves reaching that height will, in part, reflect back to the Earth along the original path. The physics is complex, but in short, this means that right- and left-hand polarized signals enter the ionosphere at slightly different times and thus the return (reflected) signal takes a slightly different path. The 'ordinary' ray is independent of the magnetic field but the other, known as the 'extraordinary' ray, slows down depending upon the strength of the Earth's magnetic field along its path. If you have ever looked at your reflection in a bathroom with mirrors both in front and behind you, you will have an idea of this multiple energy reflection. You see myriad 'me' images, each smaller and slightly displaced to the side relative to the previous image. The image recedes into infinity in the mirrors. Is this not like the ever-smaller and slightly lateral circles and crescents found in some crop formations?

CROP CIRCLE EFFECTS ON HUMANS

While noting the effects reported by hundreds of visitors to crop formations, it is salutary to remember that virtually all of the following have been experienced at ancient sacred sites at various times over the centuries and are sufficiently unusual to have been reported by those experiencing them. It should also be pointed out that many crop formation reports are from scientists, doctors, teachers and biologists, etc., all of whom must have been very sure of what they felt to put their comments down on paper, and that crop circle hoaxers now use biolocation (dowsing rods) to locate the most powerful energy leys in which to make their patterns.

What seems to be critical is the place or site in the formation, whether there has been a clockwise or anticlockwise spin to the crop, the immunocompetence of the individual, and possibly their height and build. Disorientation is very common; as is utter exhaustion, which can lead to

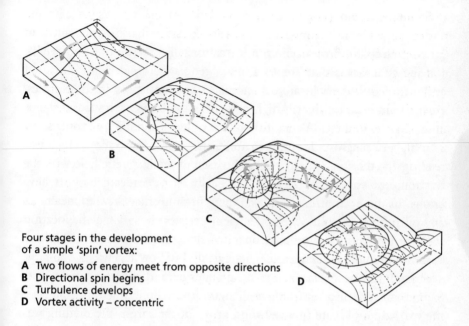

Four stages in the development
of a simple 'spin' vortex:

A Two flows of energy meet from opposite directions
B Directional spin begins
C Turbulence develops
D Vortex activity – concentric

Figure 71: Four stages in the development of a theoretical crop circle formation.

literal collapse; sudden voracious hunger; the onset of menstrual bleeds; tingling of the hands and feet, 'like being in a bed of nettles'; a sudden sensation of great heat; very slow or very rapid heartbeat (bradycardia and tachycardia); breathlessness; a 'tinny' taste at the back of the throat; great emotional changes (including total love for the universe/fellow man); terror; panic; great surge of energy; relief from the pain of rheumatism and arthritis; falling asleep; hearing one's name being called; time loss and short-term memory loss; and dyscalculia (the inability to count).

Most of these signs and symptoms are explicable in terms of deep eddy currents in the brain and stimulation from external (exogenous) sources of, for example, the parietal lobe, the motor strip of the cortex, brainwave shifts and spikes. If subjected to external stimuli, the brain stem – the motorway into and out of the brain and nervous system – can lead to many strange and fugitive effects.

External magnetic fields, however sourced, penetrate into deep brain space. Certain parts of the brain are extremely sensitive to kindling by external fields, including the temporal lobes, especially the sub-cortical components, the amygdala and the hippocampus. Certainly, the field work of Salvatore Trento in the USA at sacred Native American sites in California and the Pacific north-west has recorded quite remarkable parallels in human effects to those from crop formations and sacred sites in the UK. But the vital fact is that Trento, using a geomagnetometer, has measured and recorded the very local field anomalies and 'hot spots' in these places. He has found extraordinarily high shifts over as little as a few yards distance at sacred sites in the USA and, it should be noted, these shifts not only show a far higher background reading in milliGauss, but can also show a far lower reading. In addition, the angle of inclination of the magnetic field with the horizon, known as 'dip', varies dramatically. For decades geologists have known of these variations and used them in innovative ways to locate gas and oil sumps. As Trento writes, 'Ancient peoples chose a specific location for their inscriptions, standing stones and stone chambers. Many sites have been built on top of aberrant magnetic fields, but how and why?'[7]

To quote one example, the mean background magnetic field near Santa Cruz in California is 480 milliGauss at 50° dip. But within 6 feet (1.8 metres), at an old site in a redwood grove in the forest, the reading was 4,570 milliGauss (457,000 nanoTesla) with a 59° dip. Trento checked this several times to be certain. Of special note to those interested in human effects of Earth energy are the following facts: at this site a cabin had been built and just by the entrance, most people feel nauseous. Many lose their balance and sense of co-ordination and otherwise feel very strange. Local folklore says that a meteorite crashed here over 2,000 years ago. In addition, there is a fault across the area, but in 1939 a potential buyer of the land found, with his surveyor, that not only did the compass swing unaccountably in the area, but that 'on returning down the little canyon, we felt very light-headed or top-heavy, as if something was trying to force us right off the hill'. Those interested in following further down Trento's road are recommended to read his books and emulate his work in the UK with geomagnetometers.

An excellent starting-point would be Fountains Abbey in Yorkshire, where in September 1998 a visitor felt as though he were 'standing on a million volts'.[8] This man is very sensitive to seismic energies, so he had an idea of what to expect at the site as he approached it, but his preconceptions turned out to be totally wrong. He had felt these energies elsewhere on many occasions, 'but when I walked into it, I felt as though I was standing on a million volts and would not have been surprised if I had caught fire and disappeared in a cloud of smoke'. Even more curious, he met another person who is also sensitive to these energies and who told him that after visiting Fountains Abbey some years previously, she had to spend the next three days in bed, feeling extremely weak and with no energy at all.

THE LASER

New Physics is at the forefront of basic research that is likely to have a big impact on our lives in the years ahead. The same can be said of quantum optics, which involves the best known example of spontaneous self-organization, the laser.

Shortly after the first lasers were made, they were described as 'an invention looking for a use'. Today they have, of course, a multitude of uses, ranging from burglar alarms to telephone communications. Lasers, however, are very much more than just gadgets – they offer a means to explore some very fundamental aspects of quantum electrodynamics.

In an ordinary electric bulb, photons are emitted independently from each atom. The wave pulses overlap at random to produce continuous light. However, if the system is driven far from equilibrium, it can suddenly undergo a transition to the lasing mode, where all the atoms co-operate and emit their photons precisely in synchronization, producing a giant coherent wave train in which all the individual wavelets are exactly in step.

This transition to the lasing mode is what physicists call a 'phase transition'. We are familiar with many in our daily lives, such as the change from ice to liquid water or water vapour, or the onset of ferromagnetism in iron when it cools below the Curie temperature. The fact that matter and energy do have a tendency to self-organize into coherent structures and patterns has only very recently been appreciated by physicists.

A simple example is in a boiling pan of water. While the water is heating, the surface is flat and featureless. However, when a certain temperature is reached, the liquid abruptly organizes itself into a coherent pattern of collection cells or rolls. In this convecting mode, vast numbers of molecules move in unison as though to some unseen command.

To illustrate this, imagine you are on a mountain top looking down at a distant city square on market day. The crowd is milling about at random and each individual is doing something different – from that distance it is very difficult to make out precisely what. Now suppose, however, that it is not market day but the day of a military parade and the crowd is replaced by a battalion of well-drilled soldiers. Now every soldier is doing the same thing at the same time. It is very much easier to see, and indeed to hear, from a distance, what that is. The analogy in physics is that a normal system is like the market day crowd – every atom is doing something different – whereas in a laser the atoms are all forced to be in the same quantum state and therefore resemble the well-drilled soldiers. Every atom must do exactly the same thing at exactly the same time.

The Beautiful Mandelbrot Set

Iteration simply means that an equation, a movement or a computer simulation will, when repeated *ad infinitum*, produce images of incredible symmetry and beauty. The Mandelbrot Set is one example; the Julia Set, first reported on 7 July 1996 in a field close to Stonehenge, measuring 900 feet by 500 feet (274 metres by 152 metres), is another. This formation was comprised of 151 circles and was apparently imprinted in the space of about 30 minutes in broad daylight.

Depending on the equation, or energy input and number and type of iteration, a picture will be built up, with points seemingly added at random. As the points accumulate, an image emerges with symmetry and structure. Indeed, it is surprising to find that a totally regular checkerboard pattern rather like a miniature chessboard can be generated by the chaotic vibrations of the surface of a fluid.[9]

THE EDGE OF CHAOS

Another recurring theme in the physics of complexity is the edge of chaos. Systems that are poised between two extremes of utter regular motion and chaotic motion behave in a way which shows hints of pattern. Simple motions generate simple patterns – the swirl of leaves chasing one another is one example. Chaos theory predicts, however, that simple but non-random laws should be non-linear, that is to say, the response to change or energy input is not simply proportional to the size of such change – the whole is far greater than the sum of its parts.

When we look at crop formations, Chladni patterns or the Eidophone images *(see below)*, a common feature is that they are all driven by pumping in energy, which is dissipated or burned in an avalanche process like an earthquake. These complex systems exist in a metastable state, and tiny, apparently insignificant increments in energy input can trigger a massive avalanche, far from the equilibrium state.[10]

Earthquakes are one example. Tectonic forces inject energy into the system, and this, from being input on a large scale, transforms into a wider range of smaller scales, the energy dissipating into increasingly smaller packets. In the same way, in turbulent liquid, stirring will give a continuous input of energy and the liquid will organize itself into a structure with hundreds of tiny vortices. This is an easy experiment to try in your kitchen with a cup of black coffee and some not-too-thick cream. If you could freeze the turbulent motion you would see many of the images of the early crop circles – whorls, curls and little vortices spinning off the larger ones.

Most of the time, we think of the connections between inputs and outputs as being simple linear ones, but in reality, as such connections are in fact complex non-linear functions, we should not be surprised if unexpected effects appear.

Looking at crop circles over the decades, it is apparent that increasingly puzzling and complex forms are appearing. This may be due to hyperchaos. (Hoaxers also naturally evolve more complicated shapes over time, but we exclude them here.)

It is well known that a hallmark of chaos is its sensitive dependence on the initial conditions. Two identical but isolated chaotic systems will evolve into totally different trajectories if the original input energy differs by just a small amount.

It is interesting that much of the recent work on chaos theory relating to signal transmission has been carried out by Thomas Carroll and Lou Pecora at the US Naval Research Laboratory in Washington, DC. As Pecora writes,

Imagine that you want to transmit a secret message to your partner and you mask it with much louder chaotic noise. An eavesdropper hears only the chaos, which sounds like noise. Suppose the partner has a receiver that synchronizes with the masking chaotic system. After receiving the composite signal, he or she simply reproduces the chaos, subtracts from it the signal and listens to the message.[11]

The idea is simple and straightforward.

How does this link with crop formations? Careful map plotting has shown that formations in the UK are located not only at, or very close to, ancient sites such as Stonehenge, Silbury Hill, Cissbury Ring, etc. (again a natural target for hoaxers), but are also within beam distance of radio and microwave transmitters, which are usually situated on high ground. So we have another source of energy input to the naturally-driven system *(see Natural Earth Frequency Chart, p.259)*. The waves cover many frequencies, depending upon distant earthquakes, local fault movements and sunspot activity. Is it possible that this last and historically recent input of man-made radio frequency energies and its complex intermodulations can, on a macro scale, copy what happens in a small-scale universe, when, contrary to expectations, a pattern suddenly appears when electrons are driven to behave chaotically?

A recent conference at the Newton Institute at Cambridge[12] brought together leading world-class mathematicians to address this patterning in nature. Even more curious is the relationship between prime numbers and quantum chaos, and the Platonic Solids.

CHLADNI PATTERNS

Ultrasound and anthropomorphism – a potent mix, but what do they have to do with crop formations?

Man has a special ability to see himself or representations of himself in clouds, trees, smoke, fire, etc. When he sees such an image in sand or in water he knows it cannot be a man, therefore it must be a god. This is known as anthropomorphism.

All waves carry energy, whether they are in air (as wind), on water (as waves) or acoustic (as radio waves, microwaves or voices, or the sound of the wind in trees). But if the energy is confined, or subject to what is known as the 'boundary condition', something strange will take place. This boundary may be the edge of a well, of a threshing-floor or even a shallow opaque dish in your own kitchen, filled with water.

All sound, whether infra-, ultra- or normally-heard sound, carries energy, the amount of energy (or push) depending upon volume and frequency. Sound can cause some quite phenomenal effects. Some examples are the ultrasonic devices which render areas 'no go' for dogs, cats, mice, etc; worm charmers, who, in the same way that snakes will leave their holes

(a)

(b)

(c)

(d)

Figure 72: Chladni (b) and other patterns.

Having spent 30 years examining eyes and looking at faces one can categorically state that eyes are never round circles (the iris is round but set in an almond-shaped aperture framed by the eyelids); eyes are not set in the centre of the face, they are somewhat above a median line; the very deep near-vertical frown lines are very seldom seen and the symmetrical near-vertical lines below the mouth are also very rare. But all these are seen in the Acheropita (faces not made with hands). Thus the gods always presented angry faces and, crossing many cultures and thousands of years, showed very similar images, from Nimrod in the ninth century BC (a) to the Medusa head at the Roman city of Sulis Magna (Bath) (c) and later the Green Man (d). Why should this image form so consistently? When isochronous (simultaneous) progressive waves meet each other from opposing directions, turbulent vortices are produced which will exhibit, when driven to chaotic states, remarkable symmetrical patterns. When plane waves of the same frequency and amplitude, wavelength and speed meet at one point in space when they are travelling in opposite directions, a standing wave, with nodes and anti-nodes, will form.

below ground prior to an earthquake, can cause worms to surface by pat-
ting or treading rhythmically on the earth; and the deep 'thrumming' beat
of pop music, to which some people are extremely sensitive – they can feel
its resonance in their heads. This is not surprising, as the skull acts as a res-
onator. To visualize this, imagine an oval billiard table. A very fast shot will
send the ball, with its energy, ricocheting around the cushions in a random
fashion, imparting more energy to any ball it chances to meet in its path.
Likewise, energies inside the human skull will eddy around, stimulating any
nerves, neurones and structures, like the pineal gland or the hypothalamus,
en route. Sound in all its forms carries energy, phonons, in the same way
that light carries photons.[13] The classical billiard problem is taken as the
motion of a charged positive particle inside a plane enclosure in a uniform
and constant magnetic field. The trajectory of the 'billiards' (particles) con-
sists of circular arcs between the points of specular reflection.

In 1787, Prof. Gustav Chladni, a Hungarian scientist, experimented with
sound produced from a violin bow, using sand sprinkled on a glass plate.
We do not know what notes he played, but he left a record of the extraordinary images that the sound waves produced *(see Figure 72b)*.

Sound waves need a medium in which to travel, whether air, brain tissue
or water. They do not travel in a vacuum. If a square metallic tray with
its four sides acting as a boundary is made to vibrate by subjecting it to
acoustic energy, then sand in it will arrange itself into patterns, now called
Chladni figures. The sand naturally forms nodes and anti-nodes, gathering
in some regions and shunning others.

At the University of Texas, Austin, Paul Umbanhowar, Francesco Melo
and Harry Swinney have been experimenting with sand piles in trays. They
are using the acceleration amplitude to check the patterns that arise. At low
frequencies and amplitudes the sand just sits on the bottom of the tray, but
as more energy (shaking) is input, strange patterns emerge. Stripes, squares,
and hexagons are all clearly visible once the amplitude reaches two and a
half times the acceleration of normal gravity. Above 40 Hz, light and dark
stripes appear; below 40 Hz, there are arrays of small squares.

If the acceleration amplitude is increased to a threshold of about four
times normal gravity, yet another pattern appears – an array of tiny hexagons. Stepping it up still further, stripes, squares, spirals, hexagons and triangles appear. It is now time to remember the statement of the late Richard
Feynman, the brilliant American physicist who demonstrated to the world
the reason for the self-destruction of the *Challenger* spacecraft (the silicon

o-rings joining critical parts of the rocket casing became brittle and fractured at a low temperature). Feynman said that natural effects found on the micro scale could be replicated on the macro scale. So, if we put these factors together, we see that nature on her own, with sufficient energy input and with certain other conditions, is perfectly capable of making elegant patterns in whatever medium is suitable.

Prof. Chladni used sand on a glass plate and in the US in the nineteenth century Margaret Watts-Hughes used her own voice and lycopodium grains, sand, powder and a 'singing tube' to produce fantastic visual images (Eidophone Voice Figures). Now, in the late twentieth century, with the combination of radio frequency, microwave, man-made and Earth energy, we are seeing precisely the same apparently magical combinations of triangles, circles, arcs and lines in crops on the landscape. Just to take two examples: 'the Dragonfly' and 'the Poppyflower' symbols in Wiltshire in July 1998 and 'the Torus Knot' at Alton Barnes in 1997 are explicable by this theory. However, some of the 'accessories' may not fit.[14] Two authors from the Centre of Nonlinear Dynamics and Dept. of Physics at the University of Texas produced a further paper which appeared in *Nature* in 1996, explaining the apparently spontaneous formations of images, including stripes, hexagons and squares.[15]

Thus, two possibilities are currently the subject of research. First, as described above, complex energy inputs from multiple angles, sources, at an enormous range of frequencies and polarizations, can cause marvellous symmetrical and fractal shapes to appear. This impacts on mathematics, and Prof. Hawkins (of the Stonehenge analysis) and James Lyons at York University have both been working on applied mathematics and geometry of forces for some years, the latter on five-dimensional toroids and Platonic Solids.

The second possibility is more controversial: do crop circles form at the boundary of Hertzian waves, geophysics and thought? There are now several dozen examples of people 'thinking' a shape and lo, it appears in a matter of hours close to them. We know from the work of the US Remote Viewing Unit and Professor Irwin Laszlo's work in Hungary that under certain circumstances thoughts and images can be transmitted from a sender to a 'viewer' hundreds of miles distant. This begs the question: do our thoughts spiral upwards from our brains like millions of little cottage chimneys sending smoke curling idly upwards? Do thoughts have energy, do they join up, blend together and act in unison? Can they cause spontaneous events? Is there an as yet unknown area between the Earth's surface and the troposphere (let us call it the sophosphere), where, as Isaac Newton wrote, 'We sail strange seas of thought alone'?

WATER, THE SUN GOD AND CHAOTIC SYSTEMS

The solar disc, the sun god of antiquity, is generally depicted as a yellow disc with radiant lines running radially out away from the disc itself. This image is found in many cultures throughout the ages. But a curious factor is that no eye can look directly at the sun and remain healthy. Extremely rapid damage to the retina will follow any direct gaze at the sun with the naked eye. However, there is one way in which the image of the sun may be viewed safely and this is as a reflected image on water.

Imagine now a rock pool or a well with the water level near the top. In still water the image of the sun will appear as literally a mirror image, but in water that is slightly agitated, as when movement such as dancing is taking place on the ground nearby or there are deep Earth movements or indeed distant earthquakes, the reflected image in the water will oscillate and the surface of the water will vibrate. Due to the boundary condition – the walls of the well or the rocky edges of a pool – these subtle energies, mainly in the ELF range, will set up reflected waves bouncing hither and thither on the surface of the water and what was a flat still reflected image of the sun will become chaotic.

When two chaotic systems synchronize the results can defy common sense. In our example, the central disc of the round sun will develop two round 'eyes' centrally, with sinuous waves flowing outwards to the edge. There will also be two deep 'frown' lines above the 'eyes' and two deep lines from below the eyes to the edge of the image. These four lines run at 45° from the centre of the image. In Figure 72 we see four examples of this type of image. Two thousand years ago this was known as an 'Acheropita', i.e. an image not made with hands.

A Russian scientist recently wrote that physics on a human scale offers a tremendously rewarding intellectual challenge. Research into the turbulence of chaotic systems is the province of the particle physicists who seek to study matter on ever smaller scales (ironically by building bigger and bigger particle accelerators) and the astrophysicists who probe ever more distant parts of our galaxy. But the physics of phenomena on a human scale is considered to be of lesser importance.

Dr Anne Ross, the renowned Celtic archaeologist, has pointed out that stone heads from the Celtic period strongly resemble Classical Gorgon and Medusa heads, which themselves have a very long ancestry amongst the Indo-European cultures. These staring serpent-wreathed images were held to have an evil-averting power. In the Greek and Roman periods they were placed on temple porticoes, the shields of soldiers and on the eaves of buildings. Indeed, we have a faint echo of this purpose in the proliferation of stone faces on Victorian domestic buildings in the City of London to this day. Apotropaic powers were attributed to all these 'heads' and as Ross also notes, the Medusa heads found in the UK, France and Germany tended to be associated with healing springs.[16]

If we study human faces and heads with an analytical eye it is clear that human faces, of all nationalities, simply do not have the following features, all of which are seen in the Green Man, Medusa and Acheropita images:

Round eyes with no lid aperture or eyelids
A deep 'V' line on the forehead with parallel lines to the sides
Inverted 'V' lines below the eyes again with parallel lines
Eyes set dead centre (human eyes are set in the face in proportion)

SPIN AND ENERGY

The Rubik Cube is a familiar device. Briefly, it is comprised of a number of small cubes which spin on an axis and can, with time and patience, be rotated into coloured bands and patterns. Now imagine the spin of the Rubik Cube speeded up tenfold, a hundredfold, a thousandfold. The same patterns will appear, but now in microseconds. Imagine now a spherical Rubik Cube device, but now the spins are occurring billions of times a second...

Where do the energies originate to cause such phenomenally rapid spins? At any moment in time we are all surrounded with multi-sourced energies, from the warmth of the sun to the rumble of an earthquake, the faint but none the less real signals from high masts which bring radio and television into our homes, the microwaves from satellites many miles above our heads and the incredibly faint signals which reach the Earth from outer space. Many of these were felt by the first men who walked on the planet, but some are relatively new. Satellite signals, for instance, are very new indeed.

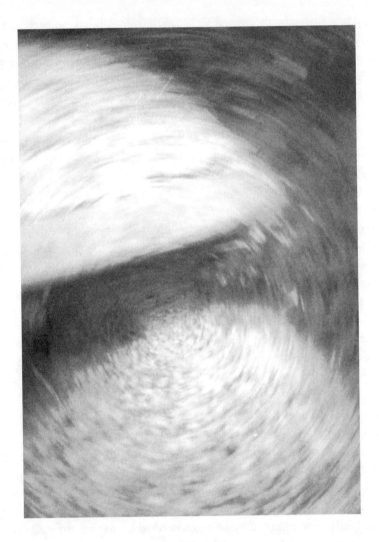

Figure 72a: The Glastonbury 'vortex'.

A further example of spontaneous self-organization is described by Fritz Capra in *The Web of Life* (HarperCollins, 1996). Liquid in a Petri dish (or even olive oil in the frying pan) will, when being heated, at one point develop a hexagonal array of patterns. This is called a Benard cell. This is just one easy way to check an example of spontaneous self-organization in which millions of molecules move coherently.

In July 1998 Grace Greaves of Carmarthen was visiting Glastonbury and paused halfway up the Tor to take some photographs of the view, using her 'point and shoot' camera. She stopped by a seat and focused her camera on the tower at the top of the Tor. She felt slightly dizzy, but nevertheless took her photo. It was not until the roll of film was developed in Carmarthen that she saw that of the whole film one image clearly showed a vortex-like feature *(see Figure 72a)*. All the other pictures were perfectly clear and well focused. The picture has been shown to several photographic specialists, who are baffled, but when the recent work in Russia by Dr Boris Artamonov and in the UK by Dr Terry Cox is considered, 'thoughtography' may not be so unlikely. Remember that the human brain and eyes are emitting electromagnetic radiation of varying frequencies all the time, as is the Earth, especially at the special sites, the *genius loci*, of the Romans, of which Glastonbury itself is certainly one. Remember also that in photographic film, with its multiple layers of chemical emulsion, each layer is a tiny factory which converts light and energy into a photographic image.

QUANTIZED VORTICES

When a cylindrical container of superfluid is rotated about its axis, as the rotation speed increases, the vortex patterns become more complex.

When a parameter is increased beyond a critical value, metals snap, smoothly flowing liquids become turbulent and chemical concentrations become chaotic. These are some of nature's non-linear manifestations. A University of Chicago biophysicist, Dr Connor, postulates bifurcations in the neuroelectric activity of the brain, cranked up past a certain threshold, when 'travelling and rotating waves' occur. Brains, computers and crops can all be tipped into chaos.

'Break time' is the crucial feature which distinguishes between classical and quantum predictions of chaotic systems. Prior to break time, quantum systems mimic the behaviour of classic systems by looking essentially random. But after break time, the system simply retraces its path. It is now no longer random, but stuck in a repeating loop, albeit one of considerable complexity.

Lasers are capable of many 'special effects' depending upon the strength, circuitry and wavelength of the emitted beam. If one wishes to decorate natural phenomena in crops with what might be thought of as 'twiddly bits', what more suitable device is there? A recent advertisement in a US science journal gave details of a hand-held laser, which, with different 'thread-on tips', projects 10-foot (3-metre) high images at 100 foot (30 metres) distance. Imagine what one could do with a far more powerful device, for, what shall we say, target practice? The 'Translight Art Pointer' advertises that it can enable such images as a 10-foot (3-metre) high reclining figure, an arrow, a head, depending upon the thread-on tip, to appear like phantoms in the distance.

An essential feature of any non-linear system is that many different states can exist under the same operating conditions. In Taylor Couette Flow, where contra-rotating fluids are held within a boundary, these states would have different numbers of cells or waves, or both. Thus, if the system is large, there may be literally thousands of different states available, all of which can interact with one another.

Chaos theory and crop circles present us with new applications in the laws of physics, with the difference that now the energy input to every place on Earth mounts steadily year by year. How the phenomenon is interpreted depends, as with all natural phenomena, from lightning (the thunderbolts of the gods) to the spin of the compass needle or indeed a metal dish (magnetic field), on the mindset of the individual.

REFERENCES

1   Personal correspondence to Anne Silk.

2   Ibid.

3   G. T. Meadon, 'Sheep in circular flocks: is there a meteorological, or some other, connection?', *Journal of Meteorology* 14:54, 1989

4   Ibid.

5   M. Belcher, personal communication

6   *Electromagnetic Fields, 300 Hz–300 Ghz*, World Health Organization, Geneva, 1993

7   S. Trento, *Field Guide to Mysterious Places of the Pacific Coast*, H. Holt, New York, 1997

8   Personal communication to Anne Silk.

9   M. Field and M. Golubitsky, 'Symmetries on the edge of chaos', *New Scientist*, 91–193

10 Ibid.

11 Lou Pecora, US Naval Res. Lab., 'Hyperchaos harnessed', *Physics World*, May 1996

12 M. du Sautoy, 'Pattern in the chaos', *The Times*, 14 July 1997

13 M. Robnik, 'Regular and chaotic billiard dynamics in magnetic fields. Non linear phenomena' in S. Sarkar (ed.), *Non-linear Phenomena and Chaos*, Royal Signals and Radar Establishment, Malvern, 1986

14 M. C. Cross and P. C. Hohenberg, 'Pattern formation outside of equilibrium', *Reviews of Modern Physics* 1993, 65 ii, 851

15 P. Umbanhowar *et al.*, 'Localised excitations in a vertically vibrated granular layer', *Nature* 382, 29 August 1996

16 Dr Anne Ross, *Pagan Celtic Britain*, Constable, 1967

21

THE DEVIL'S FOOTPRINTS IN THE SNOW

A World-Wide Phenomenon

> While I see many hoof marks going in,
> I see none coming out.
>
> AESOP, *THE LION, THE FOX AND THE BEASTS*, 550 BC

Legends abound all over the world of the strange footprints caused by mythical one-legged creatures. In the UK they are known as 'the Devil's footprints'. A typical example comes from the Exeter, Exmouth, Totnes, Torquay and Bicton area in Devon, covering some 100 square miles (260 square kilometres), where such marks appeared in 1855. They were carefully sketched and written up by many people in the area, with *The Times* and *Illustrated London News* devoting pages to the phenomenon. The steps ran in straight lines, were very deep and showed only a crescent outline cut as if with a diamond or branded with a hot iron in the snow. These were no animal pad marks, as would be found with four-legged creatures running on the ground, and no claw marks, as would be found with birds.

Suggested reasons at the time of the steps were: badger, crane, kangaroo, great bustard, donkey, very large birds hitherto unknown to science, green plover, reptile, toad, rat, hare and cat, but not one of these covers the facts of the linear continuation over the ground, over barns, through solid walls and across rivers – this is a logical impossibility.

The steps were reported as going under fruit trees and gooseberry bushes, and in many places were observed to start and stop in the middle of a garden or path. In Dawlish and Lympstone, there was 'hardly a garden where his footprints are not observable. In this parish he gambolled with inexpressible activity.'

It is of some significance to the theory of seismic activity that the weight of snow and ice in the area were reported as 'enormous'. Even the Exe and the Teign rivers were frozen over at the time and people could walk across them.

Similar reports well predate even these early West Country observations. In Glen Orchy, to the south of Glen Lyon in 1840 *(see chart on p.306)*, 12 miles (19 kilometres) of identical steps were found, and in 1840 Sir James Ross, at Kerguelen Island in Antarctica, was astonished to find singular steps of a pony or ass *(see chart)*. In all, 27 incidences have been found in a literature trawl. Doubtless there are many other instances in foreign journals waiting to surface for some future researcher, but what might be producing these mysterious tracks?

Though there is no unipedal creature in nature (the nearest might be the seahorse, who rides in the waves on his curly tail, but he was never a land creature), reports of one-legged beings occur world-wide. In Assyria, Utukku was a vengeful spirit with the powers to terrorize and destroy. Alu was one of his main forms and he appeared as a phantom with one leg. The leprechaun of Irish legend is derived from *leith bhrogan* (the one-shoe maker). Why should he make single shoes only, unless single footprints had been observed? The Scottish boobrie, a mottled white water-horse which had hooves pointing to the rear and could change its shape on a whim, is also very strange, as it is alleged to leave footprints 'the length of a house' on the muddy shoes of Loch Argyll and by the freshwater streams in that area.

For the present, however, this interim report puts forward a hypothesis involving seismic (Earth) energy, rather than mythical beings. We should remember that the steps appeared on rooftops and barns, in gardens and fields, and traversed buildings, passing over them, but not through them. The energy source, therefore, must logically be either from above (solar or cosmic), or below, as (Earth) seismic energy. What form of life could do this or what type of energy?

One pointer is given by 'Chips' Barber, who quotes a report of phenomena in the vicinity of St Anne's Well, Brewery Yard, below the Iron Bridge:

Such spectacles as large iron bars of great weight ... hurling themselves about, hosepipes suddenly whiplashing themselves into the air, and even more disconcertingly, large unaccountable footsteps appearing in sand lying on the floor.[1]

The atmosphere was so strange that six of the men refused to work night shifts. In 1993 Barber referred to the genre of the 'Nouveau Beasties' – a telling phrase.

THE DISTANCE BETWEEN STEPS

The distance between steps, whilst largely the same in a given area, does vary when the totality of steps is considered. If we consider the cause to be seismic energy wavelengths, these vary between 8.5 inches (214 mm), 12 inches (300 mm) and 14 inches (350 mm).

During the eighteenth century, and even earlier, on the Isle of Man on New Year's Eve in many of the upland cottages it was the custom for the ashes from the fire to be spread out on the floor last thing at night, as the shape of a foot might be seen on the floor in the morning. The same procedure was followed in north-east of Scotland. On New Year's morning a search was made for a mark like a human foot. We have to ask ourselves, why should footprints be sought in ash on the floor? It can only be that periodically, such step-like shapes had been previously observed.

An interesting figure in Scottish folklore is Auld Clootie, who is considered to be the harbinger of evil and is best avoided. A cloot is a cloven hoof, thus Auld Clootie may be anglicized as 'Old Cloven Hoof'. The logical reason behind such tales is that such an apparently mysterious manifestation did occur on occasion. We should also note that the Isle of Man and the north of Scotland are also volcanic, and highly faulted.

STEPS IN THE SNOW IN RUSSIA AND WALES

The Russian journal *Aura Z* (Issue 1, March 1993), reported a further case of steps in the snow at Sosnino, near Vicenza, northern Italy. On 24 January 1992, the snow near a military camp was up to the knees of walkers. Steps were observed in the snow 6 inches (16 cm) wide and 7.5 inches (20 cm) deep. Strange creatures were seen, 'but the soldiers did not believe their eyes'.

Curiously, after the event some soldiers felt so ill they reported to the Medical Officer at the camp. One witness was rendered speechless, only recovering his speech after several days. Equally strange was the fact that a

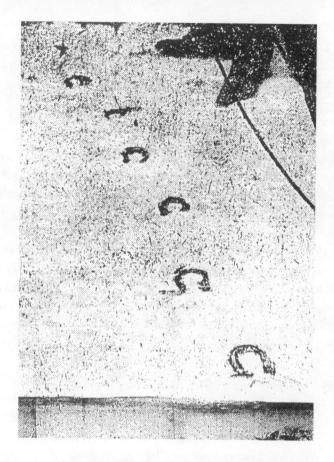

Figure 73: The Devil's footprints in the snow. (Fortean Library)

wolf was observed to approach the steps, but appeared to be unable to cross them, running back the way he had come. Ultrasound can produce a sonic barrier which so badly affects the brain of people or animals in its path that they are unable to proceed, while nausea, severe headaches and disorientation are experienced at a magnetic level of 60 milliTesla.

Wales, too, has curious steps in both sand and snow. In 1971, at a sandy beach at Llanaber, north of Barmouth, two people saw a line of steps 12 inches to 18 inches (30 cm to 45 cm) across at the water's edge. Just 4 miles (6.4 kilometres) from there in 1975, steps in the sand were seen at Penmaenpool toll bridge, 'each larger than a dinnerplate'. It is noteworthy that these places are right on the Bala Fault at Barmouth Bay, the very scene of the Welsh revival.

TRACKS OF THE DEVIL

James Alan Rennie, in his book *Romantic Speyside*, related how he discovered tracks about a mile from Cromdale in Lower Speyside:

> They were running across a stretch of snow-covered moorland, each print 19 inches long and about 14 inches wide, and there must have been all of 7 feet distance between each stride. There was no difference between a right foot and a left foot, and they proceeded in a straight line. Like the Devon tracks they were bi-lobal in shape and although there were no stone walls in the vicinity for them to climb, they did leap across a sunken roadway at one point for a distance of 30 feet or so. I followed the tracks for about half-a-mile, until they terminated at the foot of a pine, for all the world as if the strange creature making them had leaped up into the foliage of the tree. Yet they did not end here, for about 20 yards further on ... I picked them up again. They traversed the little white field, plunged down the hill to the river's edge and disappeared opposite the village churchyard.[2]

Later, one local ghillie stated bluntly that they were 'Bodach' (old man or devil) tracks.

Tracks Appeared before his Eyes

Some years later, in 1924, Rennie was working in Canada and one day was snow-shoeing across a frozen lake when he came upon strange tracks which puzzled him and 'reduced [his] companion to a state of gibbering terror'. The prints ran across the icy surface in an almost straight line, but between each step was a distance greater than the length of a tall man. His companion, a French-Canadian dog skinner, was almost paralysed with fear, crossing himself and praying in voluble French, muttering about the 'Wendigo'.

Some time later Rennie returned to the lake and crossed it again, this time alone. The snow-covered lake gleamed brightly in the frosty air, but half a mile from the shore he saw the tracks for a second time, only now they were being made before his eyes!

'I stood stock still, filled with reasonless panic. The tracks were being made within 50 yards of me – 20 – 10, then smack! I shouted aloud as a large blob of water struck me full in the face.'[3] Brushing the water from his eyes, Rennie turned to watch the tracks continuing across the lake.

His own theory as to the cause was that a freak current of warm air coming into contact with the low temperature had created condensation and as the water blobs landed in the snow, they left tracks, although this is a little unlikely to happen twice in the same place.

Rennie may have been looking at the problem upside-down, so to speak. I would suggest that we consider the effect from the bottom up, that is to say, instead of the energy in the form of water descending, think of it as energy emanating vertically from the Earth, using the ice as a waveguide for seismic energies. This is not as off-beat as it sounds, as some of the haunted places we have already encountered and shall encounter shortly are on geologically active areas: Cromdale, where climbers and hillwalkers are occasionally followed by phantom footsteps, has Ben Macdhui a few miles to the south, with its stories of 'the Big Grey Man of Ben Macdhui', and is on the Spey Valley fault; Kinlochewe is on a thrust plane; and Llanaber, north of Barmouth in Wales, where two people saw footprints in the mud near a river, is on the Bala fault. Further, the Dorset coast is traversed with faults running into the sea, Kerguelen Island is a volcanic outcrop, Exeter has three volcanic outcrops from the Permian period, with many faulted areas, and so on; earthquakes were recorded at Exmouth in 1813, 1865, 1871 and 1883.

RESERVOIRS AND LAKES CAUSE GEOLOGICAL STRESS

Many abnormalities are found near man-made lakes and reservoirs. Large artificial lakes and bodies of water impose very great strains on the underlying rocks and marked piezoelectric effects are noted as the lakes and reservoirs fill up. For example, in 1972 a new dam was built at Talbingo in the Snowy Mountains of New South Wales, Australia, creating a 730,000-acre (295,420-hectare) lake. Magnetometer readings at 15 survey points taken before and after filling showed +2.2 gammas before and −8.0 after filling.[4] So it is logical to analyse whether the energy to make the steps comes from above or below, and it is feasible that, as with many processes in nature, the same or similar effects can have more than one cause.

Here are some theories:

Impossible

- A multitude of invisible animals or birds leaping along, often for many miles, with a pace which never varies and leaves no indication other than the spoor – a common theory, but very unlikely!

Possible

- Energy from above, i.e. a freak current of warm air meeting a cold front, causing condensation, and blobs of water falling. This would accord with the steps in the Exeter, Dawlish, Exmouth group which marched over roofs and fences.
- Part of an icy comet entering the Earth's atmosphere and melting, projecting a trail of water. This would be more likely to be scattered over a fairly wide area than to appear as individual prints.
- Energy from below, an uprising of seismic energy, at a warmer temperature than the ambient temperature, sufficient to melt the snow in step-like shapes. Infra-red or microwave energy would melt the snow, but is unlikely to surface in lines.
- Energy above the ground or ice/snow surface, bounding along with a regular wavelength, as a ground wave, just above the surface, with sufficient energy to melt the snow.

Probable

- Energy within the layer of snow, with a crust on the horizontal plane, so that it would bounce along constantly, internally reflected, like a waveguide along a fibre optic, as with communications signal energy, which, given certain conditions, can travel for extremely long distances by this method with no loss of impetus.

IMPACTED SNOW – A NATURAL WAVEGUIDE

A search for complexity will only generate complexity. Experience has shown that the route to a valid discovery can lie in a simple approach, the marshalling of perceived facts. Literally, the answer to this puzzle may lie, once again, beneath our feet. We shall take a look at the last theory above: energy waves within the snow/ice layer.

Shear waves in Earth sciences are always polarized. The polarization may be horizontal, vertical, elliptical or circular. Shear waves are variable in strength (amplitude) and wavelength (elastic waves), and can and do impart their carried energy in a variety of ways. Thus reports of snow 'cut like a diamond' are explicable. Unpolarized waves contain waves orientated in any plane, but light reflected or transmitted from a surface such as water, glass, metal, etc., is dominated by waves of one particular alignment and is said to be plane polarized, that is to say that the elastic behaviour of the crystals under stress, strain or pressure will send energy in one direction only, the plane of polarization.

The standing waves, then, would 'see' the snow in one plane only, as a thin vertical line of snow crystals, bounded at the upper surface by the air or the harder frozen surface of the snow and at the lower surface by the ground. The waves would be unaware of the horizontal dimension, being themselves plane polarized.

In seismology, if a wave demonstrates polarization it must be transverse. Put very simply, imagine holding a skipping rope in your hand. Now imagine yourself waving it about at random and the rope (waves) oscillating in several meridians. Now place a board with a vertical slot cut in it over the rope and again wave it about at random. The rope downstream of the board will only wave vertically; it cannot exhibit its previous wild random movements (*Figure 6, p.17, shows a standing stone emitting a polarized wave*).

Optical fibres can transmit energy from one end of the line to the other. They are now used by BT and cable companies to transmit TV information and messages. The system relies on the fact that a wave inside the cable will bounce along, internally reflected, for very long distances at the boundary between the core (of glass) and the cladding, with no loss of reflection. However, it is essential for this internal reflection that the inner core has a higher refractive index than the outer cladding.

To return to the Devil's footprints, we find this requirement fulfilled exactly. The heavy snow, formed of crystals of frozen water, has three special properties: first, it has a higher refractive index than air; secondly, it forms a thick parallel waveguide for transmitted energy; thirdly, seismic energy is polarized. In optics and physics, waves are always reflected where they meet a barrier they cannot penetrate.

Hollow optical waveguides in communications work by heating the gas at the outer edge of the tube, so that it expands, reducing the refractive index to that of the cooler gas in the centre of the tube. In effect this is exactly what we have in the steps in the snow. Is it then logical to ask whether the Devil's cloven hooves of folklore are marks of seismic energy?

Whilst mean Earth magnetic fields are often quoted, recent papers by American seismologists have reported field strengths 300 times more than background prior to the Parkfield earthquake of December 1994. Another researcher, Dr Erling Strand, a Scandinavian geophysicist working in Australia in 1996, recorded a magnetic field 1,000 times stronger than mean prior to deep Earth movements in 1996 at Kimberley in northern Australia.

Crystals, when under pressure, exhibit aelotropy, itself an enormous and under-studied subject which has relevance to many other phenomena. An elliptical wave would hit the roof of the waveguide, in this case the crusty upper snow surface, with spin, and then would leave a horse-shoe shaped mark in a linear fashion. In age-old human tradition, we have to reconcile such an anomalous image with something we understand – the Devil's footsteps.

Figure 74: A ground wave, spinning between the ground and the icy surface of the snow, forming 'steps'.

We may, then, be seeing in the 'steps in the snow', a rare combination of polarized shear waves, ground waves and P and S waves traversing a solid with totally internally reflected waves between surfaces like the ground, the snow crystals and the air.

HORSES WITH RED-HOT HOOVES

In *The City of God* St Augustine records an invisible battle on the Plains of Campania. A noisy battle between the evil spirits was heard and the footprints of horses were seen on the ground, although no horses were there. Nearer home, at Ranworth Hall in Norfolk, there were also ghostly horses, but after they bolted down the drive, 'the stench of burning brimstone' (sulphur) was smelled. Here, the hooves were considered to be red hot as they left steam in their wake, and the trail vanished in steam and spray in the Mere. Again, this gives a very strong indication of a combination of Earth energy, outgassing, sulphur and acoustic effects.

Interestingly, a report in the *Rhondda Leader* on 14 February 1996 carried a comment by Mrs Rae Meddick to the effect that for a year, a patch of land in the Fach, Rhondda, Wales, remained free of snow, whilst all around was snow-covered. Further, she states that 'when it rains, steam rises from the ground' at this point. There are two possible explanations for this: first, infra-red seismic energy emitted along a geological fault, and secondly an underground thermal source. The former is more likely, as any fire below the surface would emit smoke and fumes, if not flames, and there is no mention of this anomalous effect.

'LONG LEGGITY BEASTIES'

The Highlands of Scotland have cornered the market, so to speak, where ghostly steps are concerned. A Gaelic poem from Scotland states:

The serpent will come from the house on the brown day of Bride
[1 February], though there should be three feet of snow on the flat
surface of the ground.
The Goddess Bride sleeps all winter and comes forth on this date.[5]

Figure 75: The mythical one-legged monster of Highland Scotland.

Also lurking in the Highlands is the Baobhan Sith (wizard), an extremely dangerous female who often haunts rivers and is capable of evoking a curse on others. Her feet may take the form of hooves and if she is seen, people should flee. She also wails like a banshee and anyone who is struck by her may be rendered childless.

The *eachan uisge*, the water horse, or boobrie, as we have already seen, is an evil monster which reputedly drowns children and travellers near the lochs it frequents. If seen, one could also die of heart failure. Rather similar was the *direach ghlinn eitidh*, a curious animal with one eye and, more importantly in the context of this work, one leg sticking out of its haunch. This was a seductive creature which lured the unwary to their doom.

Then there is the story of the phantom horse at Ranworth: 'When he is killed, nothing remains but a pool of water ... his strange inverted pad leaves [a footprint] the reverse of those in normal horses.'[6] This identifies it as a type of boobrie.

The Isle of Man meanwhile boasts 'Jimmy Squarefoot', whose very large feet are swathed in calico bands. He reputedly used to cause a lot of damage, but nowadays he apparently wanders the countryside doing no harm.

Reports of 'Steps in the Snow' from Published Literature

Year	Location	Snow/Sand	Other Features
1840	Glen Orchy, near Glen Lyon, Tayside	Snow	Very deep; continued for 12 miles (20 kilometres)
1840	Kerguelen Island, North Antarctic	Snow	3 inches (7.5 cm) long
1850	Exeter, Devon	Snow	
1852	Norfolk (no town given)	Snow	'A cloven hoof'
1852	The Cotswolds (no town given)	Snow	
1855	The Cross Pub, Rowley Regis, Birmingham	Snow	Near Hailstone quarry
1855	Pishowa Gora, Galicia, Poland	Snow/Sand	Regular yearly occurrence
1855	Inverness	Snow	Many earthquakes in area
1855	Exeter/Dawlish/ Exmouth/Devon	Snow	4 inches (10 cm) long; 1.5 inches (3 cm) wide; continued for many miles
1908	Newark, New Jersey	Snow	
1945	Everburg, Louvain, near Brussels	Snow	2.5 inches (6 cm) long; ran for 2 miles (3.2 kilometres)
1957	Hull, Humberside	Snow	4 inches (10 cm) long; part of a garden
1954	The Needles, Isle of Wight	Snow	20 inches (51 cm) long
1952	Cromdale, Speyside	Snow	19 inches (48 cm) long; 14 inches (35 cm) wide
1955	Ipplepen, near Totnes, Devon	Snow	
1924	Northern Canada	Snow	17 inches (45 cm) long; across a frozen lake
1967	Port Richey, Florida		
1968	Vicenza, Italy*	Snow	Continued for 90 feet (27 metres)
1970	Farnborough, Hants.	Snow	'Bearlike' tracks in garden

1974	Amityville, Long Island, New York	Snow	
1975	Rainhill, Merseyside		Ran for 4 feet (1.2 metres)
1985	Corrales, New Mexico	Snow	On deep block fault, a 15-foot (4.5-metre) line
1980s	Lydford, North Devon	Snow	Beside an old silver mine, on anticline
1990s	St Anne's Brewery Yard, Exeter	Sand	Line of a few feet
1991	Chingle Hall, Lancs.	Flour	Line of tiny prints; T-junction of faults
1992	Sosnino, Vicenza, Italy*	Snow	Line, 90 feet (27 metres) long
1994	Kinlochleven, Loch Leven	Snow	Straight line on Moine thrust

* 'The region between Vicenza and Verona has always posed problems of correlations because of faults ... lavas and tuffs.'[7]

Possibly Related Events

1001	Labrador. Björn Heriolfson reported a uniped, a bird with one foot.
1692–1780	Torrington Square, London. A line of 40 footsteps, 3 inches (7.5 cm) deep. No grass would grow.
1782	Yunling, China. A formless body bounded over dykes, furrowing the ground as it went.
1891	Professor Norman Collie hears the footsteps of 'Ferlas Mhor' following him on Ben Macdhui, Cairngorms.
1973	Achill Sound, Straheen, Ireland. Steps twice the size of a dog's paw on the Iltay thrust.
1950	A beach in Devon. Very deep steps in sand 'as if cut with a flat iron'.
1975	Penmaenpool, Wales. In sand, 'steps larger than a dinner plate' on Bala fault.
1971	Llanaber, Wales. In sand, steps 18 inches (46 cm) across on Bala fault.

REFERENCES

1   'Chips' Barber, *The Ghosts of Exeter*, Obelisk Publications, 1990
2   James Alan Rennie, *Romantic Speyside*
3   Ibid.
4   P. M. Davies and F. D. Stacey, *Nature* 240 (1972), 348
5   Quoted in Rennie, op. cit.
6   P. Howat, *Norfolk Ghosts and Legends*, Countryside Books, 1993
7   *A Correlation of Tertiary Rocks: Special Report No. 12*, The Royal Geological Society, 1978

CONCLUSION

Paradoxes are merely Nature's polite way of informing us –
sotto voce – that our understanding of it is
incomplete and erroneous.

THOMAS GOLD, *THE HOT DEEP*
BIOSPHERE, COPERNICUS, 1998

As science progresses we find that what were once described as paranormal phenomena begin to fade into the background and things that 'go bump in the night' or cause demonic footprints in the snow across vast tracts of country may be the result of earthquake movements and faults imperceptibly sliding along. Apparitions and demons, instead of being the terrifying forces of darkness, can be a powerful waking dream fuelled by external magnetic effects in our brain, and the ubiquitous crop circles the result of turbulent flow and chaos in areas of multi-sourced energies.

The human brain and body always have, and still do, respond to the subtle and ongoing energies from the planet, and our ancestors, in tune with nature, built their special places on geomagnetic anomaly points, where cells of magnetite, ironstone, copper ores and basalts lurk beneath the surface, giving profound effects on the minds of those who worshipped at these spots.

Our ancestors knew much about this hidden realm and added to the Earth's powerful and natural sacred groves by building a highly sophisticated network of energies from natural sources in which to place their houses and villages, using the physics of the concave lens in their megalithic structure to further amplify the faint pulsing of the planet.

The purpose must have been to produce fertility for themselves, their crops and their livestock, and build powerful places for religious ceremony, but one of their most powerful needs was to focus and amplify that same energy through their burial-grounds, and one can only surmise that they had a belief in the after-life. Given the evidence, their belief must surely have been entirely justified – our present scientific culture is one of the very few which has not believed in life after death.

And yet there is still a hard core of events which both authors have heard recounted at first hand, for which no amount of logic can determine the cause. When two people see the same ghost, are being violated by the same invisible demon or a succession of house owners see the same apparitions, then perhaps at least some of these events (barring hoaxes, of course) must involve unusual energies from otherworldly places which gravitate to these same places of energy.

We hope that this book, a lifetime's work, is a step forward in understanding some types of phenomena and also the structure of the ley system in a large part of the UK, which will eventually lead to the majority of this network being rediscovered world-wide, a network built by the giants of old.

There is a story, told on the island of Skye, that a traveller, lost and benighted, entered a huge cavern. In the darkness he was horrified to see a circle of warriors, 10 feet (3 metres) tall, clad in armour, with mighty spears. In the centre of the circle was the warrior giant Fingal himself, guarded by his knights, waiting for the clarion call to lead his people once again. Perhaps he is now beginning to stir in his sleep!

There will be some who stick stubbornly to their beliefs that poltergeists, apparitions and ley lines do not exist – but we are confident that the maps of this energy complex, rediscovered almost entirely by following the leys with divining rods (the way they were constructed) reveal to those who read this book with an open mind that what seem to be randomly placed standing stones and circles, combined with the cup-marked energy circuits, have a pattern which the author certainly could not have dreamed up.

Those who will now take the time and effort to tune into these energies, or delve into the world of unusual phenomena, will be assured of being rewarded with many a glimpse into a fascinating and hidden world, with a much richer life as a result.

Figure 76: The Dwarfie Stane, Orkney. The square stone on the right originally blocked the entrance and weighs about 1.5 tonnes. (© Charles Tait Photography)

We have tried to present a giant mirror of facts, like the brilliant light at Ward Hill, just to the north of the Dwarfie Stane, near Maes Howe in the Orkneys, which can, when the factors are right, flash off the stone as 'a broad dazzling flash of white light, more like a diamond'.[1] Seen for an hour after rain, and recorded for centuries, it illuminates the scenery like the reflection from a giant mirror, producing signs and wonders for those fortunate enough to see it.

We, too, hope to have cast some light on the signs and wonders in the world about us.

REFERENCES

1   A. W. Johnston, 'The Dwarfie Stone of Hoy, Orkney', 1896, from *The Reliquary* 2:64–86, quoted by Jeremy Harte in *3rd Stone*, January 1999

FURTHER
READING

The British Geological Survey, Murchiston House, West Mains Road, Edinburgh EH9 3LA, will send their publication list and can supply details (Memoires) of the geology of your local area on request, including faulting, water, chemicals, fossil record, mining, prehistory and much else.

The British Society of Dowsers, Secretary and treasurer: M. D. Rust, Sycamore Cottage, Tamley Lane, Hastingley, Ashford, Kent, TN25 5HW.

The society has a list of members who are experienced in their various fields, from healing to water divining. Members have access to a postal library and a very interesting book list. Their magazine is quarterly.

Albert Budden, *Electric UFOs*, Blandford Press, 1999

H. Campbell, *Introduction to Geomagnetic Fields*, Cambridge University Press, 1998
  For those interested in the physics of Earth magnetism and Earth energies.

Bruce Copen, *Dowsing for You*, Academic Publications, 1975
  An excellent and inexpensive little book which teaches the basic rudiments of water divining and dowsing to find oil, coal, missing objects, etc. There is nothing, however, about Earth energies, since it was published before the concept of using water divining techniques to find telluric energies became popular. Academic Publications are at Dane Hill, Sussex, RH17 7EX.

David Cowan and Rodney Girdlestone, *Safe as Houses?*, Gateway Books, 1996

The first part is about electromagnetic fields and their effect on our health. The second is by the author of this book and shows how Earth energies from a wide variety of sources can alter the subtle natural energies in which we all live. Briefly, the more electricity we use, the more powerful natural Earth energies become and cause illness. This book can be obtained by mail direct from the publisher: Gateway Books, The Hollies, Wellow, Bath, BA2 8QJ; Tel. 01225 835127.

Paul Devereux, *Earthlights*, Turnstone Press

Like so many people leading perfectly normal lives, an unexplainable event caused the author to delve deeply into the mysterious world. Extremely interesting account of unidentified aerial phenomena as pickets of naturally produced energy.

Electromagnetic Fields: 300 Hz–300 GHz, World Health Organisation, Geneva, 1993

A scientific analysis of the various frequency bands in the EM spectrum and the known effects of high amplitudes. How such signals are derived.

J. Havelock Fidler, *Ley Lines: Their Nature and their Properties*, Turnstone Press, 1983

Dr Fidler shows how stones may be 'charged' with energy and measured. Included are experiments of germinating seeds on lines of different energy strengths.

T. F. Gaskell, *Physics of the Earth*, Thames & Hudson, 1970

Tom Graves, *The Diviner's Handbook*, Destiny Books, 1990

Invaluable book on how to use divining rods to search for a wide variety of objects and Earth energy. Essential reading for anyone interested in man's hidden senses.

Tom Graves, *Needles of Stone Revisited*, Gothic Image Publications

Theorizes that standing stones and circles are a form of acupuncture of a living planet, working on the Chinese *feng shui* system.

Richard Gregory (ed.), *Companion to the Mind*, Oxford University Press, 1989

A clear explanation of how the brain and mind work by leading physiologists and neurologists, including some of the strange tricks our brains can play.

Sig Lonengren, *Spiritual Dowsing*, Gothic Image Publications, 1986
An interesting little book on Earth energies.

Blanch Merz, *Points of Cosmic Energy*, C. W. Daniels Co. Ltd
Very interesting book on Earth energies.

Hamish Miller and Paul Broadhurst, *The Sun and the Serpent*, Pendragon Press, 1989
An excellent and important book following the St Michael and St Mary's leys across southern England. Available from Pendragon Press, PO Box 888, Launceston, Cornwall, PL15 7YH.

Guy Lyon Playfair, *The Cycles of Heaven*, Pan Books, 1978
Although written over 20 years ago, this is a brilliant description of the totality of factors that go to make up what is known today as 'geopathic stress'. Presents many rare and unusual reports from all over the world.

Don Robins, *Circles of Silence*, Souvenir Press
Using Geiger counters and ultrasonic detectors, a group of people monitored the Rollright Stones in Oxfordshire, giving the first scientific proof that megaliths transmit energy. The author recalls how his first dawn vigils with a simple meter showed a strange pulsing effect.

Cyril Smith and Simon Best, *Electromagnetic Man*, Dent, 1989
An excellent overview of the natural electrical currents within our bodies and some of the interference effects of both natural and man-made energies. Why some are so sensitive. Includes reports from around the world and over centuries.

Helmut Tributsch, *When the Snakes Awake*, MIT Press, USA, 1983
A geophysicist describes the multitude of electromagnetic and piezoelectric phenomena generated by deep Earth movements, faults and earthquakes. Under certain circumstances the soil over a quartz vein can generate 10,000 to 100,000 v/m – ions in the air – with animal and human effects and very much more.

Alfred Watkins, *The Old Straight Track*, Abacus, 1927
This is Watkins' vision of the ancient tracks across the country, including churches, beacon hills, mounds, earthworks and moats.

Samir Zeki, *Vision of the Brain*, Blackwell Medical, 1993
How the brain and senses work at several levels, written in a way that can be read by both scientists and non-scientists.

INDEX

Thorsons

Be inspired to change your life

www.thorsons.com

The latest mind, body and spirit news

Exclusive author interviews

Read extracts from the latest books

Join in mind expanding discussions

Win great prizes every week

Thorsons catalogue & ordering

www.thorsons.com